P9-BXZ-068

# COUTURE **KNITS**

Jean Moss

# COUTURE **KNITS**

Jean Moss

Guild of Master
Craftsman Publications

Guild of Master
Craftsman Publications

First published 2006 by
Guild of Master Craftsman Publications Ltd
166 High Street, Lewes
East Sussex, BN7 1XU



ISBN-13: 978-1-86108-404-0
ISBN-10: 1-86108-404-8



A catalogue record of this book is available from the British Library.

**Managing Editor:** Gerrie Purcell
**Production Manager:** Hilary MacCallum
**Photography:** Jerry Lebens
**Additional photography:** Anthony Bailey, David Hatfull
**Editor:** Clare Miller
**Managing Art Editor:** Gilda Pacitti
**Designer:** Alison Walper

**Typeface:** Futura
Colour origination by Wyndeham Graphics
Printed and bound in China by Hing Yip Printing Co

All the designs in this book are available as knit kits or readymade online at
**www.jeanmoss.com** or phone **01904 646282.**

**Note:**
Altough care has been taken to ensure that metric measurements are true and accurate, they are only conversions from imperial; they have been rounded up or down to the nearest convenient equivalent in cases where the imperial measurements themselves are only approximate. When following the projects, use either imperial or metric measurements; do not mix units.

To all who love the knitted stitch

*'Some may knit to fill a void*
*an empty hour to patch a glove*
*a time to plan the week ahead*
*for some it is an act of love...'*

**Knitting Song**

*Jo Hamilton & Ashley Hutchings, Rainbow Chasers*

# CONTENTS

It's a fabulous time to be a knitter right now. The global knitting scene is vibrant and inspiring, both socially and creatively. There are exciting new shops and publications, drop-ins, knit-ins, knit-and-natter sessions, exhibitions and even knit theatre, as well as many inspiring new designers and makers. People are becoming tired of our wham-bam quick-fix society and there's definitely a move towards the appreciation of all things handmade. In today's hectic world, where personal time is scarce, knitting stands alongside yoga and other stress-relievers as a mantra for unwinding. Small portable projects make it easy to knit on the way to work, transporting commuters into a calmer space.

So… if you're dallying with the idea of learning or going back to knitting, procrastinate no longer! Pick up your needles right now. It doesn't matter what you knit with – if you can't find yarn, string will do, if you can't find needles, sharpen the ends of chopsticks, pencils or paint brushes and get started. Just learn the knit stitch – in, around, over and off – and join the ever-growing community of knit, textile and fibre fanatics. Not only will you make lots of new friends, but soon you'll have made more gorgeous pieces than you'll know what to do with.

Why should chic and stylish knits be the exclusive domain of the rich and famous? In Couture Knits you'll find all the tried-and-tested designer tricks-of-the-trade to transcend the homespun look and get the 'wow factor' usually exclusive to luxury couture garments.

Since I find it frustrating when I'm following a pattern to have to look up a technique in another book, I've made sure that you'll find everything you need to complete each project right here. The techniques are explained and clearly illustrated at the end of the book.

There's something for all skill levels. For beginners, once you've mastered the basic knit stitch, try Zoë. This is the simplest gilet which uses only garter stitch, has zero shaping, and can be worn inside out, upside down or any which way you want it. There are half a dozen other easy projects, such as Sophia and Sally Anne, each chosen to gradually expand your repertoire of knit skills and at the same time boost confidence. For the intermediate, keen to explore stitch patts or cables, designs such as Harriette and Rosie should fit the bill. And for those knitters who relish the challenge of colour work there's fairisle and a gentle introduction to intarsia in designs like Ella and Lizzie.

I'm a self-confessed yarnaholic and always profess good intentions of using every ball of yarn in my stash. Unfortunately, at the latest count, I would now need about five lives in order to achieve this! I'm hopelessly seduced by the fabulous new yarns which have yarn shops throbbing with colour and texture. I'm a hedonistic knitter and beautiful needles, fun stitch markers and gorgeous tactile yarns are star players in my enjoyment.

We are spoilt for choice in the yarn shops now. My favourites have always been Rowan and Jaeger, but recently I've been designing for a new company, Artesano, and I've included many designs in their lustrous alpaca. I refuse to knit in yarns which won't do justice to the time and skill invested in my knitting. I'd much rather knit a small, exquisite item in a fabulous yarn which will be cherished forever than something which disappoints through yarn economy. My favourites are wool, cotton, cashmere, silk, alpaca and natural blends. Today's busy knitters demand a quality knit experience – from yarn manufacturers who are consumer-aware, through informed and helpful yarn shops and innovative and accessible designs, to finished pieces which can be worn with confidence and pride.

People knit for many different reasons and although a knitted item was once considered to be the economy model, we all know now that to create stunning pieces, an investment of both time and money is needed. For some knitters it's not about finishing projects, they are more interested in the process. I totally applaud this. However, many are completely wracked with guilt about unfinished projects. I've never understood this. It's totally Zen to value the journey more than the arrival and the important thing is what we learn on the way. On the other hand, some knitters are serial producers of stitch-perfect heirloom pieces, which will inform and educate other generations of knitters.

There is so much to learn in knitting, yet you need to know so little to be able to knit. I see my design work as continuing education, both for myself and for those who knit my sweaters. Once you've knitted a design and loved it, I hope it will empower you to experiment and play. Don't get anxious about mistakes, often no-one else will notice – within reason of course! Knit guru Elizabeth Zimmerman always said that a repeated mistake becomes a new design, and I couldn't agree more. Take time to learn from your mistakes, they can often lead to brilliant new stitches.

For me, one of the satisfying things about teaching workshops is the exchange of ideas and the contact with other knitters. I always get a thrill when I see someone wearing one of my designs. Occasionally a knitter will add something which is just perfect. For instance, recently someone substituted beads for the colourwork in one of my sweaters and not only did it look a knock-out, but it was unique! Since I don't always have the time to develop a particular design in different ways, it's hugely satisfying to see other people's versions.

Knitting is evolving all the time and there's never been a more exciting time to start. So pick up your pins, celebrate your creativity, use your inspiration and let's knit together a better world!

Knit on,

# PART 1
# STITCH

# HARRIETTE

A good starter project for aspiring lace knitters, this sweater is straightforward to knit and versatile. Work the Fan and Feather in monotone sculptured, two-tone op art or multi-coloured stripes, then sit and watch it shimmer!

## SIZES

XS – to fit bust 32in (81cm)
S – to fit bust 34in (86cm)
M – to fit bust 37in (94cm)
L – to fit bust 40in (101cm)
XL – to fit bust 44in (112cm). See schematic for actual measurements.

## MATERIALS

Rowan Cashsoft 4-ply
197yds (180m) per 50g ball:
5[6, 6, 7, 7] balls Colour A – Loganberry (430)
2[2, 3, 3, 3] balls Colour B – Redwood (429)
One pair each 2.75mm (US 2) and 3.25mm (US 3); circular 2.75mm (US 2) or size to obtain tension

## TENSION

28 sts and 38 rows = 4in (10cm) over st st
34 sts and 42 rows = 4in (10cm) over fan and feather st

## STITCHES USED

**Stocking stitch**
**Fan & Feather stitch**
Multiple of 18 sts
**Row 1** (RS) Knit
**Row 2** Purl
**Row 3** *(k2tog) 3 times, (yo, k1) 6 times, (k2tog) 3 times; rep from *
**Row 4** Knit, Rep Rows 1–4.

**Back**

Using smaller needles and Colour A cast on 126[144, 162, 180, 198]sts and knit 4 rows. Change to larger needles and work 7½in (19cm) in fan and feather patt, working in foll 8 row stripe sequence: 4 rows Colour B, 4 rows Colour A. End on completed 4 rows of Colour B. Change to Colour A and cont to end in st st, dec 20[24, 28, 32, 36] sts evenly across first row – 106[120, 134, 148, 162] sts. Cont until work measures13.5in (34cm) from cast-on edge.

**Shape armhole**

Cast off 5[5, 6, 6, 7] sts at beg of next 2 rows. Then dec 1 st at both ends of ev row 0[0, 0, 2, 2] times, then ev alt row 0[11, 12, 17, 19] times, then ev third row 0[2, 2, 0, 0] times, then ev fourth row 2[0, 0, 0, 0] times, then ev fifth row 4[0, 0, 0, 0] times – 84[84, 94, 98, 106] sts.

AT THE SAME TIME starting on row 17[17, 19, 23, 27] of armhole dec, **Work neckline** as follows:
Work 13[15, 15, 20, 20] sts as set, k2tog, cast off the next 60[60, 70, 70, 78] sts and place the rem 15[17, 17, 22, 22] sts on holder. Working side of neck separately, dec I st at neck edge on ev row 12[12, 12, 14, 14] times in all, working armhole decs simultaneously. Cast off last st. Work other side to match.

## Front

Work as for back.

## Sleeves (both alike)

Using smaller needles and Colour A cast on 72 sts and knit 4 rows.
Change to larger needles and work 7½in (19cm) in Fan and Feather patt, working in stripe sequence as before, ending on completed Colour B stripe.
Change to colour A and cont to end in st st, inc as follows:

**XS** 1 st at both ends of ev 13th row 4 times, then ev 14th row twice – 84 sts

**S** 1 st at both ends of ev 10th row 8 times – 88 sts

**M** 1 st at both ends of ev 8th row 4 times, then ev 8th row 6 times – 92 sts

**L** 1 st at both ends of ev 7th row twice, then ev 8th row 9 times – 94 sts

**XL** 1 st at both ends of ev 6th row 5 times, then ev 7th row 8 times - 98 sts

Cont until work measures 18[18, 18½, 18½, 18½]in (46[46, 47, 47, 47]cm) from cast on edge.

## Shape sleeve cap

Cast off 5[5, 6, 6, 7] sts at beg of next 2 rows.
Then dec 1 st at both ends of next and ev row 10[14, 14, 10, 10] times, then ev alt row 9[7, 7, 10, 10] times – 36[36, 38, 42, 44] sts. Cast off.

## Finishing

Use a small neat backstitch on very edge of work for all seams (see page 129). Join raglan seams.
Join side and sleeve seams in one line.
COLLAR
Using circular needle and Colour A, starting at top of left sleeve, with right side facing, pick up and knit 42(42, 45, 50, 50) sts along top edge of sleeve, 93(93, 108, 112, 112) sts across front, 42(42, 45, 50, 50) sts along top of right sleeve, and 93(93, 108, 112, 112) sts across back – 270(270, 306, 324, 324) sts.
Working in the round, work 4in (10cm) in striped fan and feather st, ending on a completed Colour A stripe as follows:

**Round 1** Knit
**Round 2** Knit
**Round 3** *(k2tog) 3 times, (yo, k1) 6 times, (k2tog) 3 times; rep from *
**Round 4** Purl
Cast off firmly.

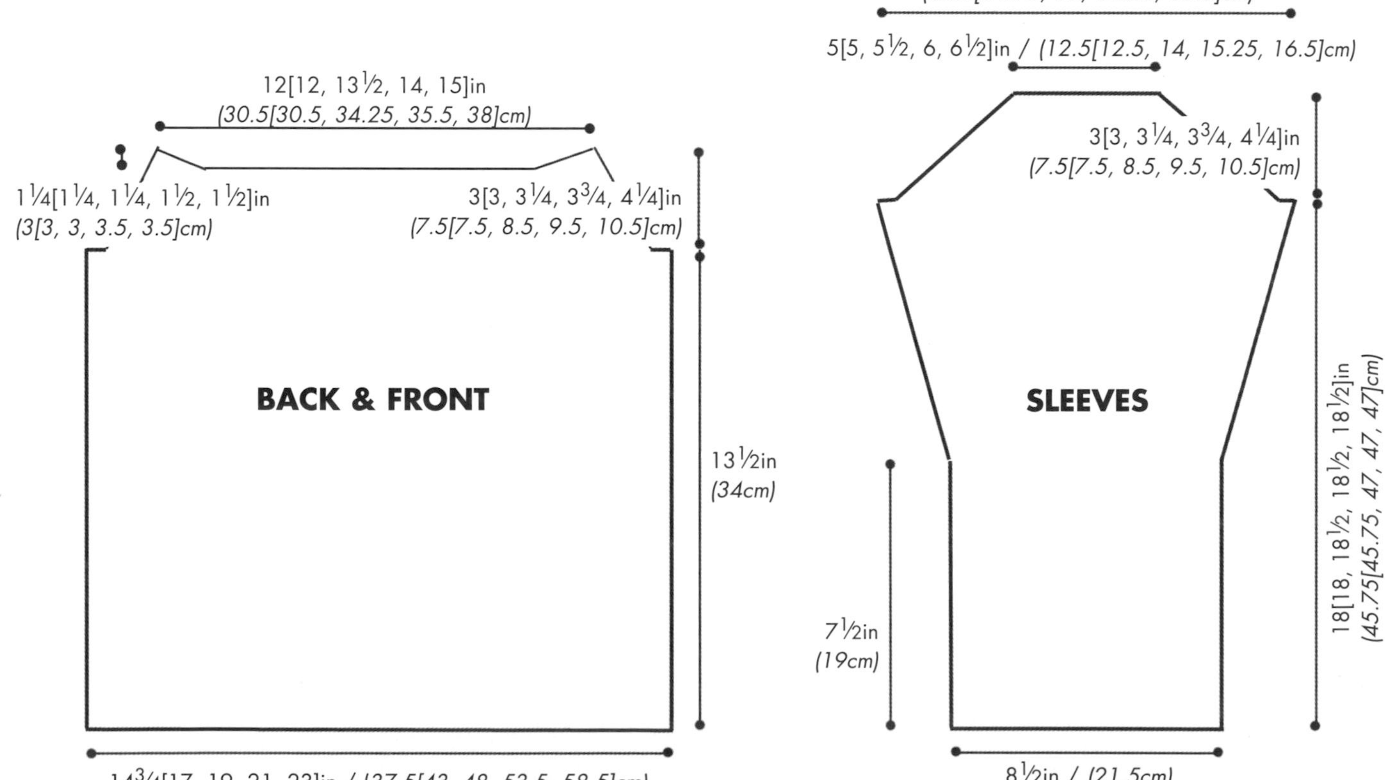

# SOPHIA

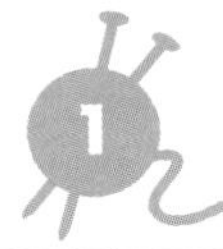


If you haven't knitted Fan and Feather before, Sophia would be a good project to complete before tackling **Harriette**. If you prefer a multi-coloured shawl, play with the length of each band of colour and create your own take on Missoni.

## SIZES

One size approx.
20½in wide x 72in long
(52 x 183cm)

## MATERIALS

Artesano Alpaca
131yds (120m) per 50g ball:
7 balls Teal (61)
Two-colour version:
4 balls Colour A, 3 balls Colour B
5mm (US 8); or size to obtain tension
Stitch markers

## TENSION

19 sts and 28 rows = 4in (10cm) over Old Shale Stitch patt when blocked.

## STITCHES USED

**Old Shale stitch**
Multiple of 18sts
**Row 1** (RS) knit
**Row 2** purl
**Row 3** *(k2 tog) 3 times, (yo, k1) 6 times, (k2 tog) 3 times; rep from *
**Row 4** purl
**Rows 5, 6, 7 & 8** as rows 1, 2, 3, and 4 respectively
**Rows 9, 10 & 11** as rows 1, 2, and 3 respectively
**Row 12** knit
Rep rows 1 – 12

## To make the shawl

**Monotone version**
Cast on 98 sts and knit 4 rows. Refer to Old Shale st and repeat the 12 rows, centring patt as follows:
**Row 1** K4, (18 sts of Old Shale patt) 5 times, k4
**Row 2** K4, (18 sts of Old Shale patt) 5 times, k4
Cont as set in Old Shale patt with garter st edging until shawl measures approximately 72in (183cm) ending on a full patt rep.
Knit 2 rows and then cast off.

**Striped version**
Cast on as above in Colour A and cont until 1 Old Shale patt has been worked. Change to Colour B and work 12 rows, then alt colours ev 12 rows, until work measures approx. 72in (183cm) ending with Colour A. Knit 2 further rows in Colour A and then cast off.

## Finishing

Weave in ends along same colour rows, or into side edges.
Press flat to size.

72in (183cm)

20½in (52cm)

# ANNABEL

Try this simple drop-stitch pattern and discover just how easy it is to make this luxurious gossamer scarf. Once you're familiar with the stitch, experiment with stripey versions. Use alternate 2-row stripes and the contrast colour frames the lacy ripples.

## SIZES

One size 7in wide x 62in long (17.75 x 157.5cm)

## MATERIALS

Artesano Alpaca
131yds (120m) per 50g ball:
Monotone – 2 balls Lilac (508)
Striped – 1 ball each:
Olive green (402), Colour A
Light grey (009), Colour B
4mm (US 6) 5mm (US 8); or size to obtain tension, markers

## TENSION

17 sts and 24 rows = 4in (10cm) over Ripple Stitch patt when blocked.

## STITCHES USED

**Ripple stitch** – multiple of 10sts
**NB** Slip the first st and knit into the back of the last st on ev row to make a neat selvedge.
**Rows 1 & 2** knit
**Row 3** (RS) k8, *(yo) twice, k1, (yo) 3 times, k1, (yo) 4 times, k1, (yo) 3 times, k1, (yo) twice, k6; rep from * to last 2 sts, k2
**Row 4** knit dropping all yo's off needle
**Rows 5** and **6** knit
**Row 7** k3, rep from * of Row 3, end last rep k3 instead of k6
**Row 8** As Row 4
Repeat rows 1–8

## To make the scarf

### Monotone version

Using smaller needles cast on 30 sts and knit 1 row. Refer to Ripple Stitch and rep the 8 rows until scarf measures approx. 62in (158cm) ending on a full rep, Knit 3 rows and then cast off using larger needles.

### Striped version

Cast on as above in Colour A and cont until 3 reps of Ripple Stitch have been worked. Change to Colour B and work 24 rows, then alt colours ev 24 rows, until work measures approx. 62in (158cm) ending with Colour A. Knit 3 further rows in Colour A and then cast off using larger needles.

## Finishing

Weave in ends along same colour rows, or into side edges. Press flat to size.

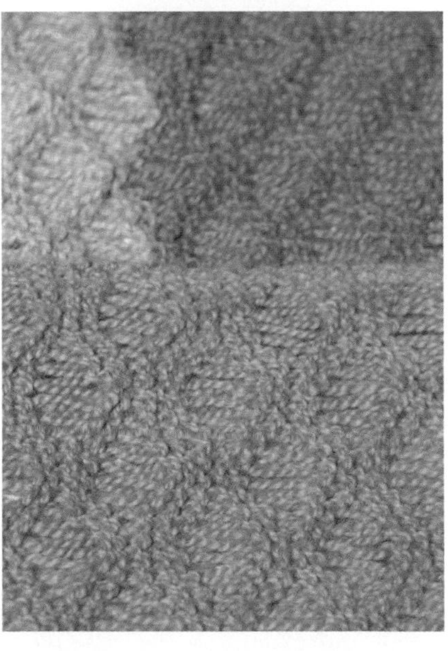

# LAUREN

This light-as-a-feather bodice is a must-have in any summer wardrobe. As there's no shaping in the cockleshell stitch this is a good project for improving lace knitters.

## SIZES

XS – to fit bust 32in (81cm)
S – to fit bust 34in (86cm)
M – to fit bust 36in (91cm)
L – to fit bust 38in (96cm)
XL – to fit bust 40in (102cm). See schematic for actual measurements.

## MATERIALS

Rowan Kid Silk Night
227 yds (208m) per 25g ball:
2[2, 3, 3, 3] balls Starlight (607)
2½yds (2.25m) of ¼in (6mm) white ribbon
One pair each 4mm (US 6); 3.75 mm (US 5);
3.5 mm (US 4); 3.75mm crochet hook
Stitch markers

## TENSION

24 sts and 30 rows – 4in (10cm) over patt

## STITCHES USED

**Garter stitch**

**Cockle Shell pattern**

Multiple of 23 sts

**Row 1** (RS) Knit

**Row 2** Knit

**Row 3** k3, yfrn, yrn, p2tog tbl, k13, p2tog, yrn, yon, k3 (25 sts)

**Row 4** k4, p1, k15, p1, k4

**Rows 5 & 6** Knit

**Row 7** k3, yfrn, yrn, p2tog tbl, (yrn) twice, p2tog tbl, k11, p2tog, (yrn) twice, p2tog, yrn, yon, k3 (29 sts)

**Row 8** k2, (k2, p1)twice, k13, (p1, k2)twice, k2

**Row 9** Knit

**Row 10** k7, k15 wrapping yarn 3 times around needle for each st, k7

**Row 11** k3, yfrn, yrn, p2tog tbl, (yrn)twice, p2tog tbl, (yrn)twice, pass next 15 sts to right-hand needle dropping extra loops, pass same 15 sts back to left-hand needle and purl all 15 sts tog, (yrn)twice, p2tog, (yrn)twice, p2tog, yrn, yon, k3 (23 sts)

**Row 12** k3, p1, (k2, p1) twice, k3, (p1, k2) twice, p1, k3

Rep these 12 rows

## Back

Using 4mm/US 6 needles and doubled yarn, cast on 79[85, 91, 96, 102] sts loosely and then change to 3.75mm/US 5 and single yarn and refer to Cockle Shell patt and rep to end, placing markers between patts and centering patt as follows:
Garter st – 5[8, 11, 2, 5] sts, rep cockle shell patt 3[3, 3, 4, 4] times, garter st 5 sts – 5[8, 11, 2, 5] sts - 79[85, 91, 96, 102] sts
AT THE SAME TIME inc 1 st at both sides of ev row 22nd row 3 times, working incd sts in garter st – 85[91, 97, 102, 108] sts.
Cont until work measures approx 10(10, 10½, 10½, 10½)in (25.5[25.5, 26.5, 26.5, 26.5]cm) from cast on edge, ending on full patt rep (WS row), then **work eyelet band**:
Purl 4 rows, then work eyelet row:

**Next row XS** k2, *k2tog, yo, k3; rep from * to last 3sts, k2tog, yo, k1

**Next row S** k2, *k2tog, yo, k3; rep from * to last 4sts, k2tog, yo, k2

**Next row M** k3 *k2tog, yo, k3; rep from * to last 4sts, k2tog, yo, k2

**Next row L** k3, *k2tog, yo, k3; rep from * to last 4sts, k2tog, yo, k2

**Next row XL** k2, *k2tog, yo, k3; rep from * to last 3sts, k2tog, yo, k1

Purl 5 rows, then using double yarn and 4mm needles, cast off loosely purlwise.

## Front

Work as for back until work measures approx 10[10, 10½, 10½, 10½]in (25.5[25.5, 26.5, 26.5, 26.5]cm) from cast on edge and **work eyelet band** as follows:
Purl 42[45, 48, 51, 54] sts, cast off 1[1, 1, 0, 0] st, place rem 42[45, 48, 51, 54] sts on holder.
Purl 3 more rows, then work eyelet row:

**Next row XS** k2, *k2tog, yo, k3; rep from * to end

**Next row S** k2, *k2tog, yo, k3; rep from * to last 3sts, k2tog, yo, k1

**Next row M** k3 *k2tog, yo, k3; rep from * to end

**Next row L** k2, *k2tog, yo, k3; rep from * to last 4sts, k2tog, yo, k2

**Next row XL** k1, *k2tog, yo, k3; rep from * to last 3sts, k2tog, yo, k1

Purl 5 rows, then using double yarn and 4mm needles, cast off loosely purlwise.
Rejoin yarn and work other side to match.

## Finishing

### Top edging

Join side seams. Join yarn to top of left side seam, with crochet hook and doubled yarn, work 1 slip st in same place as join, *miss next 2 sts, 5 treble/US double crochet (see page 120) in next st, miss next 2 sts, 1 slip st in next st, rep from * to corner, work in double /US single crochet around opening to next corner, rep from * back to left side seam. Fasten off securely.

### Straps

Make 2

Using 3.5 mm (US 4) needles, cast on 6 sts using doubled yarn and work as follows in single yarn:

**Rows 1,3** knit

**Row 2, 4** k2, p2, k2

**Row 5** k2, cast off 2 knitwise, k2

**Row 6** k2, cast on 2 sts, (working into the backs of these sts on foll row), k2

Cont rep these 6 rows until work measures 15in (38cm) or length to fit, ending on Row 4 and then cast off in doubled yarn.

Thread ribbon through each strap, then sew straps inside shell border to fit.

Thread ribbon through eyelets to tie at centre front.

14[15, 16, 17, 18]in
*(35.5[38, 40.5, 43, 45.75]cm)*

1½in
*(3.75cm)*

11½(11½, 12, 12, 12)in
*[29[29, 30.5, 30.5, 30.5]cm)*

**BODICE**

13(14, 15, 16, 17)in / *[33(35.5. 38, 40.5, 43)cm]*

# LOLA

For a hot, sultry evening, this sassy bolero in a quick-to-knit simple rib and knot stitch pattern is perfect. For a different look choose a pretty brooch to pin it together at the hem.

## SIZES

XS – to fit bust 32in (81cm)
S – to fit bust 34in (86cm)
M – to fit bust 36in (91cm)
L – to fit bust 38in (96cm)
XL – to fit bust 40in (101cm). See schematic for actual measurements.

## MATERIALS

Artesano Alpaca
131yds (120m) per 50g ball:
9[9, 10, 11, 12] balls Fuschia (57)
**Use yarn doubled**
One pair each 5mm (US 8) and 4mm (US 6); circular 4mm (US 6), or size to obtain tension, stitch holders

## TENSION

20 sts and 23 rows = 4in (10cm) over Knotted Rib St

## STITCHES USED

**Stocking stitch**
**Reverse stocking stitch**
**1 x 1 rib**

### Back

Using smaller needles cast on 83[89, 95, 101, 107] sts and work in 1 x 1 rib for 1in (2.5cm). Change to larger needles and refer to Knotted Rib Chart and rep this to end, centring patt as follows:

**XS** Rep 12 sts of chart 6 times, work first 11 sts – 83 sts
**S** Rep 12 sts of chart 7 times, work the first 5 sts – 89 sts
**M** Rep 12 sts of chart 7 times, work first 11 sts– 95 sts
**L** Rep 12 sts of chart 8 times, work the first 5 sts – 101 sts
**XL** Rep 12 sts of chart 8 times, work first 11 sts – 107 sts

| | | | | | | | | | | | | | |
|---|---|---|---|---|---|---|---|---|---|---|---|---|---|
| 12 | | | | · | | | | | | MK | | | |
| | | | | · | | | | | | · | | | 11 |
| 10 | | | | · | | | | | | · | | | |
| | | | | · | | | | | | · | | | 9 |
| 8 | | | | · | | | | | | · | | | |
| | | | | · | | | | | | · | | | 7 |
| 6 | | | | MK | | | | | | · | | | |
| | | | | · | | | | | | · | | | 5 |
| 4 | | | | · | | | | | | · | | | |
| | | | | · | | | | | | · | | | 3 |
| 2 | | | | · | | | | | | · | | | |
| | | | | · | | | | | | · | | | 1 |

**Knotted Rib Chart - 12sts**

### KEY TO CHART

Chart is read from right to left on RS rows and from left to right on WS rows.

[ ] St st – knit on RS rows, purl on WS rows

[ · ] Reverse st st – purl on RS rows, knit on WS rows

[MK] Make knot (K1, p1, k1, p1, k1) in st to make 5 sts from one, then pass 2nd, 3rd, 4th, and 5th sts, one at a time, over the first st, then slip first st onto left-hand needle and purl into the back of it.

When work measures 6½[ 7, 7, 7, 7½]in (16.5[17.75, 17.75, 17.75, 19]cm) ending on WS row.

**Shape armhole**

Cast off 4[4, 4, 5, 5] sts at beg of next 2 rows. Then dec 1 st at both ends of next and ev foll alt row 5[6, 9, 10, 11] times in all, keeping patt correct – 65[69, 69, 71, 75] sts.

Cont in patt as set until work measures 13½[14, 14½, 15, 15½]in (34.25[35.5, 37, 38, 39.25]cm) from c.o.e. ending on WS row and then shape shoulder and neck:

Work and place 7[7, 7, 7, 7] sts on holder at armhole edge on next 2 rows,

**Next row** (RS) Work and place 7[8, 7, 7, 8] sts on holder at armhole edge, work 8[8, 7, 8, 8] sts in patt, place 23[23, 27, 27, 29] sts on holder for neck and place rem 15[16, 14, 15, 16]sts on another holder.

**Next row** (WS) Work in patt as set

**Next row** (RS) Work and place rem 8(8, 7, 8, 8)sts on holder at armhole edge, turn then cast off over full 22[23, 21, 22, 23] sts.

Join second ball of yarn to other side and work in patt to end, reversing all shapings.

## Left Front

Using smaller needles cast on 31[33, 35, 37, 39] sts and work in 1 x 1 rib for 1in (2.5cm). Change to larger needles and refer to Knotted Rib Chart and rep this to end, centring patt as follows:

**XS** Rep 12 sts of ch twice, work first 7 sts – 31 sts

**S** Work the last 6 sts, work the 12 sts twice, work the first 3 sts – 33 sts

**M** Rep 12 sts of ch twice, work first 11 sts – 35 sts

**L** Work the last 6 sts, work the 12 sts twice, work the first 7 sts – 37sts

**XL** Rep 12 sts of chart 3 times, work first 3 sts – 39 sts

When work measures 6½[ 7, 7, 7, 7½]in (16.5[17.75, 17.75, 17.75, 19]cm) ending on WS row

**Shape armhole**

Cast off 4[4, 4, 5, 5] sts at beg of next row. Then dec 1 st at beg of next and ev foll alt row 5[6, 10, 10, 11] times in all, keeping patt correct – 22[23, 21, 22, 23] sts.

Cont in patt as set until work measures work measures 13.5[14, 14.5, 15, 15.5]in (34.25[35.5, 37, 38, 39.25]cm) from c.o.e. ending on WS row.

**Shape shoulder**

Work and place 7[7, 7, 7, 7] sts on holder at armhole edge. Work 1 row. Work and place 7[8, 7, 7, 8] sts on holder at armhole edge. Work 1 row. Work and place rem 8[8, 7, 8, 8] sts on holder at armhole edge.

Cast off over all 22[23, 21, 22, 23] sts.

## Right Front

Work as for left front reversing shapings and centring charts as follows:

**XS** Work last 8 sts, work 12 sts of ch once, work first 11sts – 31 sts

**S** Work the last 10 sts, work the 12 sts, work the first 11sts – 33 sts

**M** Work 12 sts of ch twice, work first 11sts – 35 sts

**L** Work the last 2 sts, work the 12 sts twice, work the first 11sts – 37 sts

**XL** Work last 4 sts, rep 12 sts of chart twice, work first 11 sts – 39 sts

## Sleeves (both alike)

Using smaller needles cast on 42(42, 42, 46, 46) sts and work in 1 x 1 rib for 4in (10cm). Change to larger needles and refer to Knotted Rib Chart and rep this to end, centring patt as foll:

**XS, S, M** Rep 12 sts of ch 3 times, work first 6 sts – 42 sts

**L, XL** Work last 3 sts of ch, rep 12 sts of ch 3 times, work first 7 sts – 46 sts

AT THE SAME TIME inc 1 st at both ends of next and then ev foll12th row 6[0, 0, 0, 0] times, ev foll 11th row 0[2, 0, 0, 0] times, ev foll10th row 0[5, 0, 0, 0] times, ev foll 9th row 0[0, 4, 0, 0] times, ev foll 8th row 0[0, 5, 6, 0] times, ev foll 7th row 0[0, 0, 4, 10] times, ev foll 6th row 0[0, 0, 0, 1] time - 56[58, 62, 68, 70] sts.

Cont in patt as set until work measures 18[18, 18½, 18½, 18½]in (45.75[45.75, 47, 47, 47]cm) from c.o.e ending on WS row.

**Shape sleeve cap**

Cast off 4[4, 4, 5, 5] sts at beg of next 2 rows. Then dec 1 st at both ends of next and ev foll 3rd row 1[0, 0, 0, 0]times, then ev 2nd row 11[12, 11, 12, 12] times, then ev row 0[1, 3, 3, 3] times, – 22[22, 24, 26, 28] sts.

Cast off 3 sts at beg of next 2 rows.

Cast off 2 sts at beg of next 2 rows.

Cast off rem 12[12, 14, 16, 18] sts

## Finishing

Join shoulder seams (see page 129). Insert sleeves placing any fullness evenly over top of sleeve cap. Join side and sleeve seams in one line.

NECKBAND

Using circular needle but working back and forth, with right side facing and starting at lower edge of Right Front, pick up and knit 80(84, 86, 90, 92) sts to shoulder seam, 1 st down back neck edge, 24(24, 28, 28, 30) sts from holder at centre back, 1 st up other side of back neck edge,and a further 80(84, 86, 90, 92) sts down Left Front – 186(194, 202, 210, 216) sts. Work 5 rows in 1 x 1 rib and then cast off loosely in rib.

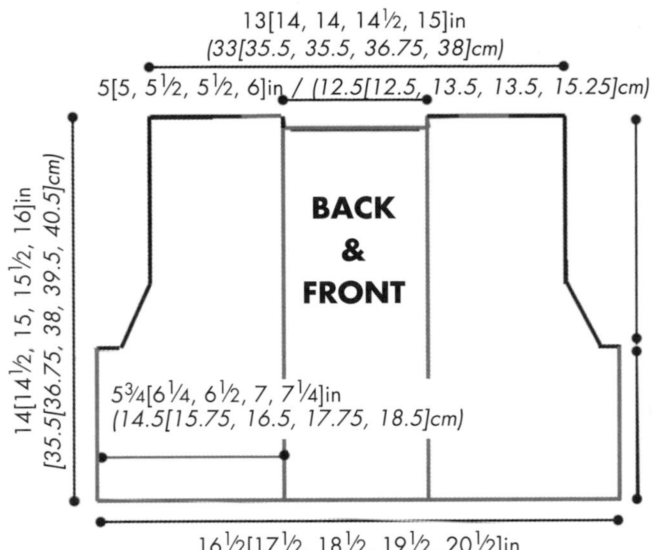
13[14, 14, 14½, 15]in
(33[35.5, 35.5, 36.75, 38]cm)
5[5, 5½, 5½, 6]in / (12.5[12.5, 13.5, 13.5, 15.25]cm)
BACK & FRONT
14[14½, 15, 15½, 16]in
(35.5[36.75, 38, 39.5, 40.5]cm)
7½[7½, 8, 8½, 8½]in
(18.5[18.5, 20.25, 21.5, 21.5]cm)
5¾[6¼, 6½, 7, 7¼]in
(14.5[15.75, 16.5, 17.75, 18.5]cm)
6½[7, 7, 7, 7.5]in
(16.5[17.75, 17.75, 17.75, 18.5]cm)
16½[17½, 18½, 19½, 20½]in
(42[44.5, 47, 48.25, 52]cm)

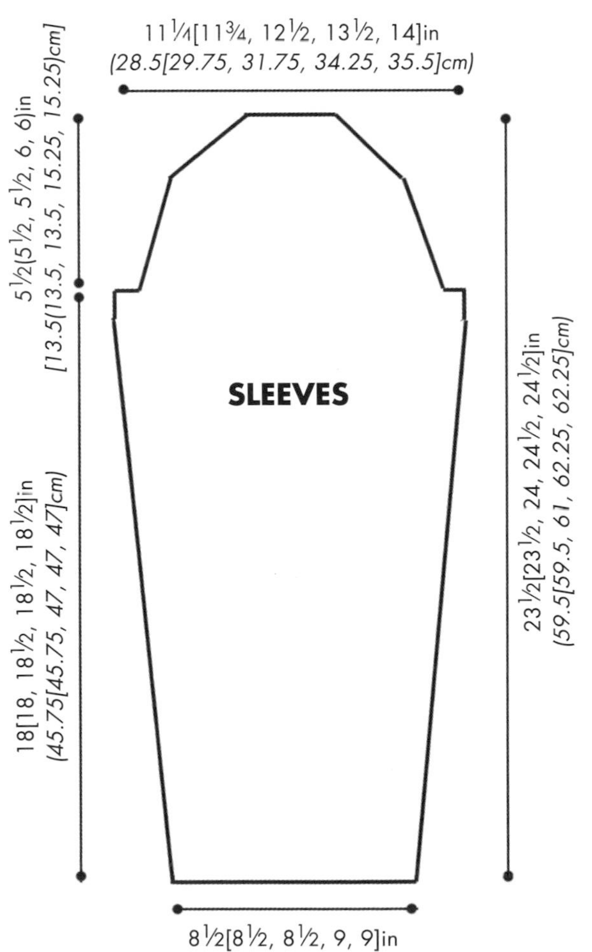
11¼[11¾, 12½, 13½, 14]in
(28.5[29.75, 31.75, 34.25, 35.5]cm)
5½[5½, 5½, 6, 6]in
[13.5[13.5, 13.5, 15.25, 15.25]cm]
SLEEVES
18[18, 18½, 18½, 18½]in
(45.75[45.75, 47, 47, 47]cm)
23½[23½, 24, 24½, 24½]in
(59.5[59.5, 61, 62.25, 62.25]cm)
8½[8½, 8½, 9, 9]in
(21.5[21.5, 21.5, 23, 23]cm)

# CHARLOTTE

A new take on the classic Aran cardy – long-line silhouette and satin ribbons add a fashionable twist. It would also look great without the cables in all-over Irish moss stitch.

## SIZES

XS – to fit bust 32in (81cm)
S – to fit bust 34in (86cm)
M – to fit bust 36in (91cm)
L – to fit bust 38in (96cm)
XL – to fit bust 40in (101cm).
See schematic for actual measurements.

## MATERIALS

Artesano Alpaca
131yds (120m) per 50g ball:
18[18, 20, 20, 22] balls
Olive Green (402)
**Use yarn doubled throughout**
4.5mm (US 7); 5.5mm (US 9); circular 4.5mm or size to obtain tension
Stitch holders and markers
2yd (1.8m) silk ribbon

## TENSION

18 sts and 24 rows = 4in (10cm) over cable patt

## STITCHES USED

**Stocking stitch**
**Reverse stocking stitch**
**1 x 1 rib**
**Irish moss stitch** (multiple of 2 + 1)
**Row 1** *k1, p1; rep from * to last st, k1
**Row 2** *k1, p1; rep from * to last st, k1
**Row 3** *p1, k1; rep from * to last st, p1
**Row 4** *p1, k1; rep from * to last st, p1
Rep these 4 rows

## Back

**NB** Yarn is doubled throughout
Using smaller needles cast on 84[88, 92, 96, 102] sts and work in 1 x 1 rib for 1¼in (3cm) ending on RS row.
Change to larger needles and refer to chart and starting on Row 1, rep the 24 rows to end, dec 1 st at both ends of ev 32nd row 3[0, 0, 0, 3] times, then ev 45th row 0[2, 2, 2, 0] times, keeping patt of Irish Moss st and cable diamond correct as set – 78[84, 88, 92, 96] sts.
Centre chart and Irish Moss st (cont to edges) on Row 1 as foll:
**NB** On 2nd (centre diamond) rep of chart, start on row 13 instead of row 1. 1st and 3rd reps start on row 1.

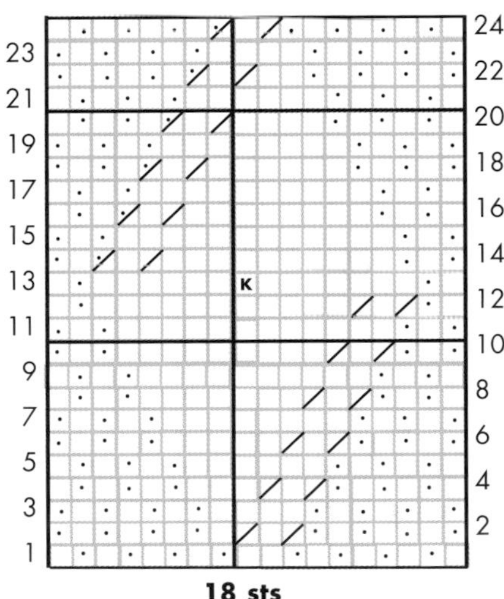


**NB** Chart starts on WS row.

- □ Knit on RS rows, purl on WS rows
- ⊡ Purl on RS rows, knit on WS rows
- ⁄⁄ Slip 1 st onto cable needle and hold at back, k2, then k1 from cn
- ⁄⁄ Slip 1 st onto cn and hold back, k2, then p1 from cn
- K Work KNOT on this st – *k1, p1, k1, p1, k1 to make five sts from one, then pass 2nd, 3rd, 4th and 5th sts, one at a time, over first st, then slip first st onto LH needle and knit into back of it

**XS** (p1, K1) 4 times, p1, *k1, p1, k1, work the 18 sts; rep from * twice, (k1, p1) 6 times
**S** (p1, k1) 5 times p1, *k1, p1, k1, work the 18 sts; rep from * twice, (k1, p1) 7 times
**M** (p1, k1) 4 times p1, *k1, p1, k1, p1, k1, work the 18 sts; rep from * twice, (k1, p1) 7 times
**L** (p1, k1) 5 times p1, *k1, p1, k1, p1, k1, work the 18 sts; rep from * twice (k1, p1) 8 times
**XL** (k1, p1) 5 times, *k1, p1, k1, p1, k1, p1, k1, work the 18 sts; rep from * twice, (k1, p1) 8 times, k1
Cont in patt, keeping Irish Moss st between cable diamonds correct, until work measures 20[20, 19½, 20, 20]in (51[51, 49,5, 51, 51]cm) from c.o.e ending on WS row and then

**Shape armhole**
Cast off 4[4, 4, 5, 5] sts at beg of next 2 rows. Then dec 1 st at both ends of next and ev foll alt row 6(6, 8, 8, 9) times in all, keeping patt correct – 58(64, 64, 66, 68) sts.
Cont in patt as set until work measures 27½[27½, 27½, 28, 28]in (70[70, 70, 71.25, 71.25]cm) from c.o.e, ending on WS row.

**Shape shoulder and neck**
**Next row** (RS) Cast off 9[10, 10, 10, 10] sts at armhole edge, work 9[11, 10, 11, 11]sts in patt, place 22[22, 24, 24, 26] sts for neck on holder and place rem 18[21, 20, 21, 21] sts on another holder.
**Next row** (WS) Work in patt as set
**Next row** (RS) Cast off rem 9[11, 10, 11, 11]sts.
Join second ball of yarn to other side and work in patt to end, reversing all shapings.

## Left Front

**Pocket Linings**
Using larger needles, cast on 22 sts and work 6in (15cm) in st st and then leave on holder. Work 2.

Using smaller needles cast on 42[44, 46, 48, 51] sts and work in 1 x 1 rib for 1¼in (3cm) ending on RS row. Change to larger needles and refer to chart and starting on Row 1, rep the 24 rows to end, dec 1 st at outside edge of ev 32nd row 3[0, 0, 0, 3] times, then ev 45th row 0[2, 2, 2, 0] times, keeping patt of Irish Moss and cable diamond correct as set – 39[42, 44, 46, 48] sts. Centre chart and Irish Moss St as follows:
**XS** (p1, k1) 6 times, work the 18 sts, (k1, p1) 6 times
**S** (p1, k1) 7 times, work the 18 sts, (k1, p1) 6 times
**M** (p1, k1) 7 times, work the 18 sts, (k1, p1) 7 times
**L** (p1, k1) 8 times, work the 18 sts, (k1, p1) 7 times
**XL** (k1, p1) 8 times, work the 18 sts, (k1, p1) 8 times
AT THE SAME TIME when work measures 7¼in (18.5cm) from c.o.e. ending on WS row **Work pocket**
Work 11[11, 12, 13, 15] sts, place foll 22 sts on holder and work 22 sts in patt from pocket lining, work rem 11[11, 12, 13, 16]sts.
Cont in patt as set until work measures 19[19, 19, 20, 20]in (48.25 [48.25, 48.25, 50.75, 50.75]cm) from c.o.e ending on RS row.

**Shape neck**
Dec 1 st at neck edge on next and then ev foll 3rd row 0(0, 0, 0, 5) times, then ev 4th row 7(7, 11, 11, 7) times, then ev 5th row 3(3, 0, 0, 0) times.
AT THE SAME TIME when work measures 20(20, 19.5, 20, 20)" )" [51(51, 49,5, 51, 51)cm] from c.o.e ending on WS row **Shape armhole**
Cast off 4[4, 4, 5, 5] sts at beg of next row. Work 1 row. Then dec 1 st at beg of next and ev foll alt row 6[6, 8, 8, 9] times in all, keeping patt correct. Cont in patt as set until work measures work measures 27½(27½, 27½, 28, 28)IN [70(70, 70, 71.25, 71.25)cm] from c.o.e, ending on WS row.

**Shape shoulder**
Cast off 9[10, 10, 10, 10] sts at armhole edge. Work 1 row.
Cast off rem 9[11, 10, 11, 11] sts.

## Right Front
Work as for left front reversing all shapings and pocket placement.
Centre chart:
**XS** (p1, k1) 6 times, work the 18 sts, (k1, p1) 6 times
**S** (p1, k1) 6 times, work the 18 sts, (k1, p1) 7 times
**M** (p1, k1) 7 times, work the 18 sts, (k1, p1) 7 times
**L** (p1, k1) 7 times, work the 18 sts, (k1, p1) 8 times
**XL** (p1, k1) 8 times, work the 18 sts, (k1, p1) 8 times, k1.

## Sleeves (both alike)
Using smaller needles, cast on 40[40, 40, 42, 42] sts and work in 1 x 1 rib for 4in (10cm) ending on RS row. Change to larger needles and refer to chart and starting on Row 1, rep the 24 rows to end.
Centre chart and Irish Moss St as follows:
**XS, S, M** (k1, p1) 5 times, k1, work the 18 sts, (k1, p1) 5 times, k1
**L, XL** (p1, k1) 6 times, work the 18 sts, (k1, p1) 6 times
AT THE SAME TIME inc as foll:
**XS** at both ends of ev 12th row twice, then ev 13th row 4 times – 52 sts
**S** at both ends of ev 10th row once, then ev 11th row 6 times – 54 sts
**M** at both ends of ev 8th row 3 times, then ev 9th row 6 times – 58 sts
**L** at both ends of ev 7th row twice, then ev 8th row 8 times – 62 sts
**XL** at both ends of ev 6th row 6 times, then ev 7th row 6 times – 66 sts
Cont in patt as set until work measures 22[22, 22.5, 22.5, 22.5]in (55.75[55.75, 57, 57, 57]cm) from c.o.e.

**Shape sleeve cap**
Cast off 4(4, 4, 5, 5) sts at beg of next 2 rows Then dec 1 st at both ends of next and
**XS** ev 2nd row 3 times, then ev 3rd row 7 times – 22 sts
**S** ev 2nd row 6 times, then ev 3rd row 5 times – 22 sts
**M** ev 2nd row 9 times, then ev 3rd row 3 times – 24 sts
**L** ev 2nd row 10 times, then ev 3rd row 3 times – 24 sts
**XL** ev row once, then ev 2nd row 14 times – 24 sts
Cast off 2 sts at beg of next 4 rows.
Cast off rem 14[14, 16, 16, 16] sts

## Finishing

POCKETS

Using smaller needles, pick up 22 sts from holder at top of pocket. With RS facing purl 1 row to form foldline. Work 1in (2.5cm) in st st and then cast off. Fold down on inside along purl edge and slip stitch in place.

Join shoulder seams. Insert sleeves placing any fullness evenly over top of sleeve cap. Join side and sleeve seams in one line. Using an invisible stitch, sew pocket linings in place to sit on top of rib.

BAND

Using circular needle but working back and forth, with RS facing and starting at bottom Right Front edge, pick up and knit 146[146, 146, 152, 152] sts to shoulder seam, 1 st down back neck edge, 22[22, 24, 24, 26] sts from holder at centre back, 1 st up other side back neck edge and 147[147, 147, 153, 153] sts down to bottom Left Front – 317[317, 317, 331, 333] sts.

Work 5 rows of 1 x 1 rib and then cast off loosely.

Attach length of ribbon to each front at centre v neck.

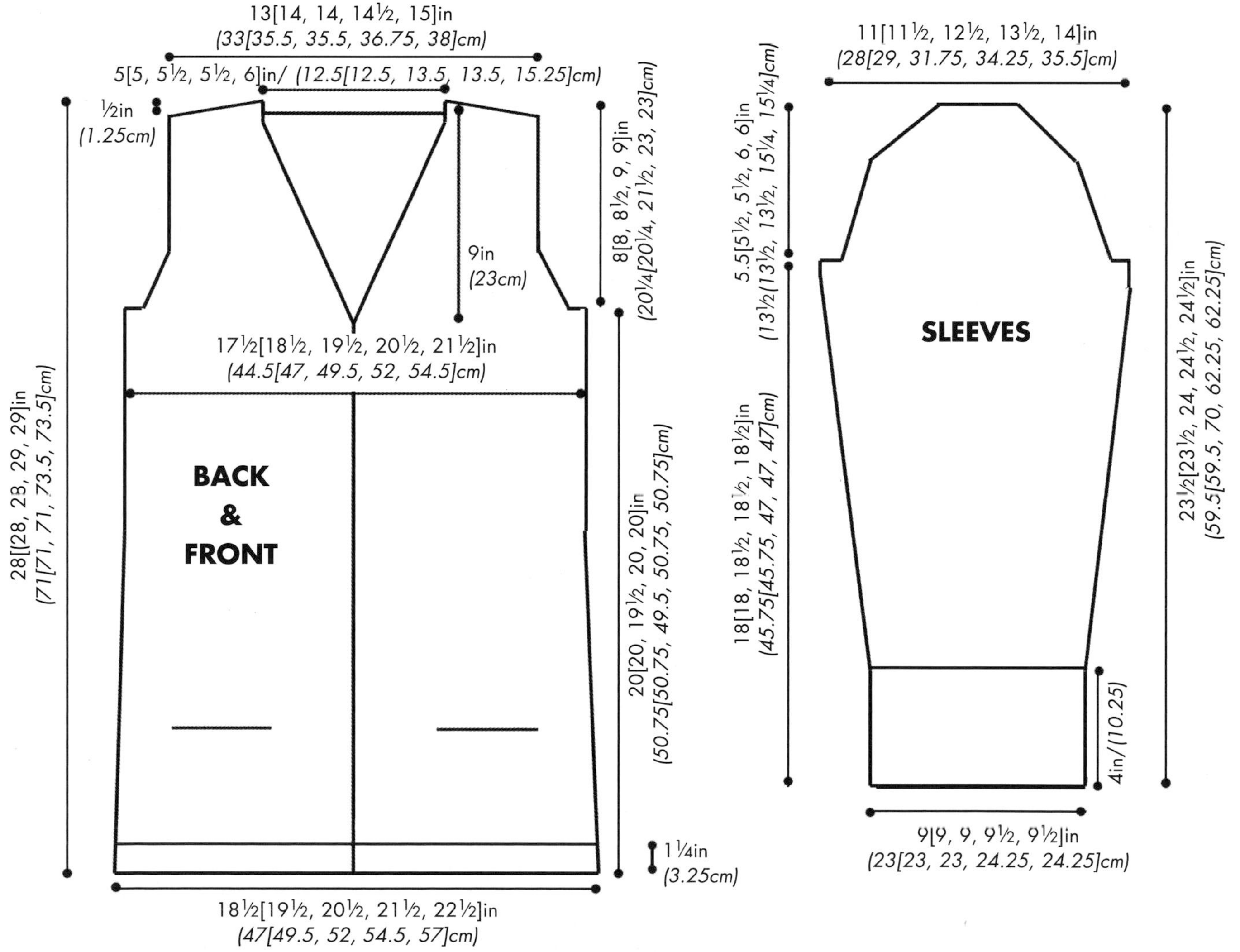

# ROSIE

Think out-of-the-box with this aran sweater with a twist. Experiment and encourage the cables to do their own thing beyond the edge!

## SIZES

XS – to fit bust 32in (81cm)
S – to fit bust 34in (86cm)
M – to fit bust 36in (91cm)
L – to fit bust 38in (96cm)
XL – to fit bust 40in (101cm). See schematic for actual measurements.

## MATERIALS

Rowan wool/cotton
approx 123½yd (113m) per 50g:
8[8, 9, 9, 10] x 50g balls in Flower (943)
1 pair each of 3mm and 3.75mm needles; 3.25mm circular needle; cable needle
4 stitch holders

## TENSION

28 sts and 32 rows to 4in (10cm) over patt.

## STITCHES USED

**Stocking stitch**
**Reverse stocking stitch**
**2 x 2 rib**
**Cables**

## KNITTING NOTE

**Neckline Shaping**

Working from chart for back and front: When shaping is at end of row k2tog twice, when at beg, cast off 2sts.

**Back and Front**

Using smaller needles work 5in (13cm) of I-cord (see page 117). On final row k2tog, k1. Leave these sts on a holder.
Work 2 lengths alike.
Using smaller needles cast on. 116(124, 130, 136, 144) sts incorporating the two cords with WS facing (so on the next row they will be knit sts) thus:
32in (81cm): sts 56/57 and 60/61
34in (86cm): sts 60/61 and 64/65
36in (91cm): sts 63/64 and 67/68
38in (96cm): sts 66/67 and 70/71
40in (101cm): sts 70/71 and 74/75
Refer to chart and work 52 rows.
Change to larger needles and work to end of chart 106[108, 112, 116, 120] rows, working all shaping (see note) as chart and leaving 42[48, 44, 46, 50] sts at centre front/back on a stitch holder.

## BACK/FRONT

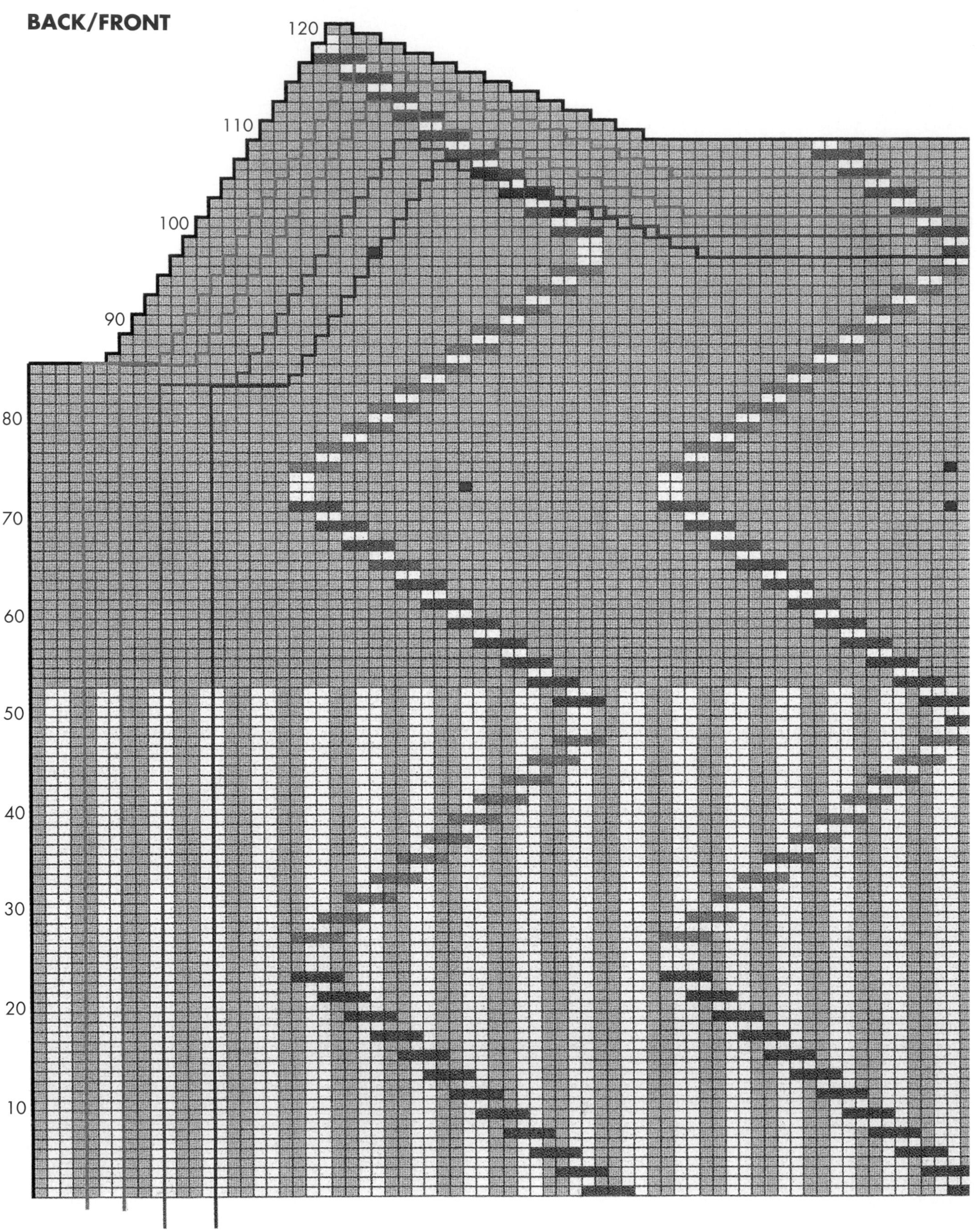

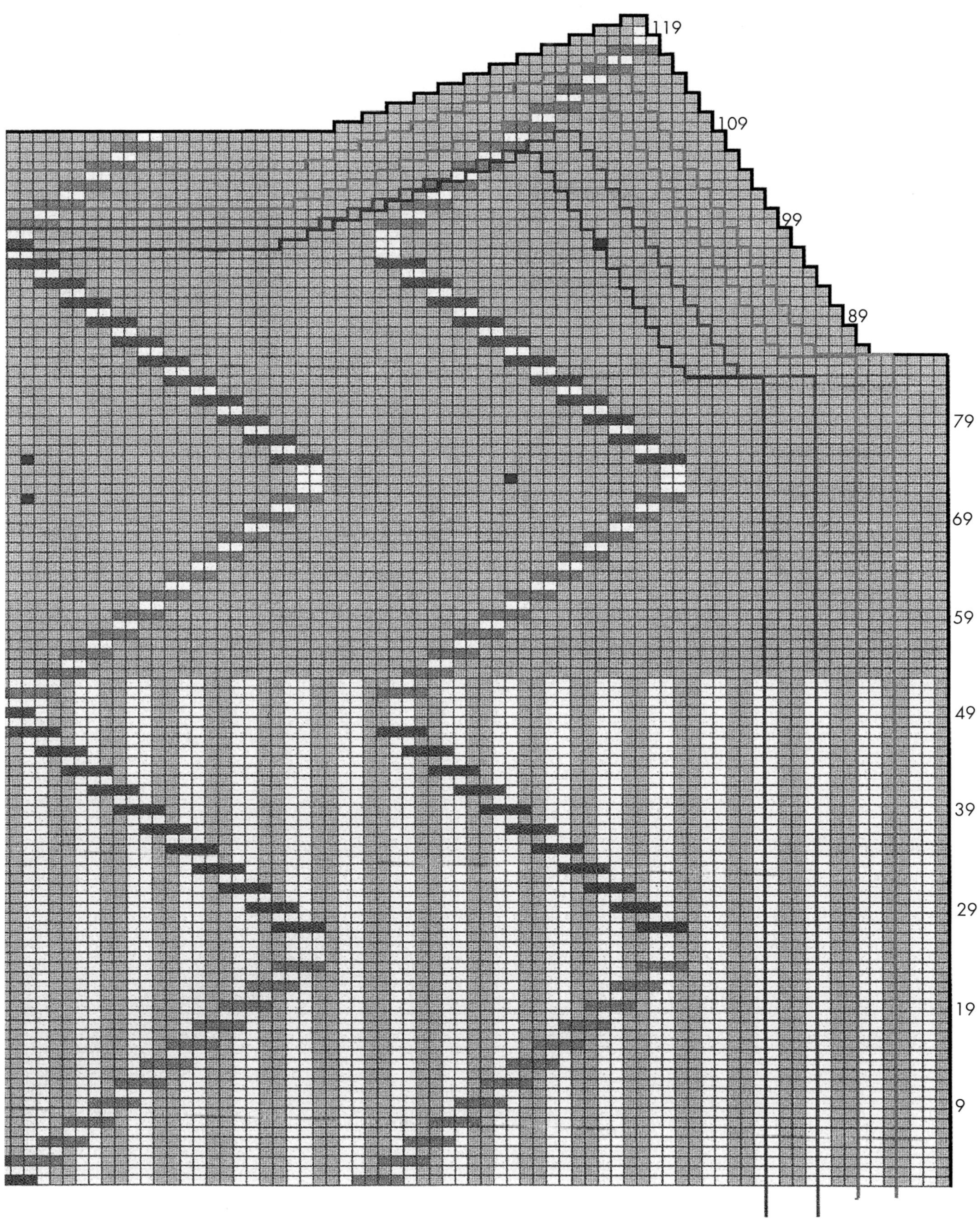
119
109
99
89
79
69
59
49
39
29
19
9

## SLEEVE

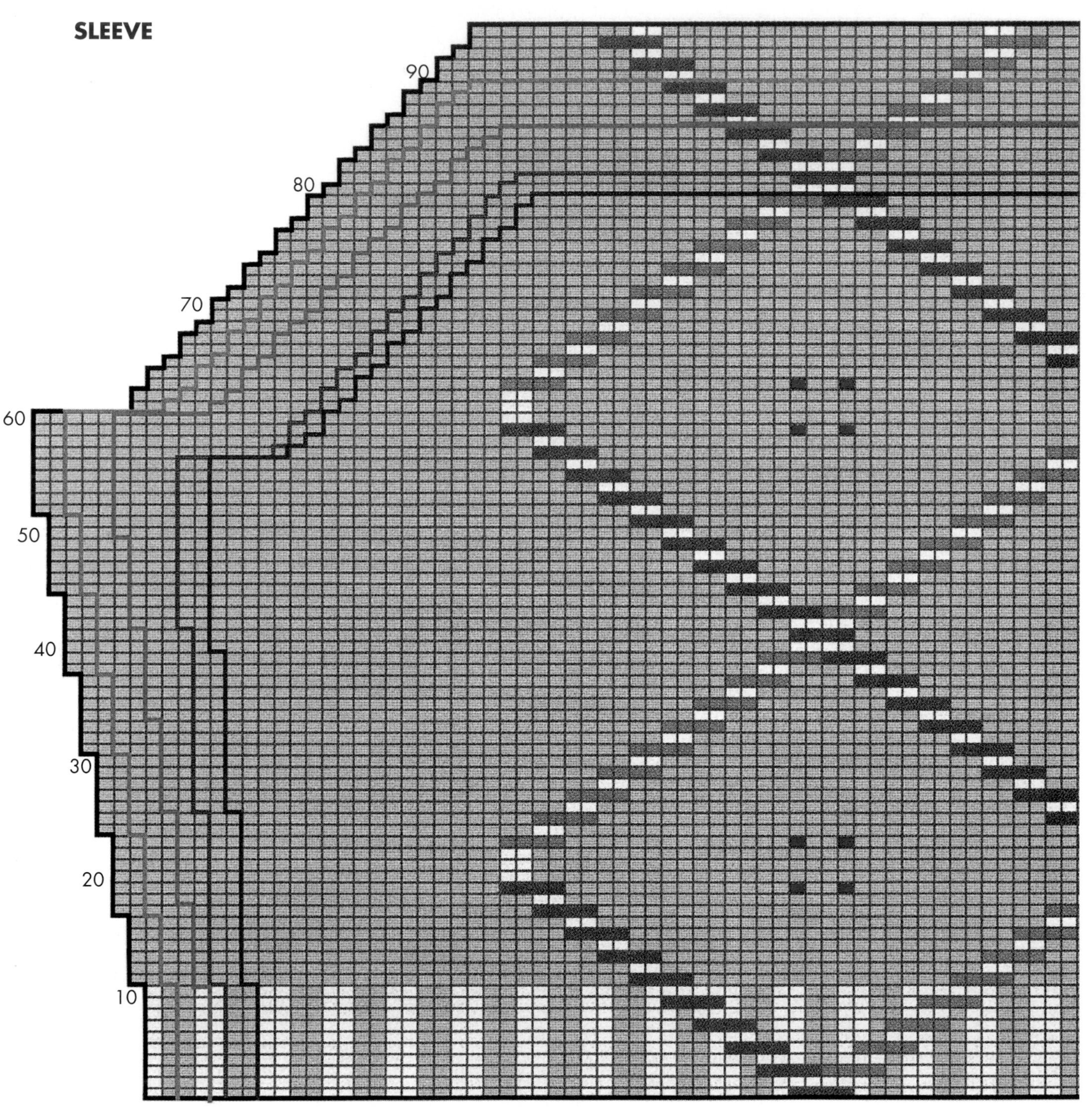

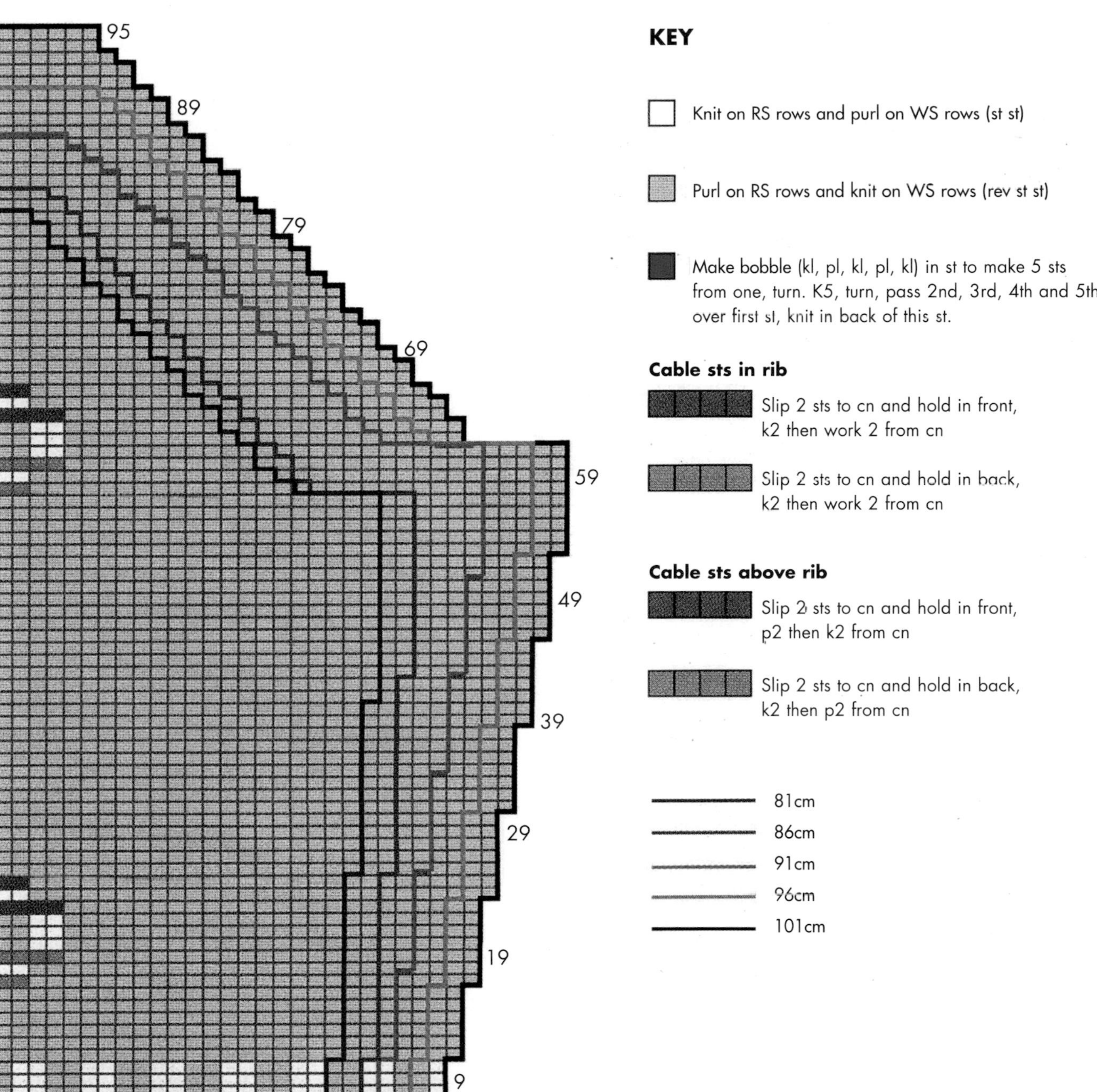
95
89
79
69
59
49
39
29
19
9
KEY
Knit on RS rows and purl on WS rows (st st)
Purl on RS rows and knit on WS rows (rev st st)
Make bobble (kl, pl, kl, pl, kl) in st to make 5 sts from one, turn. K5, turn, pass 2nd, 3rd, 4th and 5th sts over first st, knit in back of this st.
Cable sts in rib
Slip 2 sts to cn and hold in front, k2 then work 2 from cn
Slip 2 sts to cn and hold in back, k2 then work 2 from cn
Cable sts above rib
Slip 2 sts to cn and hold in front, p2 then k2 from cn
Slip 2 sts to cn and hold in back, k2 then p2 from cn
81cm
86cm
91cm
96cm
101cm

## Sleeve

Using smaller needles work 3½in (9cm) of i-cord as for back. Work 2 alike. Using smaller needles cast on 70[74, 76, 80, 84] sts incorporating the two cords with WS facing (so on the next row they will be knit sts) thus:
32in (81cm): sts 33/34 and 37/38
34in (86cm): sts 35/36 and 39/40
36in (91cm): sts 36/37 and 40/41
38in (96cm): sts 38/39 and 42/43
40in (101cm): sts 40/41 and 44/45
Refer to sleeve chart and work 10 rows. Change to larger needles and work to end of chart 80[82, 86, 90, 94] rows. Work all shaping as chart and leave 36[38, 40, 44, 44] sts at top of sleeve on a stitch holder.

## Finishing

Join raglan seams.

COLLAR

With RS facing, using circular needle, starting at top of L sleeve pick up and knit 36[38, 40, 44, 44] sts from stitch holder along top edge of sleeve, 22[22, 22, 26, 26] sts down side of neck, 42[44, 44, 46, 50] sts from holder at centre front, 22[22, 22, 26, 26] sts up other side of neck, 36[38, 40, 44, 44] sts from holder along top of R sleeve, 22[22, 22, 26, 26] sts down back side of neck, 42[44, 44, 46, 50] sts from holder across centre back and 22[22, 22, 26, 26] sts up other side of back neck 244[252, 256, 284, 292] sts. Working in the round in k2, p2 rib, work 6½in (16.5cm) and cast off loosely in rib.
Join side and sleeve seams.

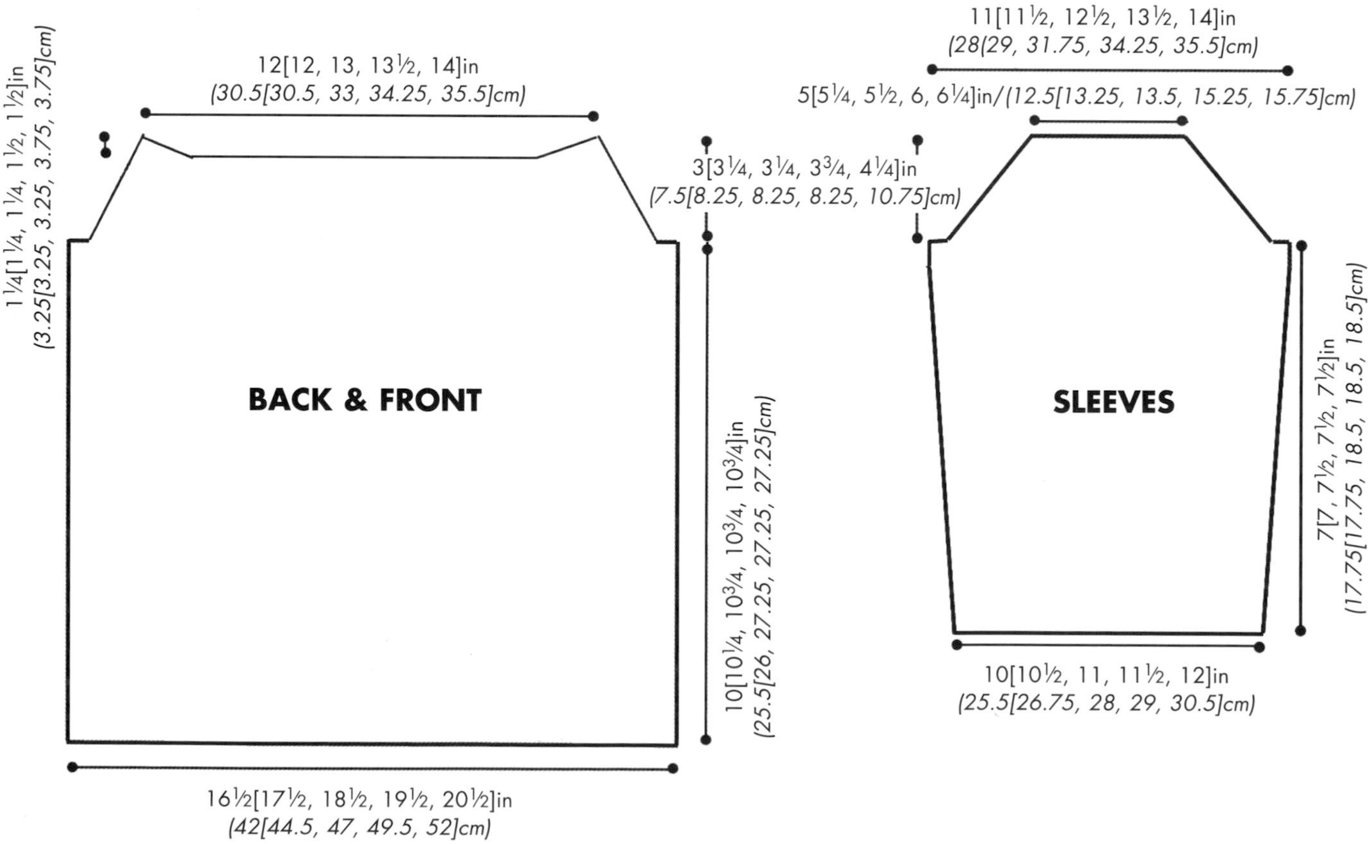

**BACK & FRONT**

12[12, 13, 13½, 14]in
*(30.5[30.5, 33, 34.25, 35.5]cm)*

1¼[1¼, 1¼, 1½, 1½]in
*(3.25[3.25, 3.25, 3.75, 3.75]cm)*

3[3¼, 3¼, 3¾, 4¼]in
*(7.5[8.25, 8.25, 8.25, 10.75]cm)*

10[10¼, 10¾, 10¾, 10¾]in
*(25.5[26, 27.25, 27.25, 27.25]cm)*

16½[17½, 18½, 19½, 20½]in
*(42[44.5, 47, 49.5, 52]cm)*

**SLEEVES**

11[11½, 12½, 13½, 14]in
*(28[29, 31.75, 34.25, 35.5]cm)*

5[5¼, 5½, 6, 6¼]in/*(12.5[13.25, 13.5, 15.25, 15.75]cm)*

7[7, 7½, 7½, 7½]in
*(17.75[17.75, 18.5, 18.5, 18.5]cm)*

10[10½, 11, 11½, 12]in
*(25.5[26.75, 28, 29, 30.5]cm)*

# PART 2
# SHAPE

# ZOË

The ultimate beginner's sweater – no shaping, no bands and minimal finishing. Garter stitch makes it reversible and you can wear it any way you like – as a gilet, or upside down as a shrug. Have fun!

## SIZES

XS – to fit bust 32in (81cm)
S – to fit bust 34inn (86cm)
M – to fit bust 36in (91cm)
L – to fit bust 38in (96cm)
XL – to fit bust 40in (101cm). See schematic for actual measurements.

## MATERIALS

Artesano Alpaca
131yds/120m per 50g ball:
2(2, 3, 3, 3) balls each of Fucshia (57), Teal (61), Royal Blue (37) & Damson (53)
**4 ends of yarn used throughout**
12mm (US 17); or size to obtain tension
Stitch markers
1 large pin

## TENSION

8 sts and 12 rows = 4in (10cm) over garter st when pressed

## STITCHES USED

Slip the first st and knit into the back of the last st on ev row to make selvedge.
**Garter Stitch**

### Back

Using four ends of yarn (same colour for monotone garment, four different colours for multi-coloured one), cast on 28[29, 30, 31, 32] sts. Work in garter st for 70[72, 76, 78, 78] rows, or until work measures 23[24, 25, 26, 26]in (58.5[61, 63.5, 66, 66])cm) when pressed. (Press flat whilst on needles, stretching slightly to shape). Cast off leaving a long tail for sewing up.

### Fronts

Make 2
Using four ends of yarn, cast on 14[15, 15, 16, 16]sts. Work in garter st for 70[72, 76, 78, 78] rows, or until work measures 23[24, 25, 26, 26]in [58.5(61, 63.5, 66, 66)cm] when pressed. Cast off.

### Finishing

Block and press pieces to shape, stretching to match dimensions on schematic.

### Mattress Stitch

See page 125.

Using schematic as guide, mattress st side seams and collar, leaving space as indicated for armhole.

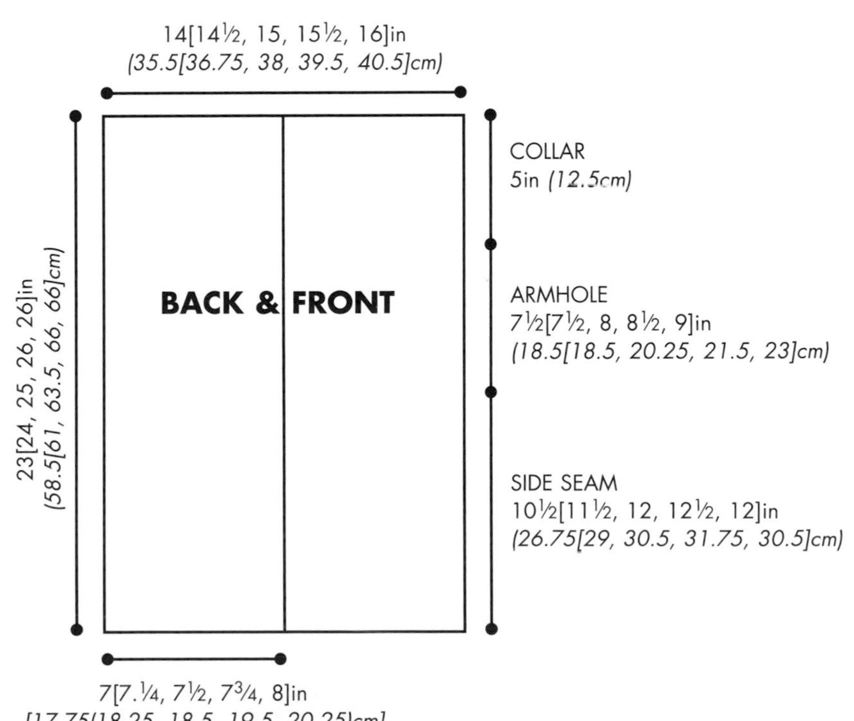

# ANYA

It's all in the shaping and the finishing with this pretty and sophisticated peplum cardigan. No special stitches are needed, just the basics done well. There's a secret scarf in here too – just work the frilled edging independently.

## SIZES

XS – to fit bust 32in (81cm)
S – to fit bust 34in (86cm)
M – to fit bust 36in (91cm)
L – to fit bust 38in (96)
XL – to fit bust 40in (101cm). See schematic for actual measurements.

## MATERIALS

Rowan Cashcotton DK
142yd (130m) per 50g ball:
7[7, 8, 8, 9] balls Geranium (604)
One pair each 3.25mm (US 3), 4 mm (US 6), long circular 4mm; or size to obtain tension
Stitch holders and markers
6 x 10mm buttons

## TENSION

22 sts and 30 rows = 4in (10cm) over st st

## STITCHES USED

**Stocking stitch**
**Garter stitch**

### Back

Using larger needles cast on 80[86, 90, 96, 102] sts and work in st st to end, inc 1st at both ends of ev 10th row 0[0, 2,2, 0] times, ev 11th row 5[0, 4, 4, 0] times, ev 12th row 0[5, 0, 0, 0] times, ev 13th row 0[0, 0, 0, 0, 5] times - 90[96, 102, 108, 112] sts. Cont in st st as set until work measures 8½[9, 9½, 9½, 9½]in (21.5[23, 24, 24, 24]cm) from c.o.e. ending on WS row.

**Shape armhole**

Cast off 5[5, 5, 6, 6] sts at beg of next 2 rows. Then dec 1 st at both ends of next and ev foll alt row 4[4, 7, 8, 9] times in all – 72[78, 78, 80, 82]) sts.

Cont until work measures 15¼[15¾, 16¼, 16¾, 16¾]in (38.75[40, 41.25, 42.5, 42.5]cm) from c.o.e. ending on WS row.

**Shape shoulder and neck**

Work and place 7[8, 8, 8, 8] sts on holder at armhole edge on next 2 rows.

**Next row** (RS) Work and place 7[8, 8, 8, 8] sts on holder at armhole edge, work 8[9, 8, 9, 9] sts, cast off 28[28, 30, 30, 32] sts for neck and place rem 15[17,16,17, 17] sts on holder.

**Next row** (WS) Purl

**Next row** (RS) Work and place rem 8[9, 8, 9, 9] sts on holder at armhole edge, turn then cast off over whole 22[25, 24, 25, 25] sts.

Join a second ball of yarn to other side and work to end, reversing all shapings.

### Left Front

Using larger needles cast on 4[7, 7, 10, 13] sts and work in stocking st to end, inc 1st at outside edge (on right with RS facing) of ev 10th row 0[0, 2,2, 0] times, ev 11th row 5[0, 4, 4, 0] times, ev 12th row 0[5, 0, 0, 0] times, ev 13th row 0[0, 0, 0, 0, 5] times. AT THE SAME TIME using cable cast on (see page 115), cast on 2 sts at inside edge (on left with RS facing) ev alt row 18[18, 19, 19, 19] times. When incs are completed, continue in st st on these 45[48, 51, 54, 56]sts until work measures 8½[9, 9½, 9½, 9½]in (21.5[23, 24, 24, 24]cm) from c.o.e. ending on WS row.

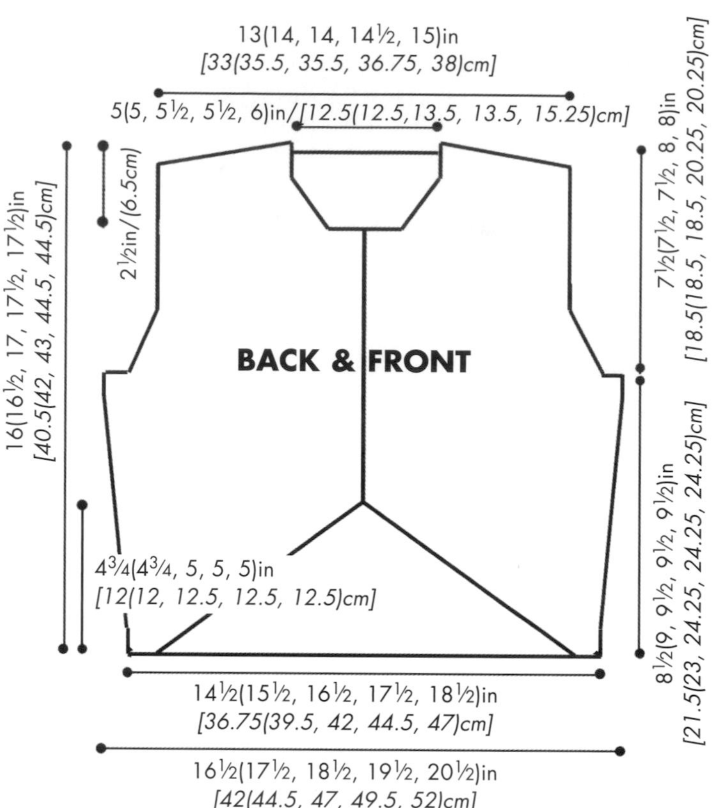


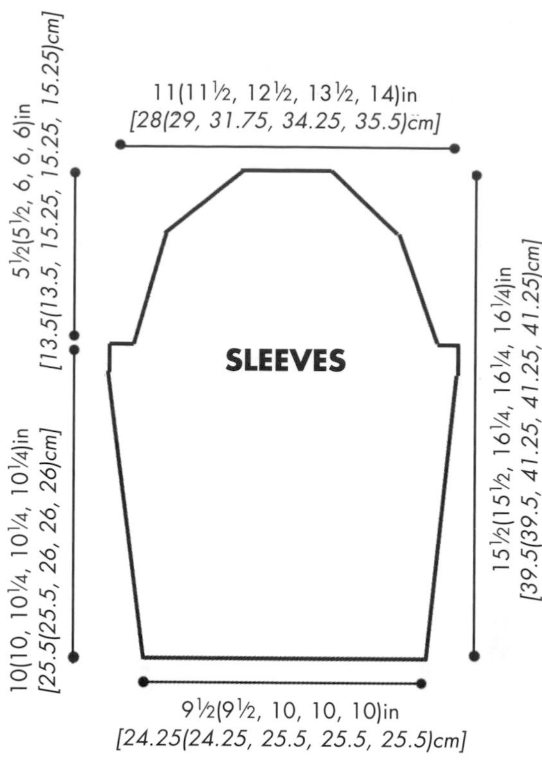


**Shape armhole**

Cast off 5[5, 5, 6, 6] sts at beg of next row. Work 1 row, then dec 1 st at armhole edge on next and ev foll alt row 4[4, 7, 8, 9] times in all – 36[39, 39, 40, 41] sts.

Cont until work measures 13½[14, 14½, 15, 15]in (34.25[35.5, 37, 38, 38]cm) ending on RS row.

**Work neck shaping**

Cast off 7[7, 8, 8, 9] sts at beg of next row. Work 1 row, then dec 1 st at beg of next and ev alt row 7 times – 22[25, 24, 25, 25] sts.

Cont in patt as set until work measures 15¼[15¾, 16¼, 16¾, 16¾]in (38.75[40, 41.25, 42.5, 42.5]cm) from c.o.e. ending on WS row.

**Shape shoulder**

Work and place 7[8, 8, 8, 8] sts on holder at armhole edge. Work 1 row.
Work and place 7[8, 8, 8, 8] sts on holder at armhole edge. Work 1 row.
Work and place rem 8[9, 8, 9, 9] sts on holder at armhole edge.
Cast off over all 22[25, 24, 25, 25] sts.

**Right Front**

Work as for left front reversing all shapings.

**Sleeves (both alike)**

Using larger needles cast on 52[52, 56, 56, 56] sts, sts and work in st st to end, inc 1st at both ends of ev 6th row 0[0, 0, 0, 7] times, ev 7th row 0[0, 0, 2, 4] times, ev 8th row 0[0, 0, 7, 0] times, ev 11th row 0[6, 2, 0, 0] times, ev 12th row 0[0, 4, 0, 0] times, ev 16th row 4[0, 0, 0, 0] times - 60[64, 68, 74, 78] sts. Cont in st st as set until work measures 10[10, 10¼, 10¼, 10¼]in (25.5[25.5, 26, 26, 26]cm) from c.o.e ending on WS row.

**Shape sleeve cap**

Cast off 5(5, 5, 6, 6) sts at beg of next 2 rows. Then dec 1 st at both ends of next and then ev foll 3rd row 12[10, 12, 10, 8] times, then ev foll alt row 0[3, 2, 5, 8] times – 26[28, 30, 32, 34] sts.

Cast off 3 sts at beg of next 4 rows.
Cast off rem 14[16, 18, 20, 22] sts.

**Finishing**

Join shoulder seams.

Insert sleeves placing any fullness evenly over top of sleeve cap.

BUTTON BAND

Using smaller needles cast on 3 sts and working in garter st, knit band to fit centre front straight edge.

**NB** Overstitch the band in place on WS as you knit.

Leave sts on holder at neck edge.

Mark position of 6 buttons: top one 5in (12.5cm) down from neck edge, bottom one ¼in (1cm) up from bottom, other 4 spaced evenly between.

BUTTONHOLE BAND

Work as for Button Band, but when positions of buttons are reached, leave a ¼in (1cm) gap for buttonhole.

COLLAR

Using smaller needles, with right side facing starting centre right front, pick up and knit 3 sts from buttonhole band holder, 7[7, 8, 8, 9] sts along horizontal neck edge, 20[20, 20, 22, 22] sts up to shoulder seam, 2 sts down back neck, 28[28, 30, 30, 32] sts from centre back, 2 sts up other side back neck, 20[20, 20, 22, 22] sts down left side neck edge, 7[7, 8, 8, 9] sts along horizontal left neck edge and 3 sts from button band holder – 92[92, 96, 100, 104] sts. Work 1¼in (3cm) in garter st, ending on RS row, then starting on a purl row, work 1¼in (3cm) in st st. Cast off loosely in st st. Fold back collar onto inside and slipstitch in place. Neatly slip stitch side edges of collar.

FRILLED EDGING

Using circular needle, but working back and forth in garter st, with RS facing, starting at centre front bottom of button band, pick up and knit 58[60, 62, 64, 66] sts to side seam, 81[87, 91, 97, 103] sts across back and 58( 60, 62, 64, 66) sts to centre front buttonhole band – 197[207, 215, 225, 235] sts. Work 1 row.

**Frill row 2** K3, *k1, m1 in next st by knitting into front and back, rep from * to last 4 sts, k4 – 292[307, 319, 334, 349] sts

**Row 3** Knit

**Row 4** Knit

**Row 5** Knit

Rep these 4 rows twice more, 435[457, 475, 498, 520] after first rep, (rep from * to last 3 sts when row has an even number of stitches). Work 1 further row, then cast off 649[682, 709, 744, 777] sts.

CUFF EDGING

Using larger needles and working in garter st, with RS facing, pick up and knit 53[53, 57, 57, 57] sts at cuff edge. Work 1 row.

**Frill row 2** *k1, m1 in next st by knitting into front and back, rep from * to last st, k1 – 79[79, 85, 85, 85] sts

**Row 3** Knit

**Row 4** Knit

**Row 5** Knit

Rep these 4 rows twice, 118[118, 127, 127, 127] after first rep, work 1 further row, (14 rows in all for frill) and then cast off 177[177, 190, 190, 190] sts.

**NB** Never inc on last st.

Join side and sleeve seams in one line. Attach buttons opposite buttonholes.

# TABITHA

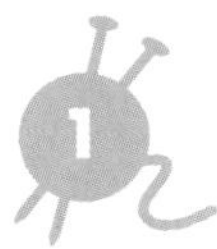

Sharpen your short-row shaping skills and end up with this helix-shaped scarf. Using the same technique, add more stitches and work fewer rows and it becomes a cape!

## SIZES

One size 4in (10cm) wide x 48in (122cm) long

## MATERIALS

Artesano Alpaca
131yds (120m) per 50g ball:
3 balls Fuchsia (57)
4.5 mm (US 7); or size to obtain tension

## TENSION

20 sts and 30 rows = 4in (10cm) over st st

## STITCHES USED

**Stocking stitch**
**Garter stitch**
**Wrapping a stitch**
see page 123

## Making the scarf

Cast on 20 sts.
**Row 1** Knit
**Row 2** k2, p16, k2
Work shaping as foll**:
**Rows 3 & 4** k2, wrap next st, turn and k2
**Rows 5, 7 & 6** k3, picking up wrap on third st and knitting it with st above, wrap next st, turn, p1, k2
**NB** On all subsequent RS rows before turning wrap next st, picking up wrap on foll RS row.
**Rows 7 & 8** k4, turn, p2, k2
**Rows 9 & 10** k5, turn. p3, k2
**Rows 11 & 12** k6, turn, p4, k2
Cont in this way working across 1 more st on ev alt row, keeping 2 sts in garter st at both sides until the 35th and 36th rows have been worked which read k18, turn, p16, k2.
**Rows 37 & 38** k17, turn, p15, k2
**Rows 39 & 40** k16, turn, p14, k2
Cont as set working 1 st less ev alt row until rows k2, turn, k2 have been worked.
**Next row** Knit, picking up all the wraps.
**Next row** k2, p16, k2 ***
Rep the last 2 rows 3 more times****

Rep from ** to **** 26 times in all, end last rep at ***.
Cast off.

## Finishing

Weave in ends along same colour rows, or into side edges. Press to size.

# JOSEPHINE

I love godets for the stylish way they introduce feminine shape and movement. Knit this lacy cropped cardy and add the techniques to your repertoire.

## SIZES

XS – to fit bust 32in (81.25cm)
S – to fit bust 36 (91.5cm)
M – to fit bust 40 (101.5cm)
L – to fit bust 44 (111.75cm)
XL – to fit bust 48 (122cm). See schematic for actual measurements.

## MATERIALS

Rowan 4-ply
approx 184 yd (170m) per 50g ball:
8[8, 9, 9, 10] 1.75 oz (50g) balls of Tan (111)
Sizes US 2 and US 3 (2.75 and 3mm) circular needles, 24in (60cm) long
One pair US 3(3mm) needles
Five ½in (13mm) buttons
Stitch holders

## TENSION

28 sts and 42 rows to 4in/10cm over st st using larger needles
25 sts of chart patt to 3.75/9.5cm using larger needles or size to obtain tension.

## STITCHES USED

**Moss stitch**
**Stocking stitch**

### Body

With larger circular needle, cast on 316[351, 386, 421, 456] sts. K1 row on WS.
Beg chart patt
**Row 1** (RS) Work 35 sts of chart 9[10, 11, 12, 13] times, then work first st of chart once more.
Cont in patt as established (note omit small half-diamond design, chart rows 46–50, at beg and end of row) through chart row 56–226[251, 276, 301, 326] sts. Cont to rep chart rows 25-56 until piece measures 9[9½, 9½, 9½, 10½]in /23[24, 24, 24, 26.5] cm from beg, end with a WS row.
Divide for armholes
**Next row** (RS) Cont in patt, work across 49[55, 61, 68, 74] sts (right front), cast off next 14 sts (underarm), work until there are 100[113, 126, 137, 150] sts on RH needle after cast off (back), cast off 14 sts (underarm), work in patt to end (left front).
**Next row** (WS) Work 49[55, 61, 68, 74] sts of left front and place all other sts on holders.

### Left Front

**Armhole and V-neck shaping**
**Next row** (RS) K1, ssk (armhole dec), work in patt to end.
Cont in this way to dec 1 st at armhole edge ev other row 8(9,10, 11, 12) times more.
AT THE SAME TIME when armhole measures ½in (1.25cm), end with a WS row and work as foll:
**Next row** (RS) Work to last 3 sts of row, k2tog (neck dec), k1.
Cont in this way to dec 1 st at neck edge ev 4th row 4[5, 11, 17, 20] times more, then ev 6th row 9[9, 5, 1, 0] times – 26[30, 33, 37, 40] sts.
Cont in patt until armhole measures 8[8½, 8½, 8½, 9]in (20.25[21.5, 21.5, 21.5, 23]cm), end with a WS row.
**Shoulder shaping**
Cast off at beg of RS rows 9[10, 11, 12, 13] sts twice, then 8[10, 11, 13, 14] sts once.

### Right Front

Place 49[55, 61, 68, 74] right front sts from holder to larger needle and work to correspond to left front, reversing shaping.

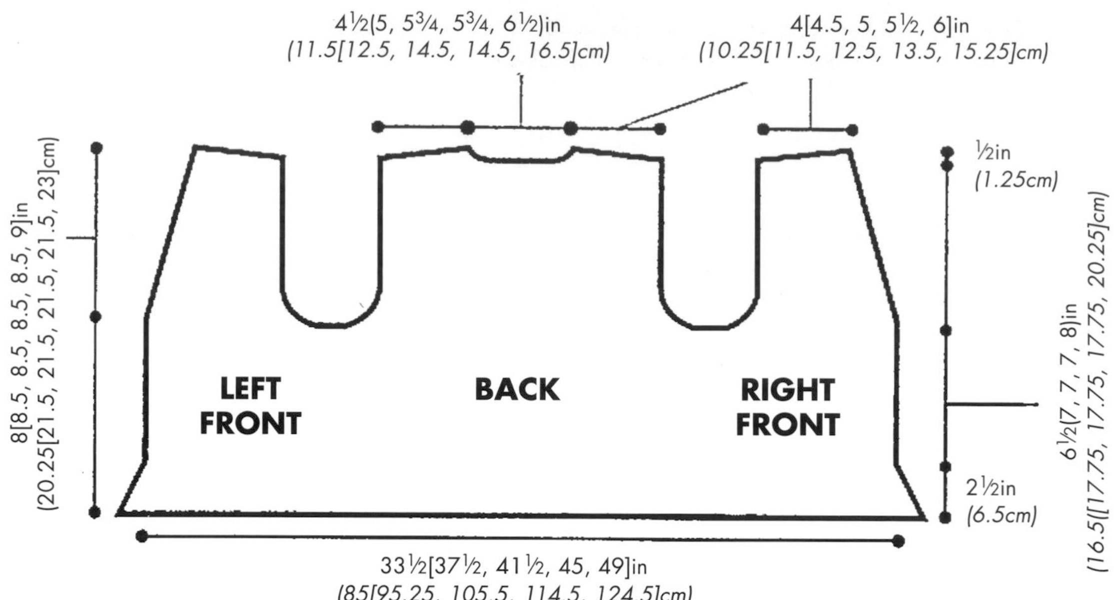


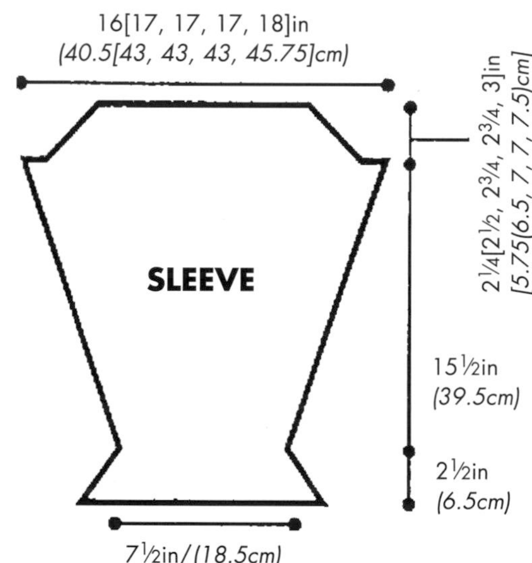

**Back**
Place rem 100[113, 126, 137, 150] back sts from holder to larger needle and shape armhole at each side as for fronts – 82[93, 104, 113, 124] sts. Cont in patt until same length as fronts to shoulder shaping.

**Shoulder and neck shaping**
Shape shoulders each side as for fronts.
AT THE SAME TIME cast off centre 22[25, 30, 31, 36] sts and working both sides at once, cast off from each neck edge 4 sts once.

**Sleeves**
With straight needles, cast on 70 sts. Knit 1 row on WS.

**Beg chart patt**
**Row 1** (RS) Work 35 sts of chart twice. Cont in patt as established through chart row 20 (50 sts). Cont in patt through chart row 56, then cont to rep rows 25–56.
AT THE SAME TIME inc 1 st each side (working inc sts into patt) on next row, then ev 4th row 10[19, 19, 19, 28] times more, ev 6th row 18[12, 12, 12, 6] times – 106[114, 114, 114, 120] sts. Cont in patt until piece measures 18in (46cm) from beg, end with a WS row.

**Cap shaping**
Cast off 7 sts at beg of next 2 rows. Dec 1 st each side of next row, then ev other row 8[9, 10, 11, 12] times more. Work 1 row even. Cast off 3 sts at beg of next 4 rows. Cast off rem 62[68, 66, 64, 68] sts.

**Finishing**
Block pieces. Sew shoulder seams.
FRONT AND NECK BAND
Place 5 markers along right front edge for buttonholes, with the first marker just below first neck dec, the last ½in (1.25cm) from lower edge, and three others spaced evenly between. With RS facing and smaller circular needle,

pick up and k66[70, 70, 70, 78] sts along right front edge to beg of neck shaping, 60[62, 62, 62, 64] sts to shoulder, 28[31, 37, 37, 41] sts along back neck, then pick up along left front edge to correspond to right front – 280[295, 301, 301, 325] sts.
Work 6 rows in moss st.
AT THE SAME TIME, on row 3, cast off 3 sts at each marker for buttonholes. On foll row, cast on 3 sts over each set of cast off sts. When 6 rows of moss st have been completed, knit 1 row on WS for turning ridge.

Then, beg with a knit row, work 6 rows in st st, working buttonholes to match those on right front band.
Cast off.
Set in sleeves. Sew sleeve seams. Fold front band to WS at turning ridge and slipstitch in place. Sew 2 sides of buttonhole together. Sew on buttons.

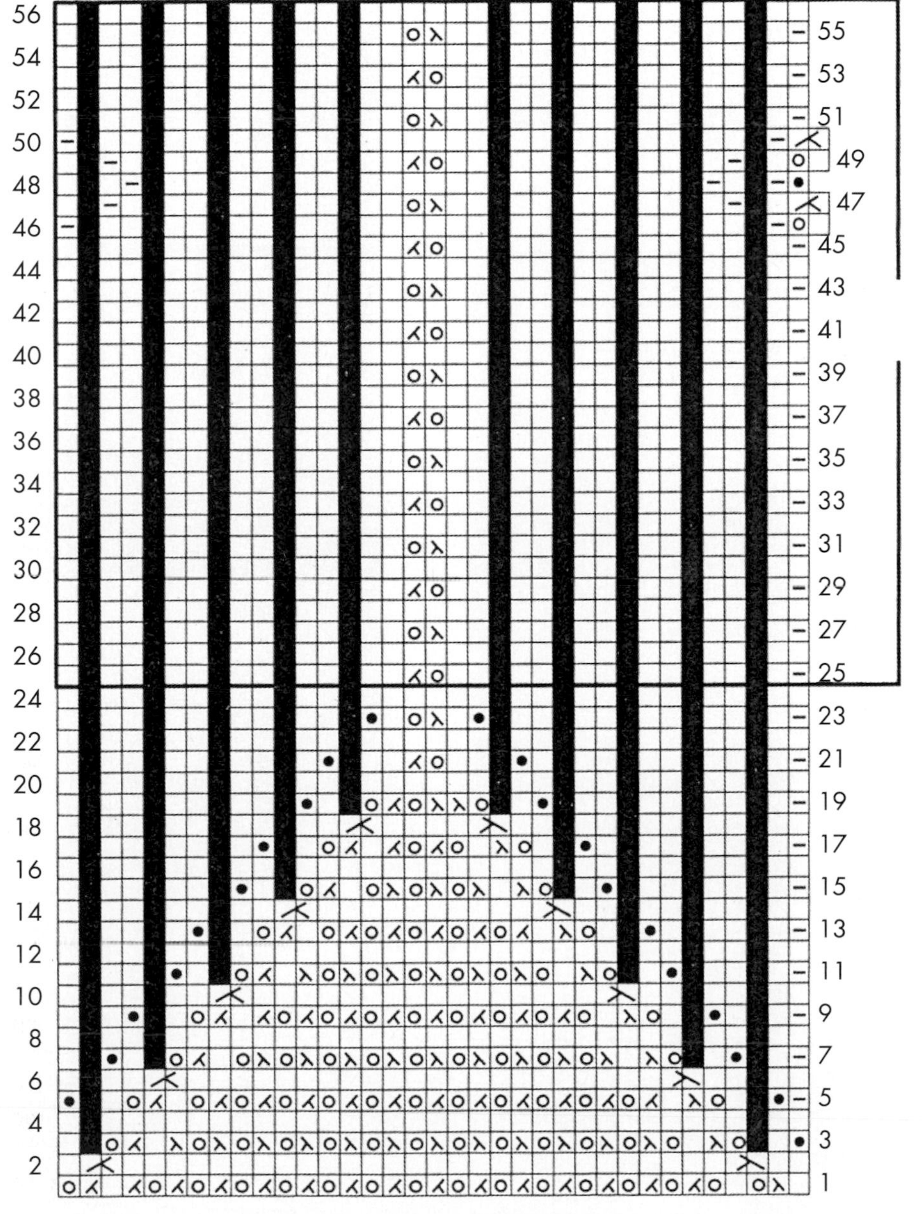


**35 sts decreased to 25 sts**

**STITCH KEY**

- K on RS, P on WS
- – P on RS, K on WS
- O yarn over
- k2tog
- ssk
- no stitch
- • MB Make bobble on RS rows: (p1, k1, p1, k1, p1) in one st to make 5 sts in this st, then pass 2nd, 3rd, 4th, 5th sts one at a time, over first st. On WS rows: (k1, p1, k1, p1, k1) in one st, then complete as for RS version.

**NB** Cardigan is knitted back and forth in one piece to armholes, then divided and fronts and back worked separately.

# ANGELICA

Chic and sexy cotton camisole knitted in lace and cable stitches. You also have the option of altering the cup size with this pattern, to ensure a perfect fit.

## SIZES

XS – to fit bust 32in (81cm)
S – to fit bust 34in (86cm)
M – to fit bust 36in (91cm)
L – to fit bust 38in (96cm)
XL – to fit bust 40in (101cm). See schematic for actual measurements.

## MATERIALS

Jaeger Siena
153 yds (140m) per 50g ball:
4[4, 4, 5, 5] balls of Blush (417)
3.25mm (US 3); 3mm (US 2);
3mm (US 2) circular needle
Stitch holders

## TENSION

28 sts and 36 rows = 4in (10cm) over patt

## STITCHES USED

**Stocking stitch**
**Reverse stocking stitch**
**Travelling (twisted) stitches**

### Back

Using larger needles cast on 98[104, 112, 120, 126] sts and work 4 rows in garter st. Refer to Chart 1 and starting on row 7[1, 1, 1, 1] work to row 106, shaping sides as chart and then leave on holder.

### Front

Work as for Back up to and including row 106 then work as foll: Place 6[6, 6, 7, 7] sts on holder, place the foll 30[33, 37, 40, 43] sts on holder, work row 107 over the next 26 sts, place rem 36[39, 43, 47, 50] sts on holder. Cont on centre 26 sts through to row 120 then cast off rem 2 sts.

### Right Cup

Using smaller needles starting at top of front on WS row, place 6[6, 6, 7, 7] sts, on holder, then purl the 30[33, 37, 40, 43] sts on holder for right cup. Then working over these 30[33, 37, 40, 43] sts refer to chart 2 and starting on RS row, work until piece measures 3[3½, 3¾, 4, 4¼]in (7.5[9, 9.5, 10.25, 10.75]cm), When lace patt occurs over last 2 sts at centre, work these sts in st st.
**NB** Choose your cup size here by adding or subtracting from these rows, ending on a WS row. Cont along left edge of piece, pick up and purl so that they are knit on RS rows 21[24, 26, 28, 31] sts – 51[57, 63, 68, 74] sts. Working across all sts, cont in patt (working added sts in st st with no lacy patt) for another 2¼in (5.75cm) ending on a WS row (this should match up along side edge of triangle at centre front). Leave sts on holder.

### Left Cup

Work as for right cup, reversing shaping by picking up sts along right edge of piece at end of a RS row.

## Chart 1

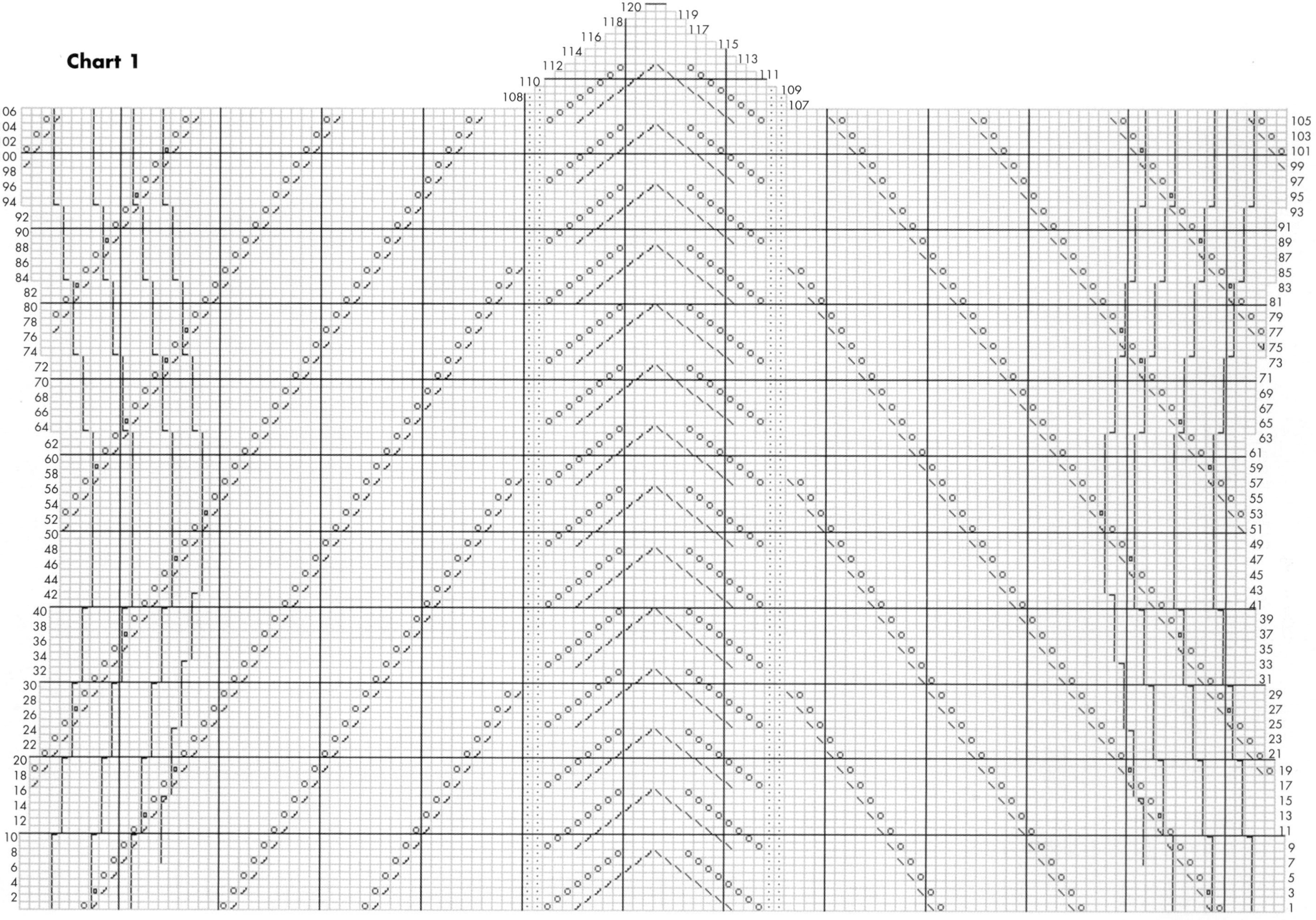

## Stitch key

- Knit on RS and purl on WS – stocking stitch
- Purl on RS and knit on WS – rev st st
- On RS rows Ssk – slip the next 2 sts knitwise, one at a time to RH needle and then knit them tog by inserting the tip of the LH needle into the fronts of these two sts from the left
  On WS rows p2tog tbl
- On RS rows K2tog
  On WS rows p2tog
- Yarn over needle to make a stitch

## Finishing

Sew cups to body – sloping edge of centre triangle along inside edge of cup. Using smaller needles and RS facing, pick up and knit sts from left cup, pick up 1 st in centre, then right cup – 103[115, 127, 137, 149] sts. Knit one row and then cast off knitwise. Join side seams. Then using circular needle with RS facing, cast on 90 sts (lengthen or shorten straps here), pick up and knit 35[37, 39, 41, 43] sts down side of right cup, 6[6, 6, 7, 7] sts from holder at armhole edge, 98[104, 112, 120, 126] sts from holder at back, 6[6, 6, 7, 7] sts from holder at other front armhole edge, 35[37, 39, 41, 43] sts up side of left cup, and then cast on a further 90 sts (again lengthen or shorten here)for other strap – 360[370, 382, 396, 406] sts. Knit 2 rows and then cast off knitwise. Cross straps at back and attach to outside edges of centre back cable. Decolletee can be adjusted by mattress stitching at centre front where cups meet.

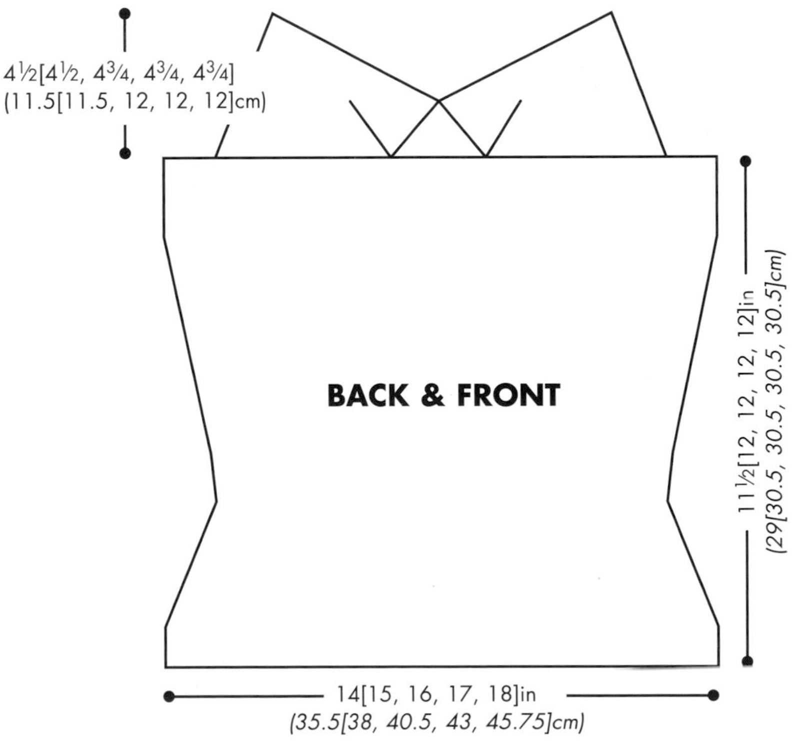


**Chart 2** **XS S M L XL**

# MIRANDA

Sculpted silk stitches with a seasonal sparkle make this an ideal party piece. If you prefer, knit the pattern monotone and trim with contrasting lurex shimmer to really glam it up!

## SIZES

XS – to fit bust 32in (81cm)
S – to fit bust 34in (86cm)
M – to fit bust 36in (91cm)
L – to fit bust 38in (96cm)
XL – to fit bust 40in (101cm)
See schematic for actual measurements.

## MATERIALS

Jaeger Silk 4-ply
186m/201yds per 50g ball:
Colour A – Tapestry (138)
5[5, 6, 6, 7] balls
Colour B – Jet (137) 1 ball
Colour C – Brilliant (144) 1 ball
Colour D – Midnight (136) 1 ball
Colour E – Cosmos (129) 1ball
Rowan Lurex Shimmer (trim)
Colour F – Claret (331) 1 ball
One pair each 3mm (US 3) and 2.75mm (US 2);
circular 3mm
28 sts and 38 rows = 4in (10cm) over st st.

## STITCHES USED

**Stocking stitch**
**Reverse stocking stitch**
**Welt pattern**
**Row 1** Knit in Colour B
**Row 2** Knit in Colour F
**Row 3** Knit in Colour C
**Row 4, 6 & 8** As row 2
**Row 5** Knit in Colour D
**Row 7** Knit in Colour E

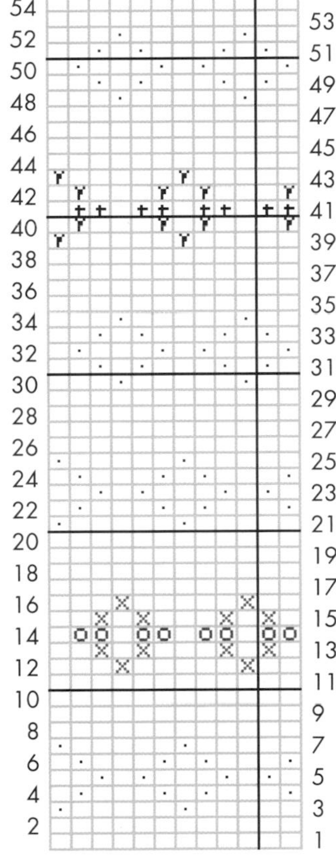


**12 sts rep**

## KEY TO CHART

MC Tapestry 138 (Colour A)
Reverse st st in MC (purl on RS and knit on WS)
Jet 137 (Colour B)
Brilliant 144 (Colour C)
Midnight 136 (Colour D)
Cosmos 129 (Colour E)

## Back

Using smaller needles and Colour A cast on 108[120, 132, 144, 156]sts. Knit 1 row in Colour F and then refer to welt patt and work the 8 rows. Change to larger needles and refer to chart and starting on chart row 1, rep the 54 rows to end of work. Set patt as foll:
**Row 1** Work the 12 sts of chart 9[10, 11, 12, 13] times.
**Row 2** Work the 12 sts of chart 9[10, 11, 12, 13] times.
AT THE SAME TIME dec 1 st at both ends of ev 8[8, 8, 9, 9]th row 5 times in all, keeping patt correct – 98[110, 122, 134, 146] sts. Work a further 10 rows in patt, then inc 1 st at both ends of next and ev foll 10[10, 10, 8,

9]th row 5 times in all, keeping patt correct – 108[120, 132, 144, 156] sts. Cont in patt as set until work measures 11½[11½, 11½, 11, 11½]in (29[29, 29, 28, 29]cm) from c.o.e ending on WS row

**Shape armhole**

Cast off 5[5, 7, 7, 7] sts at beg of next 2 rows, then dec 1 st at both ends of next and ev alt row 3[6, 10, 14, 18] times – 92[98, 98, 102, 106] sts.

AT THE SAME TIME when work measures 13½[13½, 14, 14, 14½]in (34.25[34.25, 35.5, 35.5, 37]cm) from c.o.e, ending on RS row, cease armhole shaping on left-hand side and start shaping neck edge on that side (whilst cont to dec armhole shaping at right-hand side if appropriate):

Cast off 5 sts firmly at neck edge on ev alt row 0[0, 0, 0, 1] times, then 4 sts firmly at neck edge on ev alt row 16[17, 17, 17, 20] times, then 3 sts firmly at neck edge ev alt row 0[4, 4, 4, 0] times, then dec 1 st at neck edge on ev row 10[0, 0, 0, 0] times. Cont on rem 18[18, 18, 22, 26] sts until work measures 19[19, 19½, 19½, 20]in (48.25[48.25, 49.5, 49.5, 52]cm) from c.o.e and then cast off.

## Front

Work as for back, reversing neckline shaping.

## Right Sleeve

Using smaller needles and Colour A cast on 60 sts. Knit 1 row in Colour F and then refer to welt patt and work the 8 rows. Change to larger needles and refer to chart and rep the 54 rows to end of work, starting on chart row 47[47, 43, 47, 47].

Set patt as foll:

**Row 1** Work the 12 sts of chart 5 times.

**Row 2** Work the 12 sts of chart 5 times.

Cont until work measures 5in (12.5cm) from c.o.e ending on WS row, then inc 1 st at both ends of next row, keeping patt correct as set, and then cont as foll:

**XS** inc ev foll 15th row once, then ev 14th row 7 times – 78 sts

**S** inc ev foll 13th row 5 times, then ev 12th row 4 times – 80 sts

**M** inc ev foll 10th row 10 times, then ev foll 9th row twice – 86 sts

**L** inc ev foll 8th row 6 times, then ev foll 7th row 10 times – 94 sts

**XL** inc ev foll 7th row 9 times, then ev foll 6th row 9 times – 98 sts

Cont in patt as set until work measures 18[18, 18½, 18½, 18½]in (45.75[45.75, 47, 47, 47]cm) from c.o.e ending on WS row.

**Shape sleeve cap**

Cast off 5[5, 7, 7, 7] sts at beg of next 2 rows, then dec 1 st at both ends of next row and then cont as foll:

**XS** dec ev foll 3rd row 11 times, then ev 2nd row 6 times – 32 sts

**S** dec ev foll 3rd row 9 times, then ev 2nd row 9 times – 32 sts

**M** dec ev foll 3rd row 7 times, then ev 2nd row 12 times – 32 sts

**L** dec ev foll 3rd row 7 times, then ev 2nd row 15 times – 34 sts

**XL** dec ev foll 3rd row 3 times, then ev 2nd row 21 times – 34 sts

Cast off 3 sts at beg of next 4 rows.

Cast off rem 20[20, 20, 22, 22] sts.

## Left Sleeve

Work as for right sleeve but cast off all sts when sleeve cap measures 2[2, 2½, 3, 3]in (5[5, 6.5, 7.5, 7.5]cm).

## Finishing

Insert sleeves.

Join side and sleeve seams in one line.

### NECKBAND

With right side facing and using 3mm circular needle and Colour A, starting at right shoulder seam, pick up and knit 84[90, 90, 90, 94] sts down back neck edge, 60[64, 68, 72, 76] sts across top of left sleeve and 84[90, 90, 90, 94] sts up front neck edge to shoulder seam – 228[244, 248, 252, 264] sts. Join into the round and work as foll:

**Row 1** Purl in Colour A

**Row 2** Knit in Colour F (doubled)

**Row 3** Purl in Colour A

**Row 4** Cast off knitwise in Colour F (doubled).

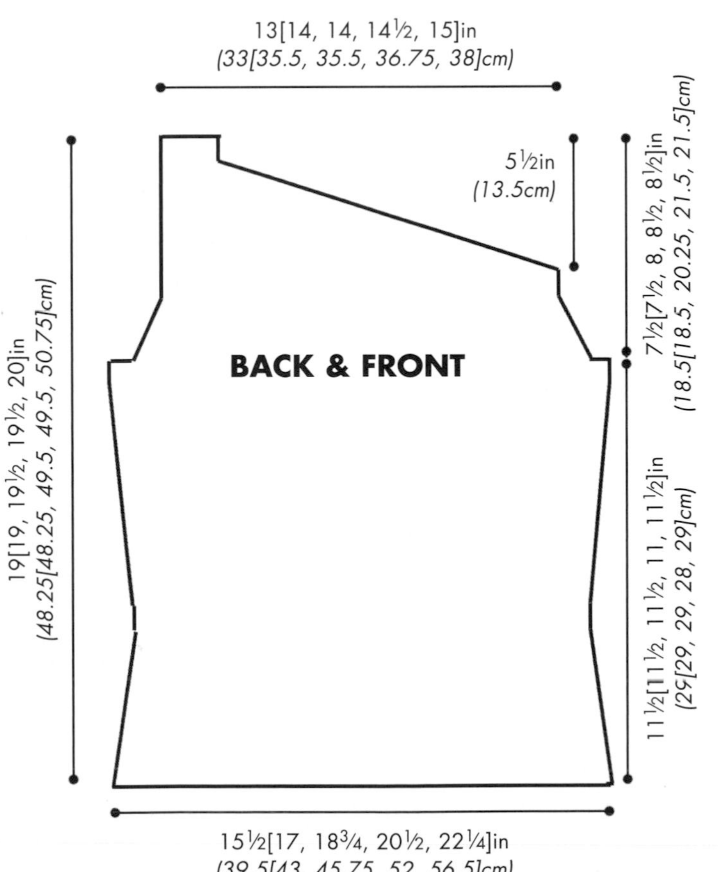
13[14, 14, 14½, 15]in
(33[35.5, 35.5, 36.75, 38]cm)
5½in
(13.5cm)
7½[7½, 8, 8½, 8½]in
(18.5[18.5, 20.25, 21.5, 21.5]cm)
19[19, 19½, 19½, 20]in
(48.25[48.25, 49.5, 49.5, 50.75]cm)
BACK & FRONT
11½[11½, 11½, 11, 11½]in
(29[29, 29, 28, 29]cm)
15½[17, 18¾, 20½, 22¼]in
(39.5[43, 45.75, 52, 56.5]cm)

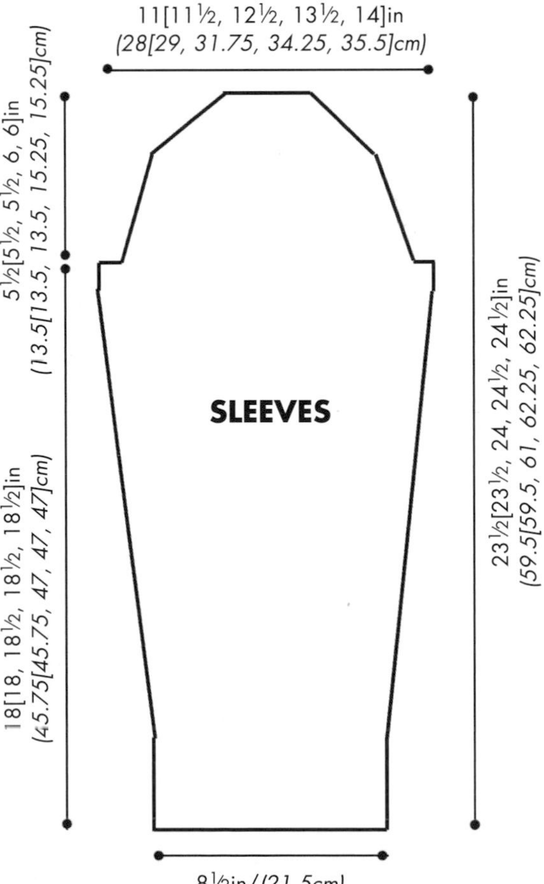
11[11½, 12½, 13½, 14]in
(28[29, 31.75, 34.25, 35.5]cm)
5½[5½, 5½, 6, 6]in
(13.5[13.5, 13.5, 15.25, 15.25]cm)
SLEEVES
18[18, 18½, 18½, 18½]in
(45.75[45.75, 47, 47, 47]cm)
23½[23½, 24, 24½, 24½]in
(59.5[59.5, 61, 62.25, 62.25]cm)
8½in/(21.5cm)

# PART 3
# DETAIL

# SALLY**ANNE**

Let your creativity run riot on the i-cord flower of this hat. Make it a big blowsy statement, a divine detail or, if you're an incorrigible extrovert, go for broke with a bouquet! The gloves are my own version of a versatile retro design that I've always loved.

## CLOCHE HAT

## SIZES

One size – to fit average size head 20in (51cm) circumference.

## MATERIALS

Artesano Alpaca
131yds (120m) per 50g ball:
2 balls Fuchsia (57) Colour A,
1 ball Damson (53) Colour B
One pair each 3.25mm (US 3); 3.75mm (US 5); or size to obtain tension
Holders and stitch markers

## TENSION

20 sts and 44 rows = 4in (10cm) over Brioche Rib

## STITCHES USED

**Garter stitch**

**Brioche rib**

Multiple of 2 sts

**Foundation row** Knit

**Row 1** *k1, k1below, rep from * to last 2 sts, k2

Repeat Row 1 throughout.

**I-cord** – see page 117.

### To make hat

Using smaller needles and Colour B, cast on 102 sts and work 8 rows in garter st.

**Next row** k3, *yarn over, k2tog, k2; rep from * to last 2 sts, k1

**Next row** purl

Work 6 more rows in garter st.

Change to larger needles and Colour A and refer to Brioche Rib and rep to end. When work measures 7¾in (19.5cm) from cast on edge ending on WS row **Shape crown**

**Row 1** work 7, slip 1, k2tog, psso, *work 14, slip 1, k2tog, psso; rep from * to last 7 sts, work 7 – 90 sts

**Rows 2, 3, 4** work in patt

**Row 5** work 6, slip 1, k2tog, psso, *work 12, slip 1, k2tog, psso; rep from * to last 6 sts, work 6 – 78 sts

**Rows 6, 7, 8** work in patt

**Row 9** work 5, slip 1, k2tog, psso, *work 10, slip 1, k2tog, psso; rep from * to last 5 sts, work 5 – 66 sts

**Rows 10, 11, 12** work in patt

**Row 13** work 4, slip 1, k2tog, psso, *work 8, slip 1, k2tog, psso; rep from * to last 4 sts, work 4 – 54 sts

**Rows 14, 15, 16** work in patt

**Row 17** work 3, slip 1, k2tog, psso, *work 6, slip 1, k2tog, psso; rep from * to last 3 sts, work 3 – 42 sts

**Rows 18, 19, 20** work in patt

**Row 21** work 2, slip 1, k2tog, psso, *work 4, slip 1, k2tog, psso; rep from * to last 2 sts, work 2 – 30 sts

**Rows 22, 23, 24** work in patt

**Row 25** work 1, slip 1, k2tog, psso, *work 2, slip 1, k2tog, psso; rep from * to last st, work 1 – 18 sts

**Row 26** work in patt

Break yarn, leaving enough to sew up hat and thread through rem sts.
Pull up tightly and secure.

### Finishing

Stitch back seam on inside from crown to ½in (1.25cm) above Col B, then stitch in outside to end so that when turned back the seam will be on the inside.

**Cord and flower**

Using Colour B and smaller needles, work 48in (122cm) of i-cord and then fasten off securely. Thread through eyelets, starting and finishing at position of flower on inside, as band will be turned back. Secure one end of i-cord to point at centre of flower and granny knot other end. Then fold and stitch the remainder into flower shape, finishing in centre with knot. Attach button or pin at centre if desired. Fold back bottom 2in (5cm) and stitch in place at back seam.

## GLOVES

### SIZES

Small – to fit small–medium hands
Large – to fit medium–large hands

### MATERIALS

Artesano Alpaca
131yds (120m) per 50g ball:
2[3] balls of Fucshia 57 (A)
1 ball of Damson 53 (B)
One pair 3.25mm (US 4); 4 double pointed 3.75mm (US 5); or size to obtain tension
Stitch holders and markers
4 x 12mm buttons

### TENSION

20 sts and 38 rows = 4in (10cm) over garter stitch
22 sts and 32 rows = 4in (10cm) over stocking stitch.

### STITCHES USED

**Garter stitch**
**Stocking stitch in the round**

### Left Glove

Using smaller needles and Colour B, cast on 39[51] sts and work 20 rows in garter st.
AT THE SAME TIME work buttonholes on rows 5 and 15:
Work to last 4 sts, cast off 2 sts, k2. Cast on these sts when you come to them on next row, knitting through backs of loops on foll row.
**Row 20** (WS) Cast off 3 sts at beg of row, knit to end.
Cont in garter st until work measures 3.5in (9cm) ending on RS row.
Change to larger needles (dpn), arrange the work evenly over three needles so that the bobbles (RS) are on the inside (RS then becomes WS) and cont working in st st in the round with Colour A to end, marking beg of round. When work measures 5½in (14cm) from c.o.e
**Shape thumb**
**Next round** K14[20], inc 1 in next st, k2 sts for thumb, inc 1 st in next st, k18[24]. Knit 1 round.
**Next round** K14[20], inc 1 in next st, k4 sts for thumb, inc 1 st in next st, k18[24]. Knit 1 round.
Cont as above inc 1 st in the same place at each of the points where you increased on the first round until you have 12[16] sts for thumb. Place these sts on holder. Knit a further 1¼ (3cm) on rem 34[46] sts then flatten knitting so that the root of the thumb is folded exactly down the middle and thumb lies on left side of the knitting.
**Shape Fingers**
Put all the stitches onto two st holders divided as foll:
Place 17[23] palm side sts on one holder, and 17[23] sts for the glove back on the other holder. Holders should open toward the thumb side.
**Index Finger**
Slip 5[7] sts from each holder onto separate dpns. Starting at the side edge, knit 5[7] sts, pick up and k2 sts from loops below last sts and first st on opposite side, knit 5[7] sts from the opposite side (12[16]sts). Knit around until finger measures 2½in (6.25cm) and then cast off by knitting 2 sts together until 1 st rem and fasten off.
**Middle Finger**
Slip the next 4[6] sts from both stitch holders onto seperate dpns. Starting next to the index finger, k4[6] sts, pick up 2[3] sts between index and middle fingers, k4[6] sts, pick-up 2 sts from the 2 picked up sts from the index finger (12[17]sts). Knit around until finger measures 3in (7.5cm) and then cast off by knitting 2 sts together until 1 st remains and fasten off.
**Ring Finger**
Slip 4[5] stitches from both holders onto 2 separate dpns. Starting next to middle finger, k4[5] sts, pick up 2[3] sts between middle and ring fingers, k4[5] from opposite-side, pick-up 2 sts from between ring and middle fingers (12[15]sts)Knit around until finger measures 2¾in (7cm) and then cast off by knitting 2 sts together until 1 st rem and fasten off.
**Little finger**
Slip 4[5] sts from each holder onto separate dpns. Starting next to ring finger, k4[5] sts, k4[5] sts from opposite-side, pick-up 2[3] sts between ring and little finger (10[13]sts).
Knit around until finger measures 2in (5cm) and then cast off by knitting 2 sts together until 1 st rem and fasten off.
**Thumb**
Place the 12[16] sts for thumb on needles and work 2¼in (5.75cm) then cast off by working decs as for index finger.

### Right Glove

Work as for left glove, reversing thumb, fingers, buttonholes and button positions.

### Finishing

Before you secure the ends of the thumb and fingers, try on your glove and make sure all the lengths are correct for you. You may need to add or delete a few rows. Bring the yarn tail to the inside of each digit, secure it and clip off excess yarn. Sew side seam on outside, so that the seam is on the inside when cuff is turned back. Attach two buttons opposite buttonholes.

# JESSICA

Chic and quick to knit, this sweater uses a short sharp burst of patterning at the hem and sleeve cap to create the zigzag edge. If you're a complete beginner, omit the scallops and replace them with a few rows of garter stitch.

## SIZES

XS – to fit bust 32in (81cm)
S – to fit bust 34in (86cm)
M – to fit bust 36in (91cm)
L – to fit bust 38in (96cm)
XL – to fit bust 40in (101cm).
See schematic for actual measurements.

## MATERIALS

Artesano Alpaca
131yds (120m) per 50g:
3[4, 5, 5, 6] balls Cream (000)
One pair each 3.25mm (US 3) and 3.75mm (US 5)]; circular 3.25mm (US 3) or size to obtain tension
Stitch holders

## TENSION

24 sts and 32 rows = 4in (10cm) over st st.

## STITCHES USED

**Stocking stitch**

**Scalloped stitch**

Multiple of 22 + 1

**Row 1** *k1, yo, k9, ssk, k9, yo, rep from * to last st, k1
**Row 2** p1 *p1, k19, p2, rep from * to end
**Row 3** *k2, yo, k8, ssk, k8, yo, k1, rep from * to last st, k1
**Row 4** p1, *p2, k17, p3, rep from * to end
**Row 5** *k3, yo, k7, ssk, k7, yo, k2, rep from * to last st, k1
**Row 6** p1, *p3, k15, p4, rep from * to end
**Row 7** *k4, yo, k6, ssk, k6, yo, k3, rep from * to last st, k1
**Row 8** p1, *p4, k13, p5, rep from * to end
**Row 9** *k5, yo, k5, ssk, k5, yo, k4, rep from * to last st, k1
**Row 10** p1, *p5, k11, p6, rep from * to end
**Row 11** *k6, yo, k4, ssk, k4, yo, k5, rep from * to last st, k1
**Row 12** p1, *p6, k9, p7, rep from * to end
**Row 13** *k7, yo, k3, ssk, k3, yo, k6, rep from * to last st, k1
**Row 14** p1, *p7, k7, p8, rep from * to end
**Row 15** *k8, yo, k2, ssk, k2, yo, k7, rep from * to last st, k1
**Row 16** p1, *p8, k5, p9, rep from * to end
**Row 17** *k9, yo, k1, ssk, k1, yo, k8, rep from * to last st, k1
**Row 18** p1, *p9, k3, p10, rep from * to end
**Row 19** *k10, yo, ssk, yo, k9, rep from * to last st, k1
**Row 20** purl

### Back

Using larger needles cast on 89[89, 89, 111, 111] sts and knit 2 rows. Refer to Scalloped st and work the 20 rows. Cont to end in stocking st, inc 1 st at both ends of ev 18[9, 6, 26, 10]th row 3[6, 9, 2, 5] times – 95[101, 107, 115, 121] sts. Cont as set until work measures11[11, 11½, 11½, 11]in (28[28, 29.25, 29.95, 28]cm) from c.o.e.

**Shape armhole**

Cast off 5[5, 5, 6, 6] sts at beg of next 2 row dec 1 st at both ends of ev row 0[2, 2, 4, 4] times, then ev alt row 8[7, 9, 8, 10] times – 69[73, 75, 79, 81] sts.
Leave these sts on holder.

### Front

Work as for back.

### Finishing

Join side seams.

ARMHOLE FACING

Using smaller straight needles, with RS facing, pick up and knit 17[17, 20, 22, 24] sts down to side seam and 17[17, 20, 22, 24] sts up other side – 34[34, 40, 44, 48] sts. Cast off these sts.

SLEEVES

Using larger straight needles, cast on 45 sts and knit 2 rows. Leave on holder. Make 2.

COLLAR

Using circular needle, with RS facing, pick up and knit 45 sts from sleeve holder, 69[73, 75, 79, 81] sts from front holder, 45 sts from other sleeve holder and 69[73, 75, 79, 81] sts from back holder – 228[236, 240, 248, 252] sts. Working in the round, work 26 rounds as foll:

**Round 1** *k1, yo, k9, ssk, k9, yo,

rep from * once, k1, (p1, k1)] 34[36, 37, 39, 40] times, p1, **k1, yo, k9, ssk, k9, yo, rep from ** once, k1, (p1, k1)34[36, 37, 39, 40] times, p1
**Round 2** *k1, p1, p19, p1, rep from * once, k1, (p1, k1) 34[36, 37, 39, 40] times, p1, **k1, p1, p19, p1, rep from ** once, k1, (p1, k1) 34[36, 37, 39, 40] times, p1
**Round 3** *k1, p1, yo, k8, ssk, k8, yo, p1, rep from * once, k1, (p1, k1) 34[36, 37, 39, 40] times, p1, **k1, p1, yo, k8, ssk, k8, yo, p1, rep from ** once, k1, (p1, k1) 34[36, 37, 39, 40] times, p1
**Round 4** *k1, p1, k1, p17, k1, p1, rep from * once, k1, (p1, k1) 34[36, 37, 39, 40] times, p1, **k1, p1, k1, p17, k1, p1, rep from ** once, k1, (p1, k1) 34[36, 37, 39, 40] times, p1
**Round 5** *kRow, k1, yo, k7, ssk, k7, yo, k1, p1, rep from * once, k1, (p1, k1) 34[36, 37, 39, 40] times, p1, **k1, p1, k1, yo, k7, ssk, k7, yo, k1, p1, rep from ** once, k1 (p1, k1) 34[36, 37, 39, 40] times, p1
**Round 6** *k1, p1, k1, p1, p15, p1, k1, p1, rep from * once, k1, (p1, k1) 34[36, 37, 39, 40] times, p1, **k1, p1, k1, p1, p15, p1, k1, p1, rep from ** once, k1 (p1, k1) 34[36, 37, 39, 40] times, p1
**Round 7** *k1, p1, k1, p1, yo, k6, ssk, k6, yo, p1, k1, p1, rep from * once, k1, (p1, k1) 34[36, 37, 39, 40] times, p1, **k1, p1, k1, p1, yo, k6, ssk, k6, yo, p1, k1, p1, rep from ** once, k1, (p1, k1) 34[36, 37, 39, 40] times, p1
**Round 8** *k1, p1, k1, p1, k1, p13, k1, p1, k1 p1, rep from * once, k1, (p1, k1) 34[36, 37, 39, 40] times, p1, *k1, p1, k1, p1, k1, p13, k1, p1, k1 p1, rep from * once, k1, (p1, k1) 34[36, 37, 39, 40] times, p1
**Round 9** *k1, p1, k1, p1, k1, yo, k5, ssk, k5, yo, k1, p1, k1, p1, rep from * once, k1, (p1, k1) 34[36, 37, 39, 40] times, p1, **k1, p1, k1, p1, k1, yo, k5, ssk, k5, yo, k1, p1, k1, p1, rep from ** once, k1, (p1, k1) 34[36, 37, 39, 40] times, p1
**Round 10** *k1, p1, k1, p1, k1, p1, p11, p1, k1, p1, k1, p1, rep from * once, k1, (p1, k1) 34[36, 37, 39, 40] times, p1, **k1, p1, k1, p1, k1, p1, p11, p1, k1, p1, k1, p1, rep from ** once, k1, (p1, k1) 34[36, 37, 39, 40] times, p1
**Round 11** *k1, p1, k1, p1, k1, p1, yo, k4, ssk, k4, yo, p1, k1, p1, k1, p1, rep from * once, k1, (p1, k1) 34[36, 37, 39, 40] times, p1, **k1, p1, k1, p1, k1, p1, yo, k4, ssk, k4, yo, p1, k1, p1, k1, p1, rep from ** once, k1 (p1, k1) 34[36, 37, 39, 40] times, p1
**Round 12** *k1, p1, k1, p1, k1, p1, k1, p9, k1, p1, k1, p1, k1, p1, rep from * once, k1, (p1, k1) 34[36, 37, 39, 40] times, p1, **k1, p1, k1, p1, k1, p1, k1, p9, k1, p1, k1, p1, k1, p1, rep from ** once, k1 (p1, k1) 34[36, 37, 39, 40] times, p1
**Round 13** *k1, p1, k1, p1, k1, p1, k1, yo, k3, ssk, k3, yo, k1, p1, k1, p1, k1, p1, rep from * once, k1, (p1, k1) 34[36, 37, 39, 40] times, p1, **k1, p1, k1, p1, k1, p1, k1, yo, k3, ssk, k3, yo, k1, p1, k1, p1, k1, p1, rep from ** once, k1, (p1, k1) 34[36, 37, 39, 40] times, p1
**Round 14** *k1, p1, k1, p1, k1, p1, k1, p1, p7, p1, k1, p1, k1, p1, k1, p1, rep from * once, k1, (p1, k1) 34[36, 37, 39, 40] times, p1, **k1, p1, k1, p1, k1, p1, k1,p1, p7, p1, k1, p1, k1, p1, k1, p1, rep from ** once, k1 (p1, k1) 34[36, 37, 39, 40] times, p1
**Round 15** *k1, p1, k1, p1, k1, p1, k1, p1, yo, k2, ssk, k2, yo, p1, k1, p1, k1, p1, k1, p1, rep from * once, k1, (p1, k1) 34[36, 37, 39, 40] times, p1, **k1, p1, k1, p1, k1, p1, k1, p1, yo, k2, ssk, k2, yo, p1, k1, p1, k1, p1, k1, p1, rep from ** once, k1, (p1, k1) 34[36, 37, 39, 40] times, p1
**Round 16** *k1, p1, k1, p1, k1, p1, k1, p1, k1, p5, k1, p1, k1, p1, k1, p1, k1, p1, rep from * once, k1, (p1, k1) 34[36, 37, 39, 40] times, p1, **k1, p1, k1, p1, k1, p1, k1, p1, k1, p5, k1, p1, k1, p1, k1, p1, k1, p1, rep from ** once, k1, (p1, k1) 34[36, 37, 39, 40] times, p1
**Round 17** *k1, p1, k1, p1, k1, p1, k1, p1, k1, yo, k1, ssk, k1, yo, k1, p1, k1, p1, k1, p1, k1, p1, rep from * once, k1, (p1, k1) 34[36, 37, 39, 40] times, p1, **k1, p1, k1, p1, k1, p1, k1, p1, k1, yo, k1, ssk, k1, yo, k1, p1, k1, p1, k1, p1, k1, p1, rep from ** once, k1, (p1, k1) 34[36, 37, 39, 40] times, p1
**Round 18** *k1, p1, k1, p1, k1, p1, k1, p1, k1, p1, p3, p1, k1, p1, k1, p1, k1, p1, k1, p1, rep from * once, k1, (p1, k1) 34[36, 37, 39, 40] times, p1, **k1, p1, k1, p1, k1, p1, k1, p1, k1, p1, p3, p1, k1, p1, k1, p1, k1, p1, k1, p1, rep from ** once, k1, (p1, k1) 34[36, 37, 39, 40] times, p1
**Round 19** * k1, p1, k1, p1, k1, p1, k1, p1, k1, p1, yo, ssk, yo, p1, k1, p1, k1, p1, k1, p1, k1, p1, rep from * once, k1, (p1, k1) 34[36, 37, 39, 40] times, p1, ** k1, p1, k1, p1, k1, p1, k1, p1, k1, p1, yo, ssk, yo, p1, k1, p1, k1, p1, k1, p1, k1, p1, rep from ** once, k1, (p1, k1) 34[36, 37, 39, 40] times, p1
**Rounds 20–26** k1, p1 rib around
Cast off.

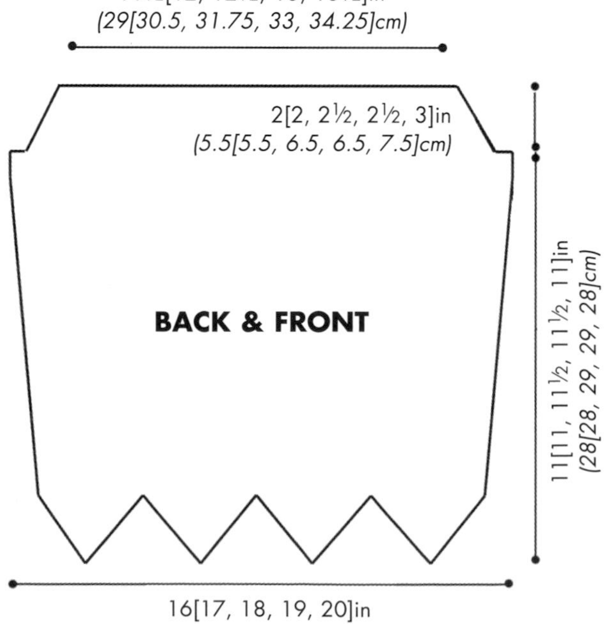

# ISOBELLA

If intarsia is not your bag, add sparkle by working the chevrons in red, silver, gold or crystal beads. For extra glamour, work them into the picot point cast off too.

## SIZES

XS – to fit bust 32–34in (81–86cm)
S – to fit bust 34–36in (86–91cm)
M – to fit bust 36–38in (91–96cm)
L – to fit bust 38–40in (96–101cm)

## MATERIALS

Rowan Wool Cotton
123yds (113m) per 50g ball:
11[12, 12, 13] balls of Colour A
Rowan Lurex Shimmer: 104yds (95m) per 25g ball: 1[1, 1, 1, 1] ball of Colour B
3 mm (US 3); 3.75 mm (US 5); cable needle, stitch holders and markers, 7 buttons

## STITCHES USED

**Stocking stitch**
**Reverse stocking stitch**
**Cables**

## KEY TO CHARTS

- Knit on right side and purl on wrong side in Colour A
- Purl on right side and knit on wrong side in Colour A
- Slip 1 st onto cn and hold at back, k1, then knit 1 from cn
- Slip 1 st onto cn and hold at front, k1, then k1 from cn
- Slip 1 st onto cn and hold at back, k1, then p1 from cn
- Slip 1 st onto cn and hold at front, p1, then k1 from cn
- Slip 2 sts onto cn and hold at back, k1 then p2 from cn

## COLOUR KEY

- Colour A Inky (908)
- Colour B Claret (331)

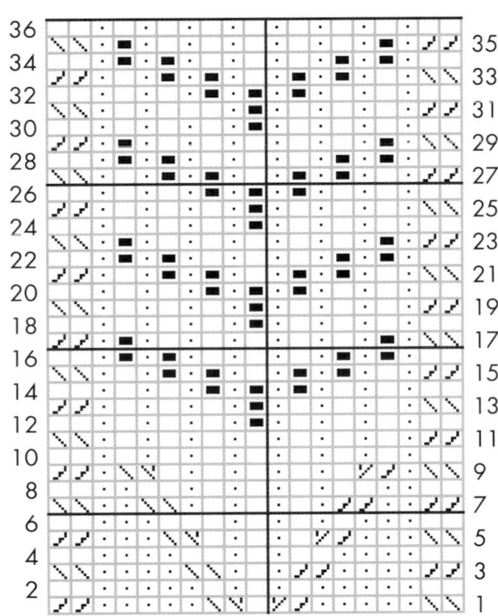

**Chart 2 (19 sts)**

## TENSION

28 sts and 32 rows = 4in (10cm) over rows 23–74 of chart
7 buttons

**Intarsia Knitting**
(See page 122)

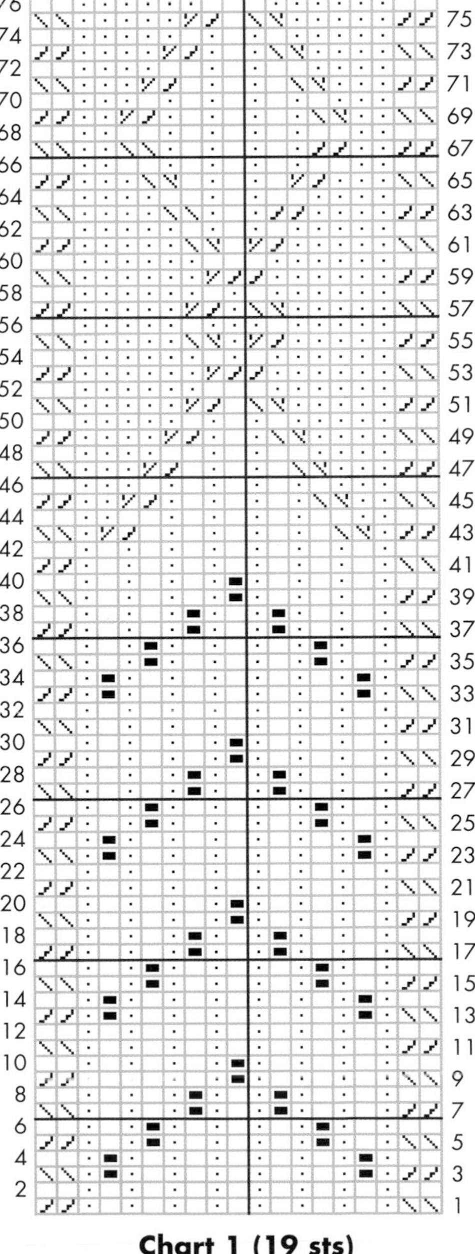

**Chart 1 (19 sts)**

**Back**

Using smaller needles and Colour A, cast on 133[141, 147, 155] sts and refer to chart 1 and work 2[2, 6, 6] rows, omitting the coloured zigzag thus: work rows 3 and 4 for sizes XS and S and rows 3, 4, 1, 2, 3 and 4 for sizes M and L, then work the first 42 row inc the coloured zigzag – 44[44, 48, 48] rows in total:

Work the last 9[13, 16, 2] sts of chart, repeat the 19 sts of chart 6 times across row, work the first 10[14, 17, 21] sts of chart.

Change to larger needles and cont with chart 1, working rows 43 to 76 and then repeating rows 53–76 twice more and then rows 53–60 once – 134[134, 138, 138] rows.

AT THE SAME TIME commencing on row 111[109, 111, 109]

**Shape armhole**

Keeping pattern correct as set:

Cast off 7 sts at beg of next 2 rows. Then dec 1 st at both ends of next and ev foll row 0[4, 6, 10 ], then ev foll alt row 10[9, 9, 8] times, keeping patt correct – 99[101, 103, 105] sts.

AT THE SAME TIME commence chart 2 on row 135[135, 139, 139] and work the 36 rows to end - 170[170, 174, 174] rows.

**Shape neck and shoulder**

Starting on row166[166, 170, 170] work 33sts, place centre 33[35, 37, 39] sts on holder, join a second ball of yarn and work to end. Working both sides

AT THE SAME TIME dec 1 st at both neck edges on next and foll alt row.

AT THE SAME TIME cast off 10 sts at armhole edge on row 167[167, 171, 171] for left back neck it will be row 168[168, 172, 172] and 10 sts on foll alt row. Work 1 row and then cast off the rem 11 sts.

**Left Front**

Using smaller needles and Colour A, cast on 67[71, 74, 78] sts and refer to chart 1 and work 2[2, 6, 6] rows, omitting the coloured zigzag thus: work rows 3 and 4 for sizes XS and S and rows 3, 4, 1, 2, 3 and 4 for sizes M and L, then work the first 42 rows including the coloured zigzag –

44[44,48, 48] rows in total:

**RS rows** Work the last 9[13, 16, 20] sts of chart, repeat the 19 sts of chart 3 times across row, p1.

**WS rows** K1, repeat the 19 sts of chart 3 times across row, work the first 9[13, 16, 20] sts.

Change to larger needles and cont with chart 1 as set, working rows 43 to 76 and then rep rows 53 – 76 twice more and then rows 53 – 60 once – 134[134, 138, 138] rows.

**Shape neckline** starting on row 107[105, 107, 105], keeping patt correct as set:

Dec 1 st at neck edge, by working together the 4th and 5th sts in from neck edge (keeping the zigzag running up the neck edge) on next and ev 3rd row 19[20, 21, 22] times.

**Shape armhole**

Starting on row 111[109, 111, 109], keeping patt correct as set:

Cast off 7 sts at beg of next row. Work 1 row. Then dec 1 st at armhole edge of next and ev foll row 0[4, 6, 10] times, then ev foll alt row 10[9, 9, 8] times, keeping patt correct.

AT THE SAME TIME commence chart 2 on row 135[135, 139, 139] and work the 36 rows to end.

**Shape shoulder**

Starting on row 167[167, 171, 171]: cast off 10 sts at armhole edge. Work 1 row. Cast off 10 sts on foll row. Work 1 row. Cast off rem 11sts.

**Right Front**

Work as for Left Front reversing all shapings. Charts should read:

**RS rows** p1, rep the 19 sts of chart 3 times across row, work the first 9[13, 16, 20] sts

**WS rows** Work the last 9[13, 16, 20] sts of chart, rep the 19 sts of chart 3 times across row, k1

**Sleeves**

Using smaller needles and Colour A, cast on 57 sts and refer to chart 1 and work 42 rows rep the 19 sts of chart 3 times across row. Change to larger needles and cont with chart 1, working rows 43 to 76 and then rep rows 53–76 to end of sleeve. Inc 1 st at both ends of row 43 and then ev 3rd row 3[7, 11, 19] times, then ev 4th row 17[14, 12, 6] times, until there are 99[101, 105, 109] sts. Work all the inc sts subsequently in rev st st.

When work measures 16[16, 16½, 16½]in (40.5[40.5, 42, 42]cm) from c.o.e. ending on WS row

**Shape sleeve cap**

Cast off 7 sts at beg of next 2 rows. Then dec 1 st at both ends of next and ev row 16[18, 22, 26) times, then ev alt row 13[12, 10, 8] times. Cast off 3 sts at beg of next 4 rows. Cast off rem 15 sts. **NB** Try to end on a cable crossing row.

**Finishing**

Join shoulder seams.

BAND (worked in one piece)

Mark position of 7 buttonholes on right front: first to start ¼in (6mm) from bottom, the last to finish at point where v-neck starts and the others spaced evenly between.

Using circular 3mm needle and Colour A, but knitting back and forth with RS facing and starting at right front bottom edge, pick up and knit 80[78, 80, 78] sts evenly to start of neck shaping, 51[53, 54, 57] sts up to shoulder seam, 2 sts down back neck edge, 33[35, 37, 39] sts across back neck, 2 sts up back neck edge, 51[53, 54, 57] sts down left neck edge and 80[78, 80, 78] sts down left side edge to bottom – 299[301, 309, 313] sts.

**NB** Each time you reach a point which corresponds to marker for button, work buttonhole on right front as foll: cast on 2 sts using backward loop method (see page 115), leave corresponding space and then cont picking up and knitting sts as above.

Knit 1 row, then cast off using picot point method:

Cast off 2 sts, *slip rem st on RH needle onto LH needle, cast on 2 sts, cast off 4 sts; repeat from * to end and fasten off rem st.

Attach 7 buttons directly opposite buttonholes. Take care that the patt lines up symmetrically across the sweater.

Set in sleeves, easing any fullness evenly across top of cap. Sew side and sleeve seams in one line.

Sew buttons opposite buttonholes.

5¾[6, 6¼, 6½]in (14.5[15.25, 16, 16.5]cm)
4¼in (10.75cm)
½in (1.25cm)
½in (1.25cm)
20¾[20¾, 21¼, 21¼]in (52.5[52.5, 54, 54]cm)
7½[7¾, 8, 8¼]in (18.5[19.5, 20.25, 21]cm)
BACK
8¼[8, 7¾, 7½]in (21[20.25, 19.5, 18.5]cm)
5½[5½, 6, 6]in (13.5[13.5, 15.25, 15.25]cm)
19[20, 21, 22]in (48.25[50.75, 53.5, 55.75]cm)


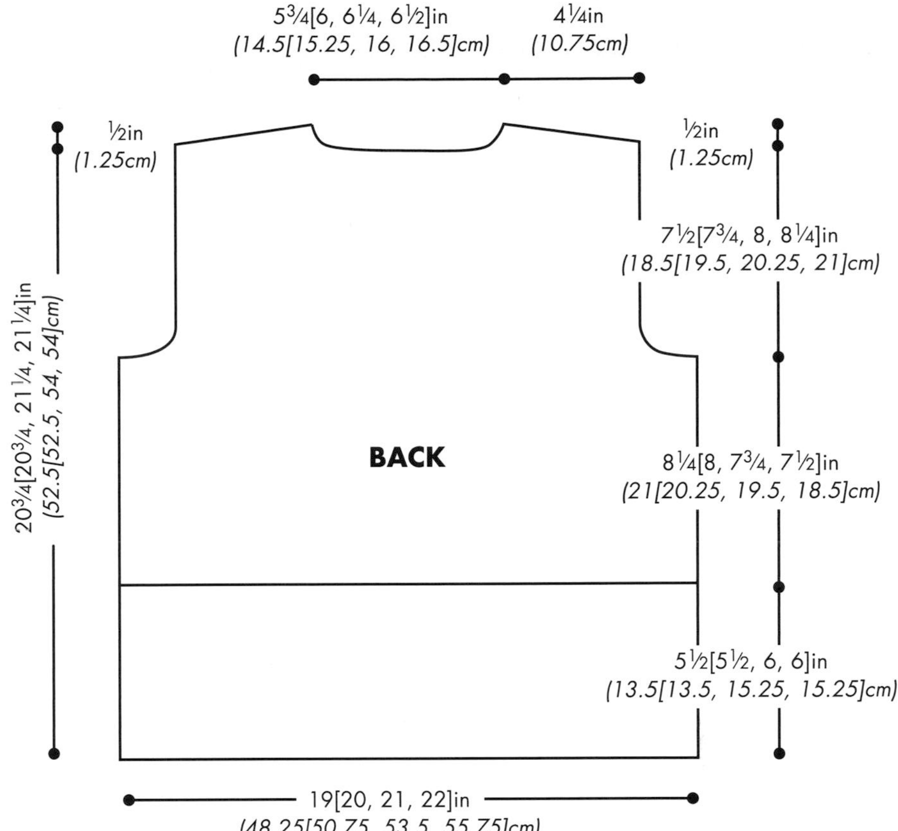

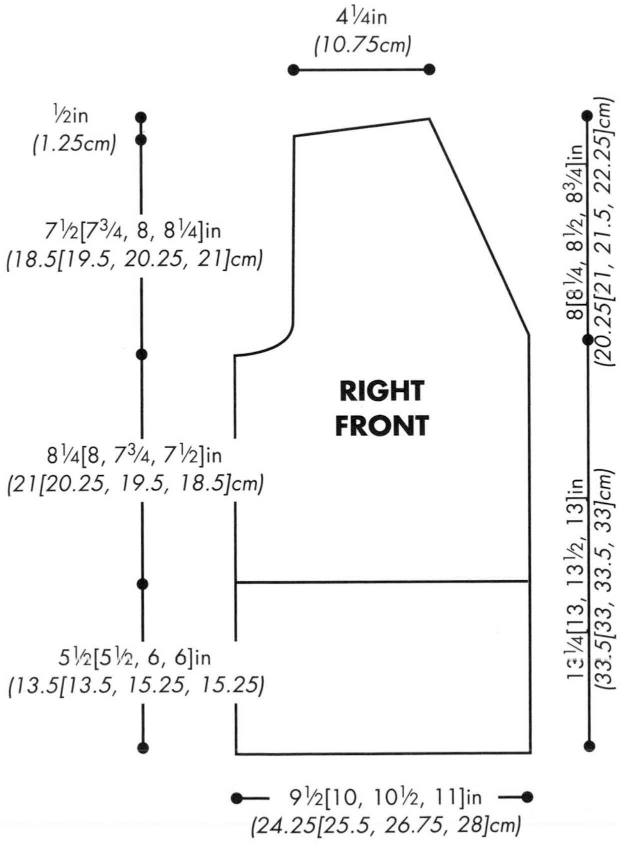

4¼in (10.75cm)
½in (1.25cm)
7½[7¾, 8, 8¼]in (18.5[19.5, 20.25, 21]cm)
RIGHT FRONT
8[8¼, 8½, 8¾]in (20.25[21, 21.5, 22.25]cm)
8¼[8, 7¾, 7½]in (21[20.25, 19.5, 18.5]cm)
13¼[13, 13½, 13]in (33.5[33, 33.5, 33]cm)
5½[5½, 6, 6]in (13.5[13.5, 15.25, 15.25)
9½[10, 10½, 11]in (24.25[25.5, 26.75, 28]cm)


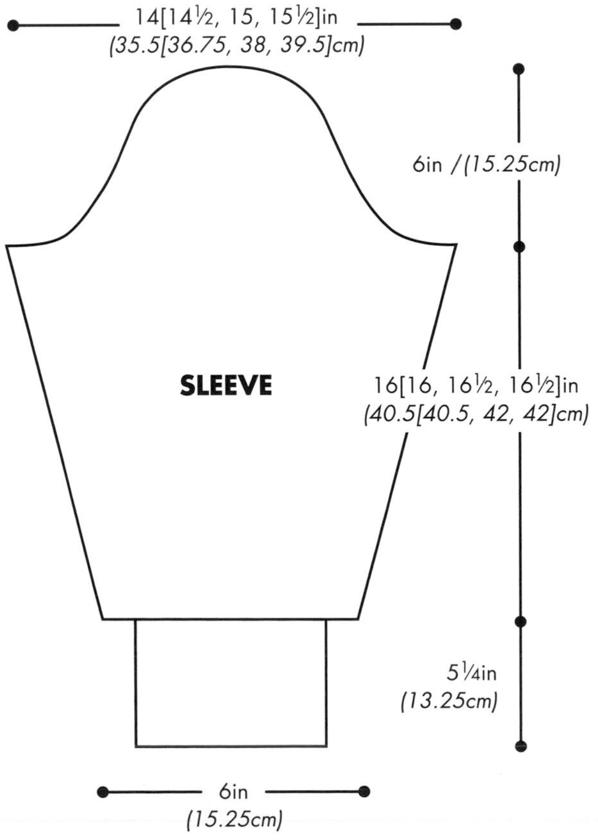

14[14½, 15, 15½]in (35.5[36.75, 38, 39.5]cm)
6in /(15.25cm)
SLEEVE
16[16, 16½, 16½]in (40.5[40.5, 42, 42]cm)
5¼in (13.25cm)
6in (15.25cm)

# IMOGEN

This glittering jacket is a new take on Elizabethan costume. The textured diagonal pattern creates a dynamic and flattering shape, emphasized by the i-cord trim. Choose contrasting lurex for extra glitz.

## SIZES

XS – to fit bust 32in (81cm)
S – to fit bust 34in (86cm)
M – to fit bust 36in (91cm)
L – to fit bust 38in (96cm)
XL – to fit bust 40in (101cm). See schematic for actual measurements.

## MATERIALS

Rowan Kid Classic
153yds (140m) per 50g ball
Lurex Shimmer
104yds (95m) per 25g ball:
8[8, 9, 9, 10] balls
A Kid Crystal (840)
3[3, 3, 4, 4] 25g
B *Lurex Pewter (333)
***Use Lurex Shimmer DOUBLE throughout**
1 pair 4.5mm (US 7) needles
2 double-pointed 4.5mm (US 7) needles
3mm (US d/3) crochet hook
Cable needle
6 buttons

## TENSION

20 sts and 30 rows to 4in (10cm) over moss stitch.

## STITCHES USED

**Stocking stitch**
**Reverse stocking stitch**
**Cables**
**Moss stitch**

### Back

Cast on 104[108, 114, 118, 124] sts using 4.5mm (US 7) needles and yarn A.
Starting and ending rows as indicated, cont in patt from chart for back as folls:
Dec 1 st at each end of 7th and ev foll 4th row until 86[90, 96, 100, 106] sts rem.
Work 9 rows, ending after chart row 48 and with a WS row.
**Row 49** (RS): Patt 41[43, 46, 48, 51] sts, slip next knit 4 sts onto a holder and, in their place, pick up and knit
4 sts from behind these sts, patt to end. 86[90, 96, 100, 106] sts.
Join in yarn B.
Using the fairisle 2-colour stranded technique (see page 121), cont in patt from chart, working rows 50 to 74 once only and then rep rows 75 to 78 throughout (these 4 rows form 2 colour moss st) until back measures 14½[15, 15, 15¼, 15¼]in (37[38, 38, 39, 39] cm), ending with a WS row.

**Shape armholes**
Keeping patt correct, cast off 4[5, 5, 6, 6] sts at beg of next 2 rows, 78[80, 86, 88, 94] sts.
Dec 1 st at each end of next 1[1, 3, 3, 5] rows, then on foll 3 alt rows, 70[72, 74, 76, 78] sts.
Cont straight until armhole measures 7½[7½, 8, 8, 8¼]in (19[19, 20, 20, 21]cm), ending with a WS row.

**Shape shoulders**
Cast off 6[7, 7, 7, 8] sts at beg of next 4 rows, then 7[6, 7, 8, 7] sts at beg of foll 2 rows.
Leave rem 32 sts on a holder.

### Left Front

Cast on 52[54, 57, 59, 62] sts using 4.5mm (US 7) needles and yarn A.
Starting and ending rows as indicated and rep the 10 row patt repeat, cont

## BACK CHART

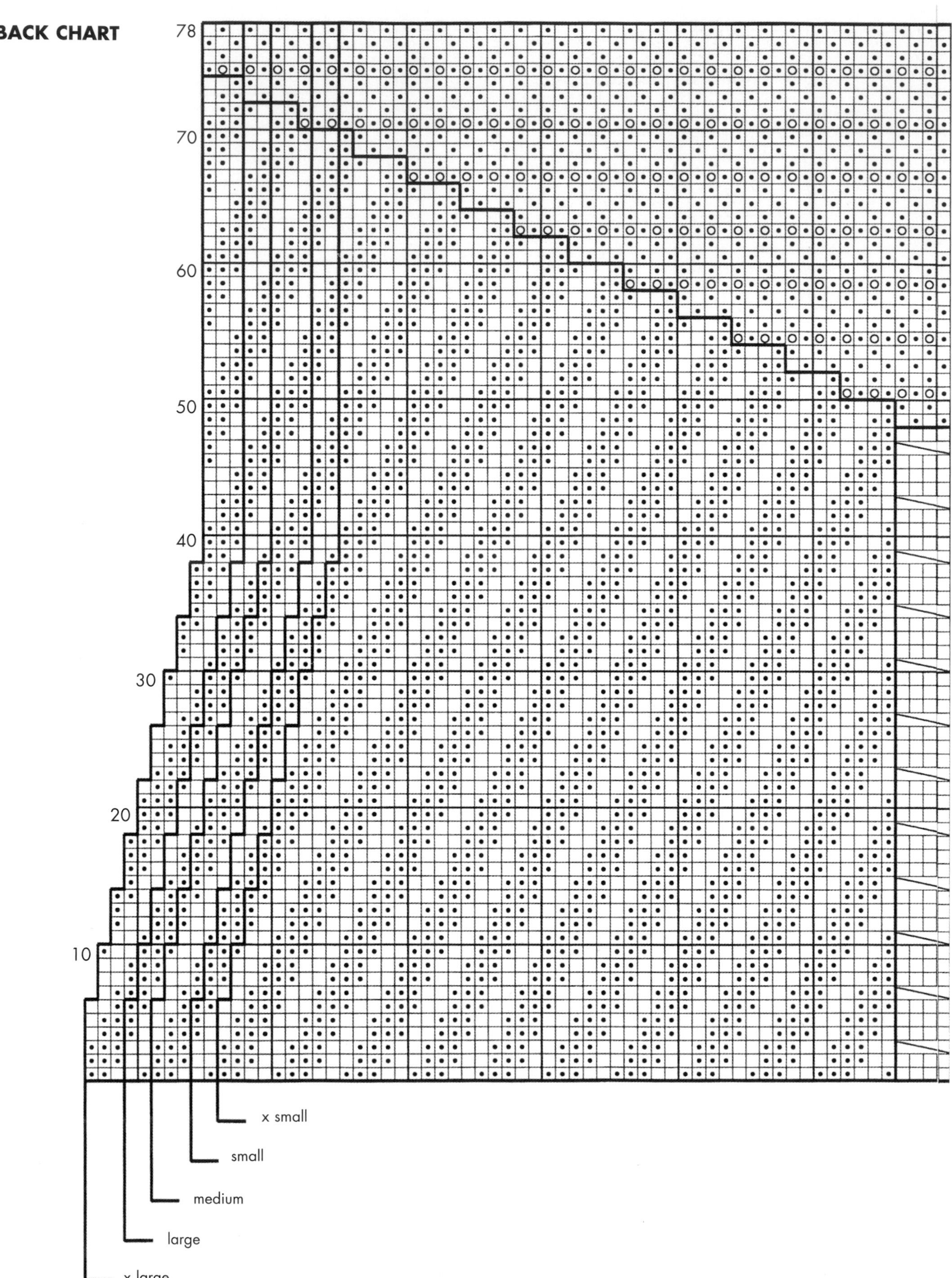

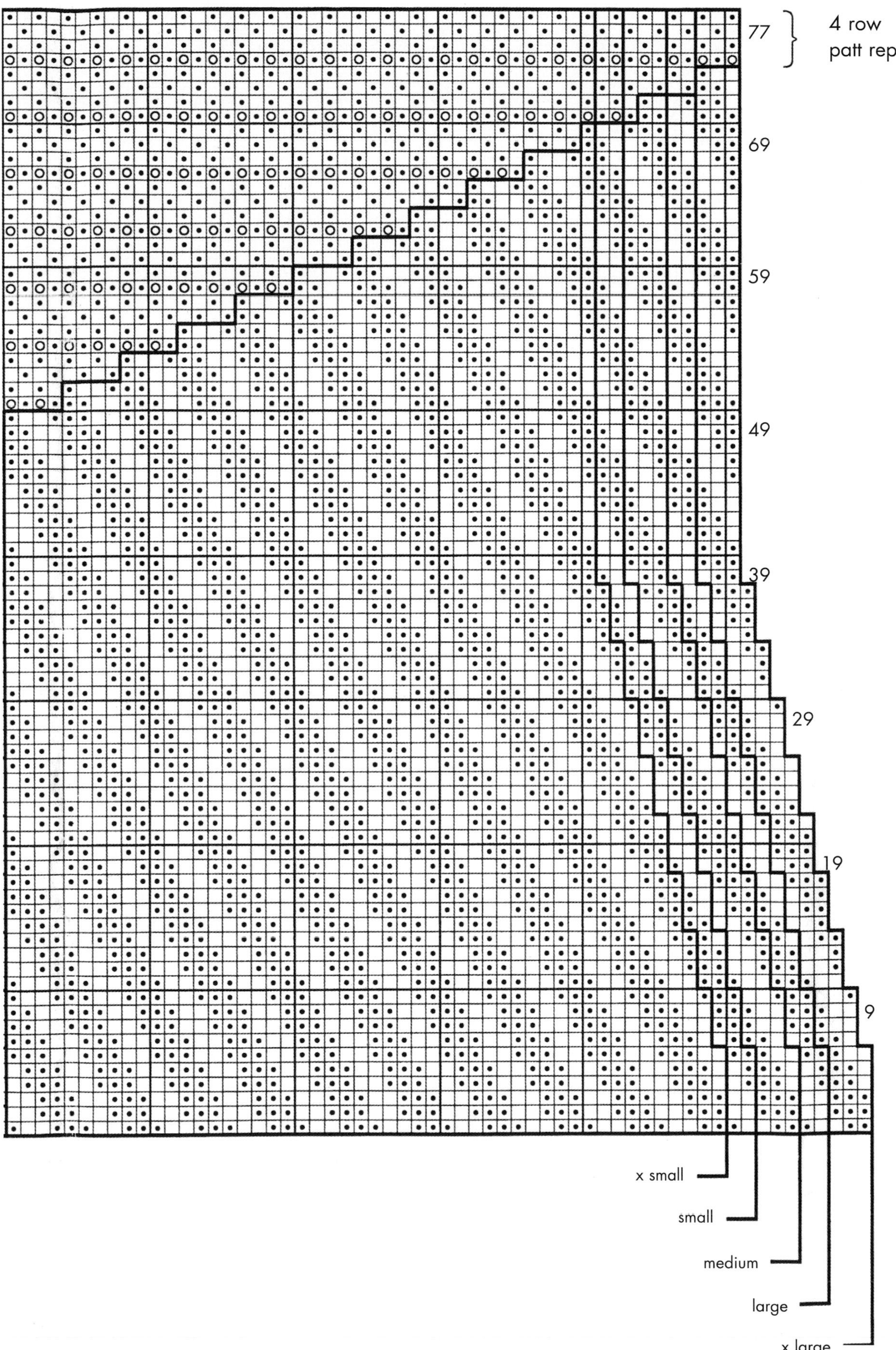
77
4 row
patt rep
69
59
49
39
29
19
9
x small
small
medium
large
x large

## SLEEVE CHART

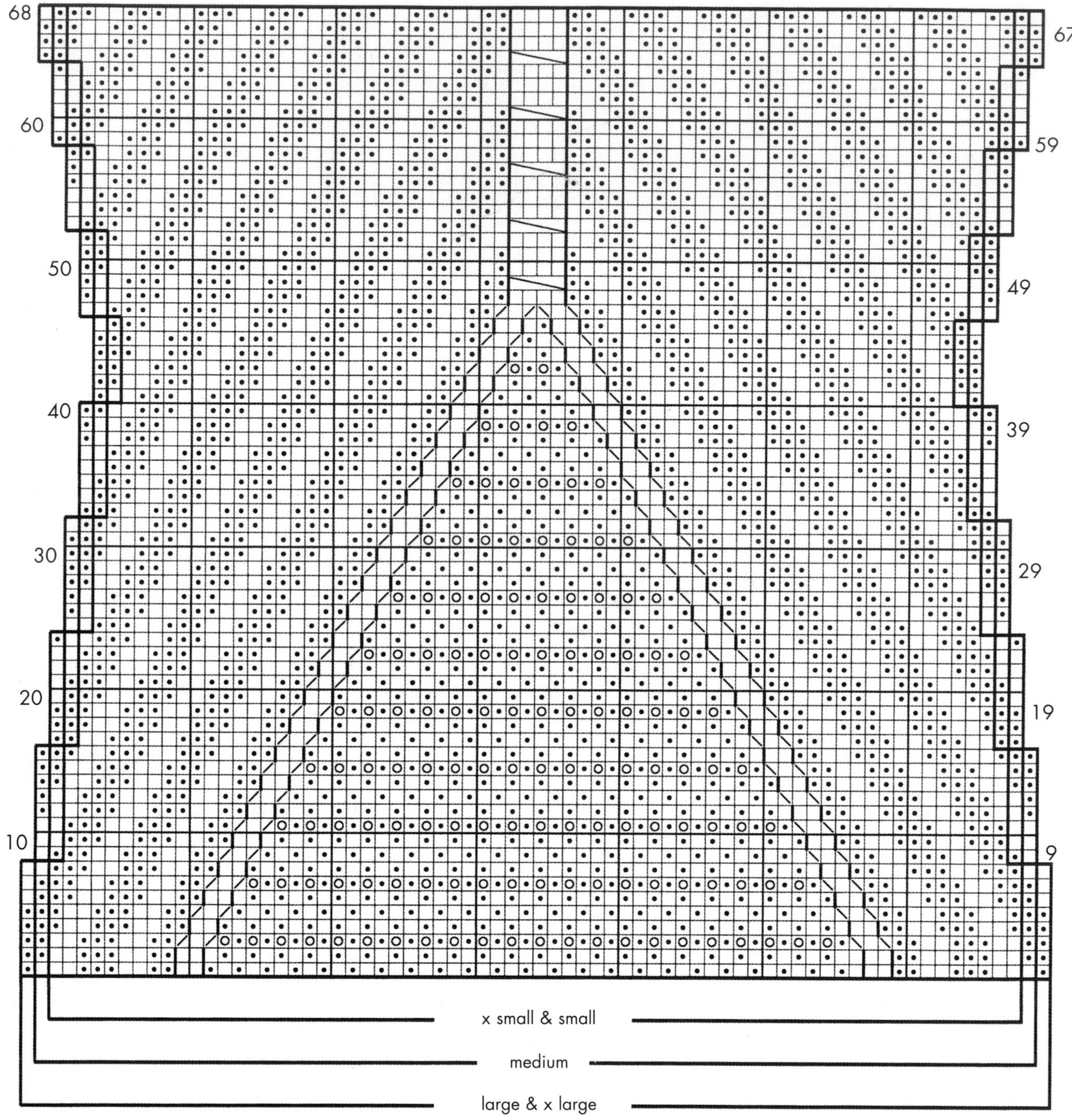


## KEY

| | | | |
|---|---|---|---|
| □ | Using A, k on RS, p on WS | | C4F (over 4 sts) – slip next 2 sts onto cn and leave at front of work, k2, then k2 from cn |
| ⊡ | Using A, p on WS, k on WS | | Cr3L (over 3 sts) – slip next 2 sts onto cn and leave at front of work, p1, then k2 from cn |
| ◙ | Using B, k on RS, p on WS | | Cr3R (over 3 sts) – slip next st onto cn and leave at back of work, k2, then p1 from cn |

in chevron patt from chart for lower left front as folls:
Dec 1 st at beg of 7th and ev foll 4th row until 43[45, 48, 50, 53] sts rem.
Work 33[33, 35, 35, 37] rows, ending with a WS row.
Join in yarn B.
Using the 2-colour stranded technique (see page 121) and keeping centre front sts correct in chevron patt, cont in patt from chart for middle left front, working rows 1 to 24 once only and then rep rows 25 to 28 throughout (these 4 rows form 2 colour moss st) until left front matches back to beg of armhole shaping, ending with a WS row.

**Shape armhole**

Keeping side edge sts correct in 2 colour moss st patt as set, working rows 1 to 32 once only and then rep rows 33 to 42 throughout, cont in patt from chart for upper left front as foll:
Cast off 4[5, 5, 6, 6] sts at beg of next row – 39[40, 43, 44, 47] sts.
Work 1 row. Dec 1 st at armhole edge of next 1[1, 3, 3, 5] rows, then on foll 3 alt rows 35[36, 37, 38, 39] sts.
Cont straight until left front matches back to start of shoulder shaping, ending with a WS row.

**Shape shoulder**

Cast off 6[7, 7, 7, 8] sts at beg of next and foll alt row, then 7[6, 7, 8, 7] sts at beg of foll alt row.
Work 1 row, ending with a WS row.
Leave rem 16 sts on a holder.

## Right Front

Cast on 52[54, 57, 59, 62] sts using 4.5mm (US 7) needles and yarn A.
Starting and ending rows as indicated and rep the 10 row rep, cont in chevron patt from chart for lower right front as foll:
Dec 1 st at end of 7th and ev foll 4th row until 43[45, 48, 50, 53] sts rem.
Complete to match left front, reversing shapings and foll charts for right front.

## Sleeves (both alike)

Cast on 68[68, 70, 72, 72] sts using 4.5mm (US 7) needles and yarn A.
Starting and ending rows as indicated and using the 2-color stranded technique (see page 121), cont in patt from chart for sleeve, working rows 1 to 48 once only and then rep rows 49 to 68 throughout, as foll:
Dec 1 st at each end of 9th and ev foll 8th row until 58[58, 60, 62, 62] sts rem.
Work 5 rows, ending with a WS row.
Inc 1 st at each end of next and ev foll 6th row to 78[74, 78, 80, 76] sts, then on ev foll 4th row until there are 80[82, 84, 86, 88] sts, taking inc sts into patt.
Cont straight until sleeve measures (17¾[17¾, 18, 18, 18]in (45[45, 46, 46, 46]cm), ending with a WS row.

**Shape top**

Keeping patt correct, cast off 4[5, 5, 6, 6] sts at beg of next 2 rows, 72[72, 74, 74, 76] sts.

Dec 1 sts at each end of next and ev foll alt row to 42 sts, then on foll row, ending with a WS row – 40 sts.

Cast off 3 sts at beg of next 2 rows, 4 sts at beg of foll 2 rows, then 5 sts at beg of next 2 rows. Cast off rem 16 sts.

## Finishing

Join shoulder seams.

COLLAR

With RS facing, using 4.5mm (US 7) needles and yarn A, patt across 33 sts from right front holder, cont in chevron patt as set by right front sts across first 16 sts from back holder, patt across rem 16 sts from back holder in chevron patt as set by sts on left front holder, then patt across 33 sts from left front holder. 98 sts. Cont in chevron patt as now set until collar measures 1½in (3.5cm). Cast off in patt. Fold facings to inside at centre front and slip stitch in place.

CORD TRIM

Slip 2 sts nearest left side seam from centre back holder onto one double-pointed 4.5mm (US 7) needle and rejoin yarn A with RS facing.

**Row 1** (RS): Inc 1 in first st, k1, work i-cord (see page 117) until cord is long enough to travel along line between chevron and 2 colour moss st patt to side seam and across front to front opening edge, up front opening edge to point where chevron patt begins again, along line between chevron patt and 2 colour moss st to neck point, then across to centre back neck, slip stitching cord in place as you go along. Cast off.

Slip other 2 sts from centre back holder onto one double-pointed 4.5mm (US 7) needle and make and attach second cord in same way, inc 1 st at end of first row.

Join ends of cords at centre back neck. Mark positions for 6 button loops along right front opening edge - top loop just below point where cord trim starts to follow chevron patt away from front opening edge, lowest loop 6in (15cm) up from c.o.e and rem 4 loops evenly spaced between.

CROCHET EDGING

Using 3mm (USD/3) hook and yarn B, rejoin yarn at base of one sleeve seam and, placing sts evenly along edge, work around cast-on edge of sleeve as folls: *3 dc, 3 ch, 1 ss into same place as last dc, rep from * to end.

Fasten off.

Starting and ending at centre back of collar, work crochet edging along collar edge, down left front opening edge, across cast on edge, up right front opening edge in same way, ensuring 3 ch loops correspond with positions marked for button loops. Attach buttons to left front to correspond with button loops, positioning buttons 3 sts in from finished edge.

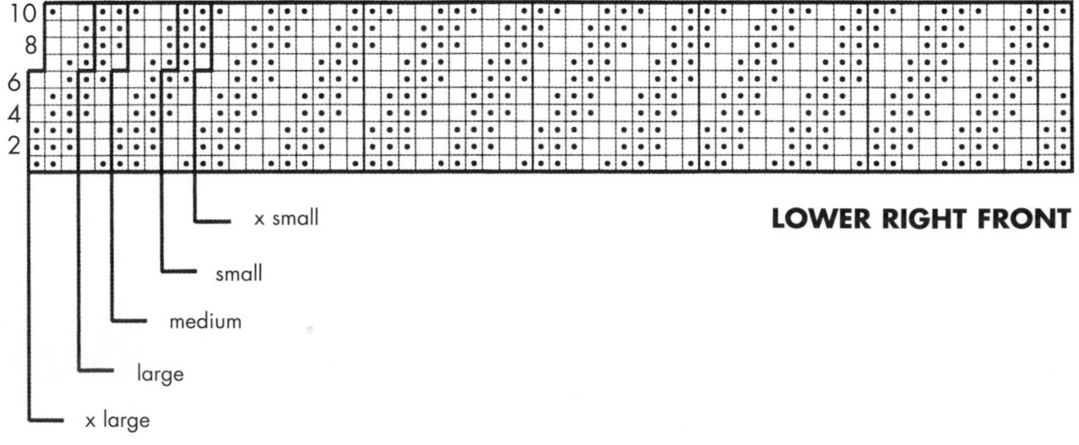


**LOWER RIGHT FRONT**

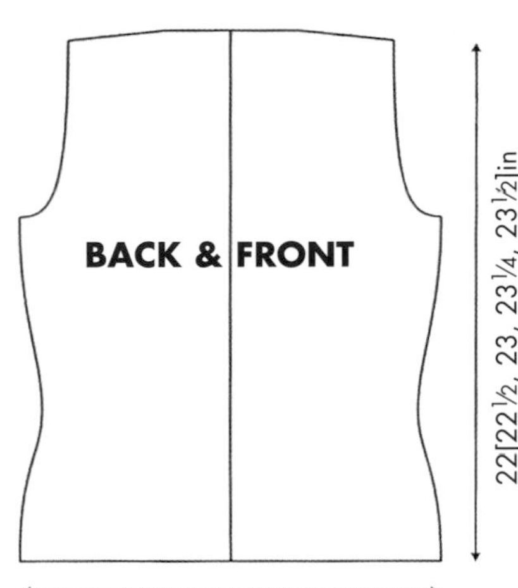

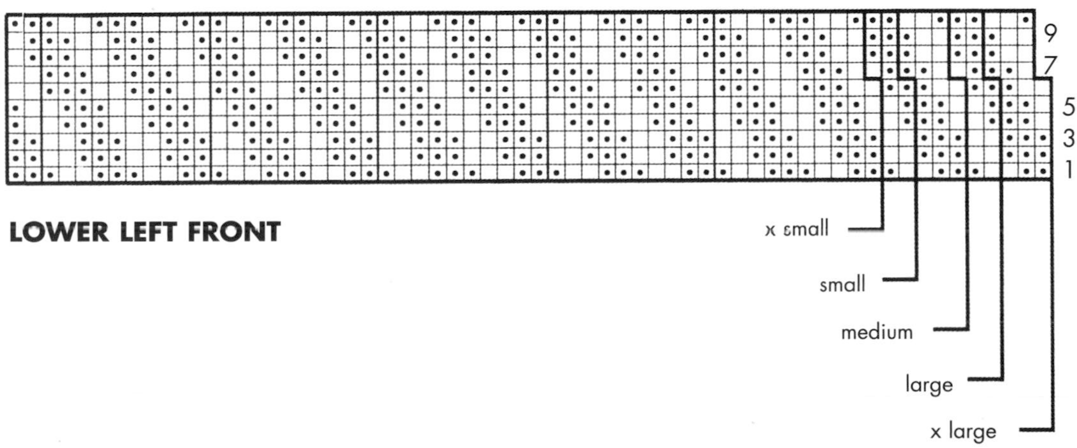


LOWER LEFT FRONT

## KEY

- A–K on RS, P on WS
- A–P on RS, K on WS
- B–K on RS, P on WS
- C4F (over 4 sts)
- Cr3L (over 3 sts)
- Cr3R (over 3 sts)

28
27
20
19
10
9
chevron pattern

**MIDDLE RIGHT FRONT**

x small
small
medium
large
x large

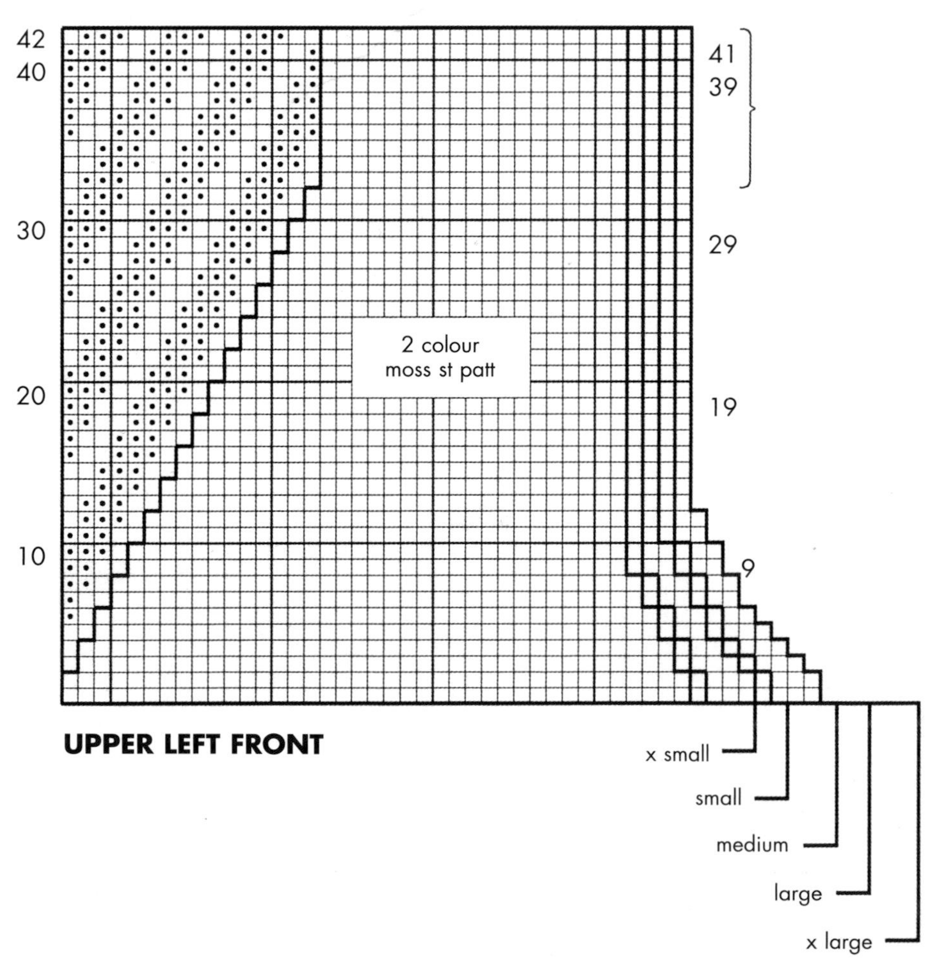


**UPPER LEFT FRONT**

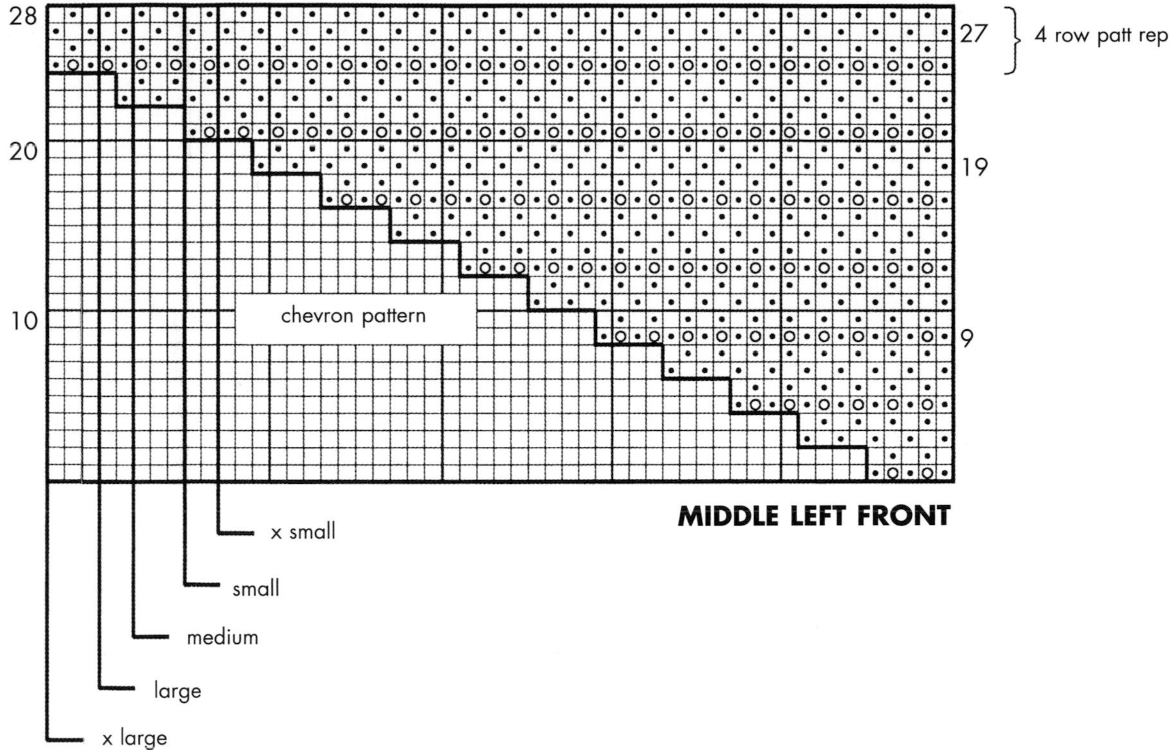


**MIDDLE LEFT FRONT**

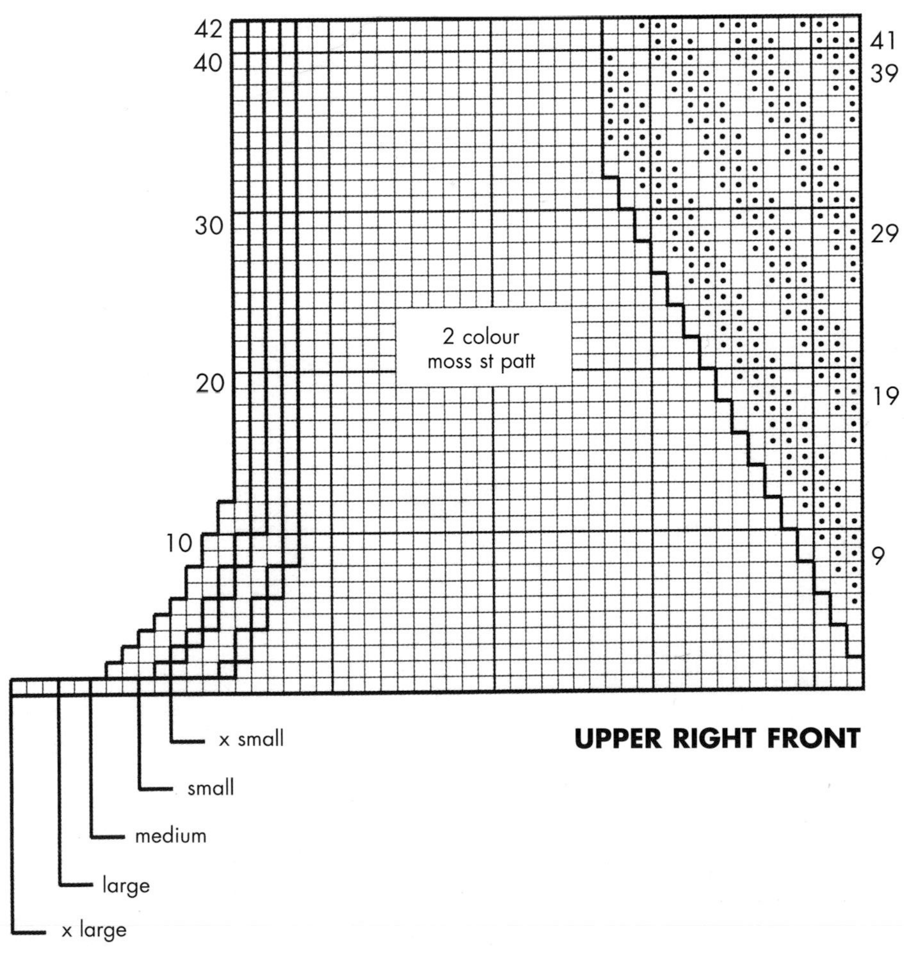


**UPPER RIGHT FRONT**

# CLARA

A celebration of all things triangular in shape, colour and stitch. Godets create the bell sleeves, with decorative decreases sculpting the v-neck, so no neckband to pick up later!

## SIZES

XS – to fit bust 32in (81cm)
S – to fit bust 34in (86cm)
M – to fit bust 36in (91cm)
L – to fit bust 38in (96cm)
XL – to fit bust 40in (101cm).
See schematic for actual measurements.

## MATERIALS

Jaeger Extra Fine Merino DK
137yds (125m) per 50g ball:
10[11, 12, 13, 14] balls of Scarlet (985),1 ball each of Cream (931), Jet (951), Tabby (974)
4mm (US 6), cable needle
Stitch holders

## TENSION

32 sts / 28 rows = 4in (10cm) over rib patt
22 sts / 30rows = 4in (10cm) over st st.

## STITCHES USED

**Stocking stitch**
**Reverse stocking stitch**
**Twists**
**Cables**

### Stitch key

**See charts**

- Knit on RS and purl on WS – st st in Colour A
- Purl on RS and knit on WS – rev st st in Colour A
- Left Twist – knit the second st on LH needle tbl, do not slip off needle. Knit the first and second sts on LH needle tog tbl, slip both sts off needle (in Colour A)
- Right Twist - Knit the second st on LH needle, do not slip off needle, knit the first st on LH needle, slip both sts off needle (in Colour A)
- C5F – place the first 2 sts on cn and hold at FRONT of work, work 3 sts, work 2 from cn (in Colour A)
- C5B – place the first 3 sts on cable needle and hold at BACK of work, work 2 sts, work 3 sts from cable needle (in Colour A)
- Slip 2 sts to cn and hold at front, p1, then k1, p1 from cn
- Slip 2 sts to cn and hold at front, k1, then k1, p1 from cn
- Slip 1 st to cn and hold at back, p1, k1, then p1 from cn
- Slip 1 st st cn and hold at back, p1, k1, then k1 from cn

### Colour key

- Colour A Scarlet (985)
- Colour B Jet (951)
- Colour C Cream (931)
- Colour D Tabby (974)

### Back

Using 4mm needles and Colour A, cast on 132[140, 148, 156, 164] sts and refer to Chart 1 and rep the 24 rowrounds until work measures 13[13, 13½, 13½, 14]in (33[33, 34.25, 34.25, 35.5]cm) from c.o.e ending on a RS row as foll:
Work 5[9, 3, 7, 1] sts in p1, k1 rib, then repeat sts 1 – 10 6[6, 7, 7, 8] times, then work sts 22 and 23, then work sts 35 – 44 6[6, 7, 7, 8] times, then work 5[9, 3, 7, 1] sts in p1, k1 rib – 132[140, 148, 156, 164] sts.
**Next Row** (WS) Keeping patt correct dec 19[22, 23, 24, 25] sts evenly before centre cables and 19[22, 23, 24, 25] sts evenly after centre cables – 90[96, 102, 108, 114] sts.

**Shape armhole**

**XS, S & L**

Refer to Chart 2 and work the 12 rows cont on 4mm needles. Centre chart as foll: work the last 1[0, 2] sts of chart, work the 8 sts 11[12, 13] times across row, work the first 1[0, 2] sts.
**Next row** Cast off 4[4, 5] sts at beg of first 2 rows, then dec 1 st at both ends of next and ev alt row 2[4, 8,] times – 78[80, 82] sts.

**M & XL**

Continuing in rib patt as set cast off 5 sts at beg of next 2 rows, then dec 1 st at both ends of next and ev alt row 5 (10) times – 82[84] sts.

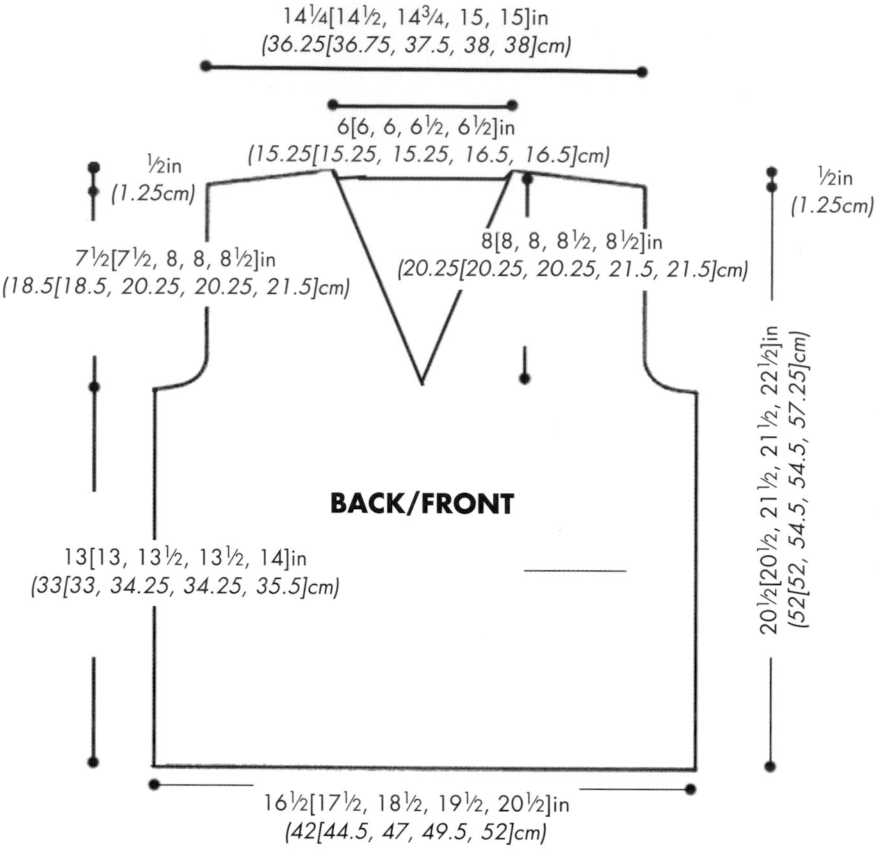

14¼[14½, 14¾, 15, 15]in
(36.25[36.75, 37.5, 38, 38]cm)
6[6, 6, 6½, 6½]in
(15.25[15.25, 15.25, 16.5, 16.5]cm)
½in
(1.25cm)
7½[7½, 8, 8, 8½]in
(18.5[18.5, 20.25, 20.25, 21.5]cm)
8[8, 8, 8½, 8½]in
(20.25[20.25, 20.25, 21.5, 21.5]cm)
½in
(1.25cm)
BACK/FRONT
13[13, 13½, 13½, 14]in
(33[33, 34.25, 34.25, 35.5]cm)
20½[20½, 21½, 21½, 22½]in
(52[52, 54.5, 54.5, 57.25]cm)
16½[17½, 18½, 19½, 20½]in
(42[44.5, 47, 49.5, 52]cm)

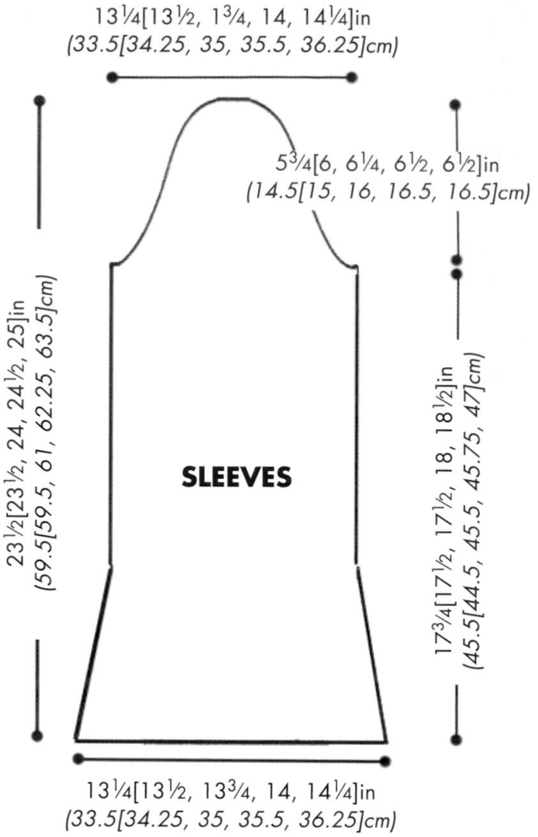

13¼[13½, 1¾, 14, 14¼]in
(33.5[34.25, 35, 35.5, 36.25]cm)
5¾[6, 6¼, 6½, 6½]in
(14.5[15, 16, 16.5, 16.5]cm)
23½[23½, 24, 24½, 25]in
(59.5[59.5, 61, 62.25, 63.5]cm)
SLEEVES
17¾[17½, 17½, 18, 18½]in
(45.5[44.5, 45.5, 45.75, 47]cm)
13¼[13½, 13¾, 14, 14¼]in
(33.5[34.25, 35, 35.5, 36.25]cm)

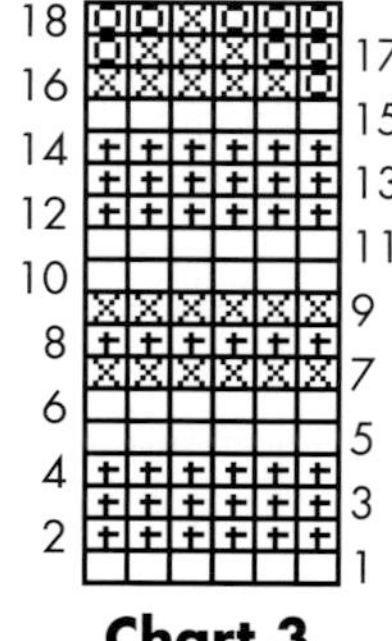

18
17
16
15
14
13
12
11
10
9
8
7
6
5
4
3
2
1

**Chart 3**

12
11
10
9
8
7
6
5
4
3
2
1

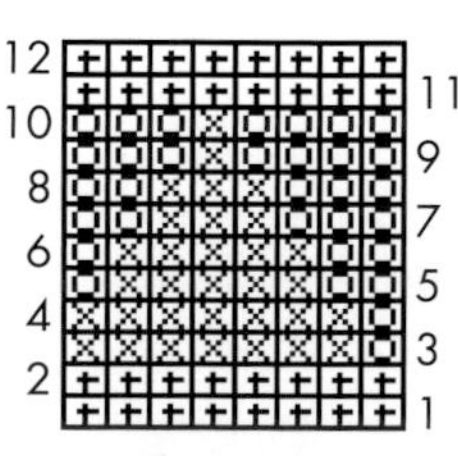

**Chart 2**

AT THE SAME TIME when 4 rows have been worked in rib patt, refer to Chart 2 and cont on 4mm needles, centre chart as foll: work the last 3[1] sts of chart, work the 8 sts 12[14] times across row, work the first 3[1] sts.

**All sizes**

AT THE SAME TIME when 12 rows of Chart 2 have been worked, refer to Chart 3 and start on row 5, rep the 18 rows to end of work, centring chart on rows 16–18 as foll:
Work the last 0[1, 2, 2, 3] sts of chart, work the 6 sts 13 times across row, work the first 0[1, 2, 2, 3] sts.
Cont in patt as set until work measures 20½[20½, 21½, 2½, 22½]in (52[52, 54.5, 54.5, 57]cm) from cast on edge ending on WS row.

**Work neck and shoulder**

Work 25[26, 27, 26, 27] sts, cast off centre 28[28, 28, 30, 30] sts, join a second ball of yarn and work to end.

Working both sides AT THE SAME TIME dec 1 st at both neck edges on next and foll alt row.
AT THE SAME TIME work and place 7[8, 8, 8, 8] sts on holder at armhole edge on next row, (for left back neck it will be foll row), and 8 sts on foll alt row. Cast off over whole 23[24 , 25, 24, 25] sts.

### Front

Using 4 mm needles and Colour A, cast on 132[140, 148, 156, 164] sts and refer to Chart 1 and rep the 24 rows until work measures 13[13, 13.5, 13.5, 14]in (33[33, 34.25, 34.25, 35.5]cm) from c.o.e ending on a RS row as foll:
Work 4[8, 2, 6, 0] sts in k1, p1 rib, then rep sts 1 – 10 5[5, 6, 6, 7] times, then work sts 11 – 34, then work sts 35 – 44 5[5, 6, 6, 7] times, then work 4[8, 2, 6, 0] sts in p1, k1 rib –

132[140, 148, 156, 164] sts. Cont as for back (inc armhole shaping) until work measures 13[13, 14, 13.5, 14.5]in (33[33, 34.25, 34.25, 35.5]cm) ending on WS row.

**Divide for neckline**

**NB** For all sizes this will be on the same row that Chart 2 commences. The centre cable splits and forms the neck edge from here – therefore work in Chart 2 up to 6 sts before neckline, then work 6 sts of cabled edging in Colour A, so that cable cont up the neck edge.

**Next row** Work to centre st, turn and work back in patt as set. Place the other half of sts on stitch holder. Then working sides separately, cont with armhole shaping, whilst working neckline by dec 1 st 6 sts in from neck edge (on inside of cable) on ev 5th row 4[4, 4, 6, 6] times, then ev 6th row 6[6, 6, 5, 5] times – 23[24, 25, 24, 25] sts.

Cont in patt as set until work measures 20½[20½, 21½, 2½, 22½]in (52[52, 54.5, 54.5, 57]cm) from c.o.e ending on WS row.

**Work shoulder**

Place 7(8, 8, 8, 8)sts on holder at armhole edge on next row, (for other side it will be foll row), and 8 sts on foll alt row. Cast off 23[24, 25, 24, 25] sts, leaving the 6 sts of cable on holder. Work other side of neck to match, reversing shaping. Cont on rem 6 sts in cable patt until the band will travel around back neckline to left shoulder, finishing to fit other side of band. Leave sts on holder.

## Sleeves (both alike)

Using 4 mm needles and Colour A, cast on 83[85, 87, 89, 91] sts and then knit 1 row. Refer to chart 4 and work the 74 rows as foll:

**XS, M & XL** Work 10[12, 14] sts in p1, k1 rib, work the 63 sts of chart, work 10[12, 14] sts in k1, p1 rib.

**S & L** Work 11[13] sts in k1, p1 rib, work the 63 sts of chart, work 11[13] sts in k1, p1 rib.

**NB** To make a neat edge in the triangular inserts, on WS rows work the first and last stitches in Main Colour.

Cont, keeping centre cable and zigzag ribs correct as set, rep rows 51–74 to end of sleeve. When work measures 17¾[17½, 17¾, 18, 18½]in (45[45, 45, 45.75, 47]cm) from c.o.e.

**Shape sleeve cap**

Cast off 4[4, 5, 5, 5] sts at beg of next 2 rows, keeping patt correct as set.

Dec 1 st at both ends of ev alt row 13[14, 16, 18, 17] times, then ev row 8[8, 6, 4, 6] times.

Cast off 3 sts at beg of next 4 rows.

Cast off rem 21[21, 21, 23, 23] sts.

**Finishing**

Join shoulder seams.

Stitch band in place around back neck ending at left shoulder. Then using 3 needle cast off (see page 116), with right sides together, knit the knit sts and purl the purl sts, casting off together the 6sts on holder at top left shoulder and those of band.

Insert sleeves, placing any fullness evenly over sleeve cap. Join side and sleeve seams in one line.

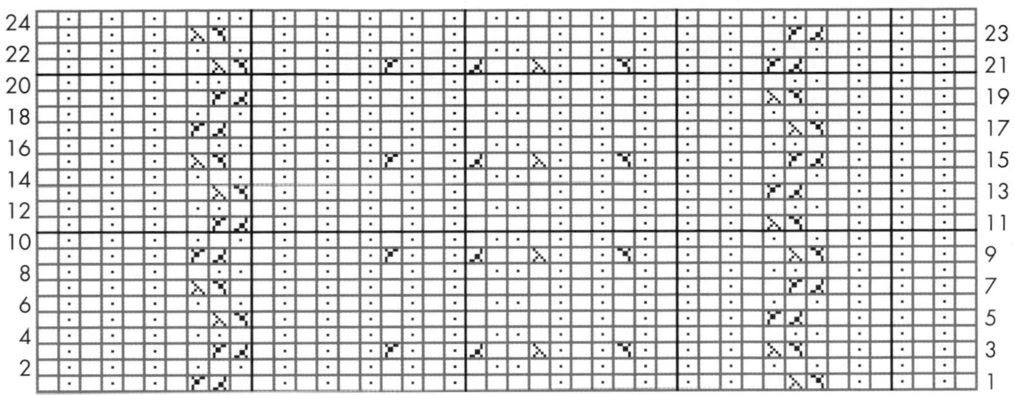

**Chart 1 (44 sts)**

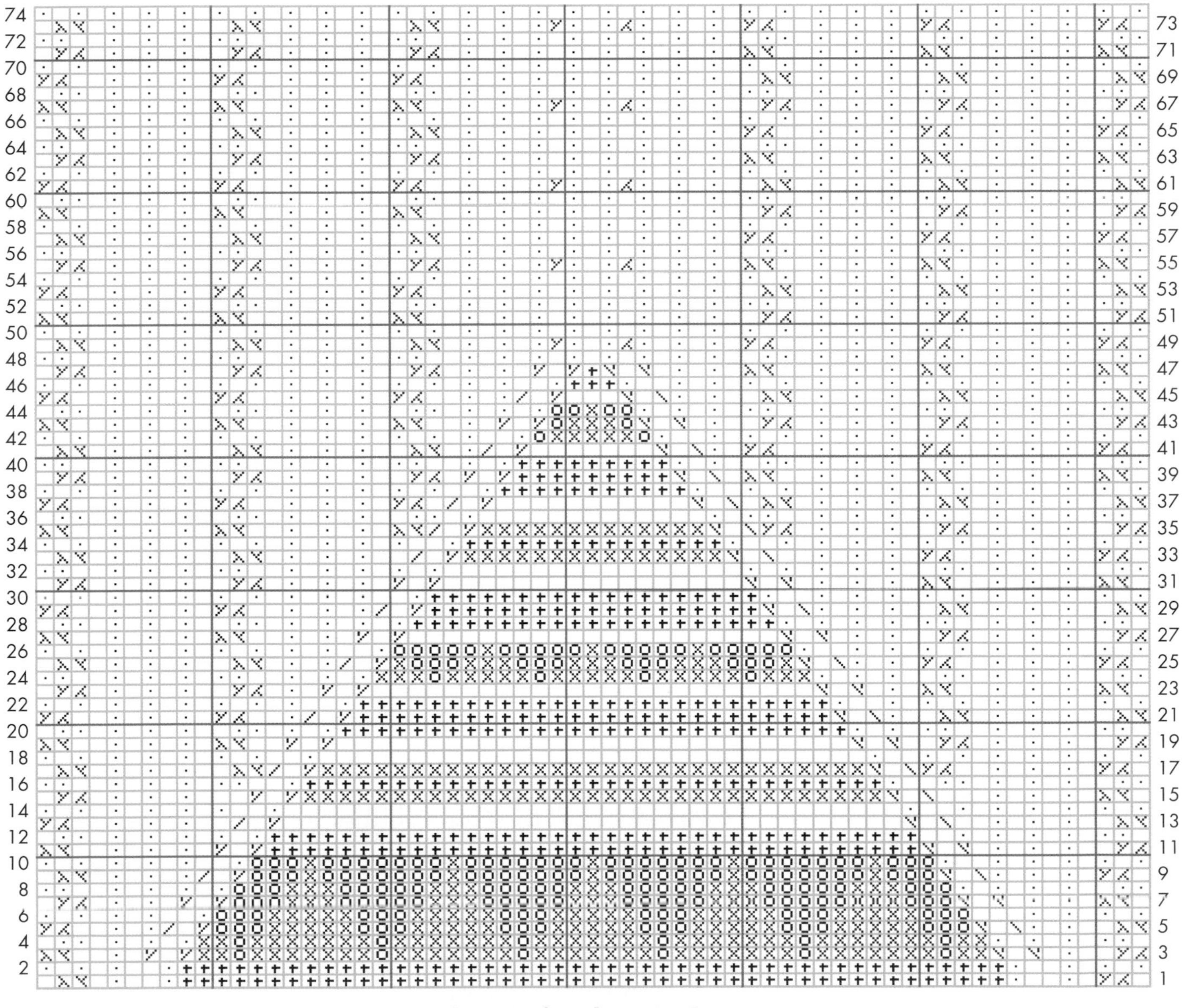

**Chart 4 (for sleeve) 63 sts**

# PART 4
# COLOUR

# LIZZIE

An early photo of Princess Elizabeth inspired this fitted jacket. If you're uncomfortable with colourwork, leave it out and instead work the welts and collar in a contrasting colour. Add fabulous buttons and a regal pin at the collar and you're set.

## SIZES

XS – to fit bust 32–34in (81–86cm)
S – to fit bust 34–36in (86–91cm)
M – to fit bust 36–38in (91–96cm)
L – to fit bust 38–40in (96–101cm)
XL – to fit bust 40–42in (101–106cm).
See schematic for actual measurements.

## MATERIALS

Rowan Wool Cotton
123 yds (113m) per 50g ball:
10[11, 12, 13, 14] balls Colour A:
2 balls Colours C, D;
1 ball Colours B, E, F & G
One pair each 3mm (US 3); 3.75mm (US 5); 4mm (US 6); 1 extra 4mm
Stitch holders and markers
3 x 24mm buttons
2 x 22 mm buttons for sleeves

## TENSION

24sts and 32 rows = 4in (10cm) over st st

## STITCHES USED

**Stocking stitch**
**Moss stitch**

## COLOUR KEY

Colour A Shipshape (955)
☐ Colour B Rich (911)
☒ Colour C Gypsy (910)
◢ Colour D Deepest Olive (907)
▣ Colour E Pumpkin ((962)
▬ Colour F Still (964)
V Colour G French Navy (909)

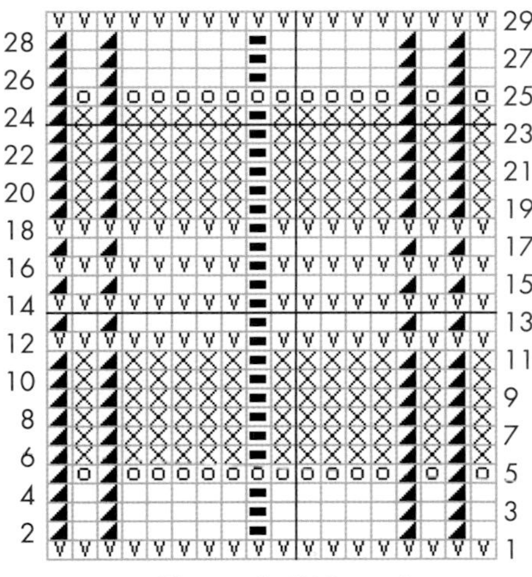


**Chart 1 (18 sts)**

## Back

Using 3mm needles and Colour A cast on 108[114, 120, 126, 132] sts and work 1¼in (3cm) in moss st. Change to 4mm needles and refer to chart 1 and work the 29 rows, centering the chart as foll:

Work last 0[3, 6, 0, 3] sts of chart, rep the 18 sts 6[6, 6, 7, 7] times across row, work first 0[3, 6, 0, 3] sts.

AT THE SAME TIME start decs on row 3 keeping chart correct, dec 1 st at both ends of row 3 and then ev 9th row 5 times in all – 98[104, 110, 116, 122] sts.

AT THE SAME TIME when 29 rows of chart are completed, change to 3.75mm needles and cont in st st in Colour A to end of work.

When above shaping is completed, work 6[10, 10, 10, 10] rows in patt as set and then commence incs:

Inc 1 st at both ends of next and ev foll 9th row 5 times in all 108[114, 120, 126, 132] sts. Cont in patt as set until work measures 12¾[13¼, 13¼, 13¼, 13¼]in (32.5[33.5, 33.5, 33.5, 33.5]cm) from c.o.e ending on WS row.

**Shape armholes**

Cast off 6 sts at beg of next 2 rows, keeping patt correct.

Dec 1 st at both ends of next and ev alt row 7[10, 12, 15, 17] times – 82[82, 84, 84, 86] sts.

Cont in patt as set until work measures 19¾[20¼,20¼, 20¾, 20¾]in (50[51.5, 51.5, 52.75, 52.75]cm) from c.o.e ending on WS row.

**Work neck and shoulder**

Work 28sts, cast off centre 26[26, 28, 28, 30] sts, join a second ball of yarn and work to end. Working both sides AT THE SAME TIME, dec 1 st at both neck edges on next and foll alt row.

AT THE SAME TIME work and place 9sts on holder at armhole edge on next row, (for left back neck it will be foll row), and 9sts on foll alt row. Cast off over whole 28 sts.

## Left Front

**Pocket Linings** (work 2)

Using 3.75mm needles and Colour A, cast on 28 sts and work 3½in (9cm) in st st, then leave on holder.

Using 3mm needles and Colour A cast on 65[68, 71, 74, 77] sts and work 1¼in (3cm) in moss st. Change to 4mm needles and refer to chart 1 and work the 29 rows, centering chart as foll:

**RS rows** Work last 0[3, 6, 0, 3] sts of chart, rep the 18 sts 3 times across row, work first 4[4, 4, 13, 13] sts,

**WS rows** Work 7 sts in Colour A in moss st, work last 4[4, 4, 13, 13] sts of chart, rep the 18 sts 3 times across row, work first 0[3, 6, 0, 3] sts

AT THE SAME TIME keeping the moss st edging up the centre of work correct, commence shaping at outside edge on row 3, dec 1 st at beg of row 3 and then ev 9th row 5 times in all – 60[63, 66, 69, 72] sts.

AT THE SAME TIME when 29 rows of chart are completed, change to 3.75mm needles and cont in st st in Colour A, with moss st edging (7 sts) at centre throughout to end of work, inserting pocket linings on first row as foll:

Moss st 7sts, p 15[16, 18, 19, 20] sts, place next 28 sts on holder for pocket tops, p across the 28 sts of pocket lining, p to end of row.

When shaping is completed, work 6[10, 10, 10, 10] rows in patt as set and then commence incs:

Inc 1 st at outside edge of next and ev foll 9th row 5 times in all – 65[68, 71, 74, 77] sts.

Cont in patt as set until work measures 12¼(12¾, 12¾, 12¾, 12¾)in (31[32.5, 32.5, 32.5, 32.5]cm) from c.o.e ending on RS row.

**Shape neckline**

Place 14 sts at beg of next row on holder – 51[54, 57, 60, 63] sts.

Work 1 row.

Then dec 1 st at neck edge on next and then ev foll 5th row 0(0, 5. 0, 7) times, then ev 6th row 9(9, 5, 10, 4) times.

Cont in patt as set until work measures 12¾(13¼, 13¼, 13¼, 13¼, 13¼)in (32.5[33.5, 33.5, 33.5, 33.5]cm) from c.o.e ending on WS row.

**Shape armholes**

Cast off 6 sts at beg of next row, keeping patt correct. Work 1 row.

Dec 1 st at beg of next and ev alt row 7[10, 12, 15, 17] times in all, keeping patt correct. When work measures 20¼[20, 25, 20, 20¾]in (51.5[50.75, 63.5, 50.75,52.75]cm) from c.o.e. ending on RS row work shoulder:

**Next row** Work to last 9 sts, turn.

**Next row** Work back in patt.

**Next row** Work to last 18 sts, turn.

**Next row** Work back in patt.

Cast off over whole 28sts.

## Right Front

Work as for Left front, reversing all shapings and pocket placements.

Chart should read:

**RS rows** Work 7 sts in Colour A in moss st, work last 4[4, 4, 13, 13] sts of chart, rep the 18 sts 3 times across row, work first 0(3, 6, 0, 3)sts

**WS rows** Work last 0(3, 6, 0, 3)sts of chart, rep the 18 sts 3 times across row, work first 4(4, 4, 13, 13)sts.

Insert 3 buttonholes when work measures 5¾(6, 6, 6, 6)in (14.5[15.25, 15.25, 15.25, 15.25]cm), 9[9¼, 9¼, 9¼, 9¼]in (23[23.5, 23.5, 23.5, 23.5]cm) and 12¼[12¾, 12¾, 12¾, 12¾]in (31[32.5, 32.5, 32.5, 32.5]cm) respectively on a RS row as foll:

Work 2[2, 2, 3] sts, cast off 3 sts, work 4[4, 4, 4] sts, cast off 3 sts, work to end of row. Cast on the sts as you come to them on the foll row, working into the backs of the cast on sts on foll row.

## Left Sleeve

Using 3mm needles and Colour A cast on 61[61, 61, 65, 65] sts and work 1¼in (3cm) in moss st ending on WS row. When ½in (1cm) is completed, ending on WS row, work buttonhole row as foll:

Work 3 sts, cast off 2 sts, work to end of row. Cast on these sts when you come to them on foll row, working into backs of sts. Work final row (WS) as foll:

Work to last 7[7, 7, 8, 8] sts and cast off these sts – 54[54, 54, 58, 58] sts.

Change to 4mm needles, rejoin yarn and refer to chart 1 and work the 29 rows, inc as foll incorporating the incs into the patt at each side.

**XS & S** Inc 1st at both ends of next and then ev foll 14th row 8 times – 72 sts

**M** Inc 1st at both ends of next and then ev foll 10th row 11 times – 78 sts

**L** Inc 1st at both ends of next and then ev foll 13th row 9 times – 78 sts

**XL** Inc 1st at both ends of next and then ev foll 10th row 12 times – 84 sts

Work the first row of chart as foll:

Work the last 0[0, 0, 2, 2] sts of chart, rep the 18 sts 3 times, work the first 0[0, 0, 2, 2] sts.

AT THE SAME TIME when 29 rows of chart are completed, change to 3.75mm needles and cont in st st to end, cont with incs as set until there are 72[72, 78, 78, 84) sts as above.

Then cont in patt as set until work measures 17[17, 17, 17½, 17½]in (43[43, 43, 44.5, 44.5]cm) from cast on edge ending on WS row.

**Shape top of sleeve**

Cast off 6 sts at beg of next 2 rows.

Dec 1 st at both ends of next and then ev foll 3rd row 12[12, 8, 8, 2] times, then ev alt row 2[2, 8, 8, 17] times – 30[30, 32, 32, 32] sts

Cast off 3 sts at beg of next 4 rows.

Cast off rem 18[18, 20, 20, 20] sts.

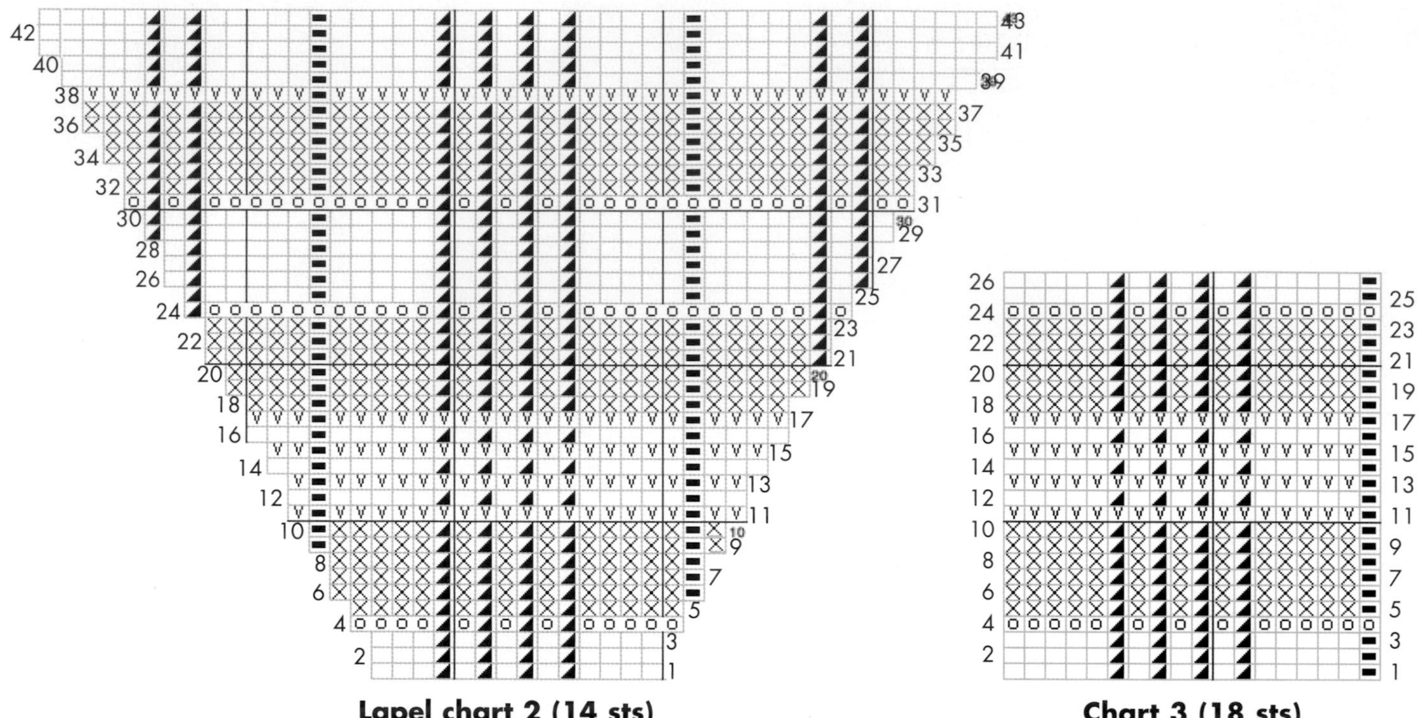


## Right Sleeve

Work as for Left Sleeve, but place buttonhole tab as foll:
Using 3mm needles cast on 61[61, 61, 65, 65] sts and work 1¼in (3cm) in moss st ending on WS row. When ½in (1cm) is completed, ending on WS row, work buttonhole row as foll:
Work to last 5 sts, cast off 2 sts, work last 3 sts. Cast on these sts when you come to them on foll row, working into backs of sts. Work final row (WS) as foll:
Cast off 7[7, 7, 8, 8] sts then work to end – 54[54, 54, 58, 58] sts.

## Lapels

Using Colour B and 4mm needles, pick up the 14sts from holder at centre front, then refer to Lapel chart 2 and work 39[39 42, 42, 42] rows, inc as indicated, incorporating extra sts as you inc as on chart.
On cast off row place half the sts on a third needle, folding the collar double with RS on outside, and work 3-needle cast off (see page 116).

## Finishing

POCKET TOPS
Using 3mm needles and Colour A, pick up the 28 sts from holder and work ½in (1cm) in moss st and then cast off. Slipstitch pocket linings in place on inside and also sides of pocket tops.
Join shoulder seams. Set in sleeves, placing any fullness evenly across the top of sleeve cap. Join side and sleeve seams neatly, leaving buttonhole tab at bottom of sleeve overlapping on RS. Stitch button directly beneath tab on moss st cuff. Fold back the moss st edgings at centre fronts to inside and slipstitch in place. On Right Front, stitch together the edges of the two layers of buttonholes. Attach 3 buttons directly opposite buttonholes on Left Front. With WS facing stitch the lapels in place (they should end 3in (7.5cm) from shoulder seam) and then slipstitch other side of lapel in place on right side.

COLLAR
Using Colour B and 4mm needles, cast on 44 sts and refer to chart 3 and work 105 rows, rep the 26 rows 4 times, then working row 1 again, so that the patt matches up at start and finish. Cast off. Centre the chart as foll: Work the last 13 sts, work the 18 sts once, work the first 13 sts.
Fold the collar double with RSs facing and oversew along the short cast on and cast off edges.

Oversew lapels to jacket, placing right side of one thickness of lapel to wrong side of jacket, then folding over and oversewing the other side on top of the first seam, so that when the collar is turned back on the right side, the seam is invisible. Attach collar around neck edge in same way, starting where lapels finish and making sure that centre of collar is lined up with centre back neck. Slipstitch the collar to the lapel for about 1½in (4cm) from centre front.

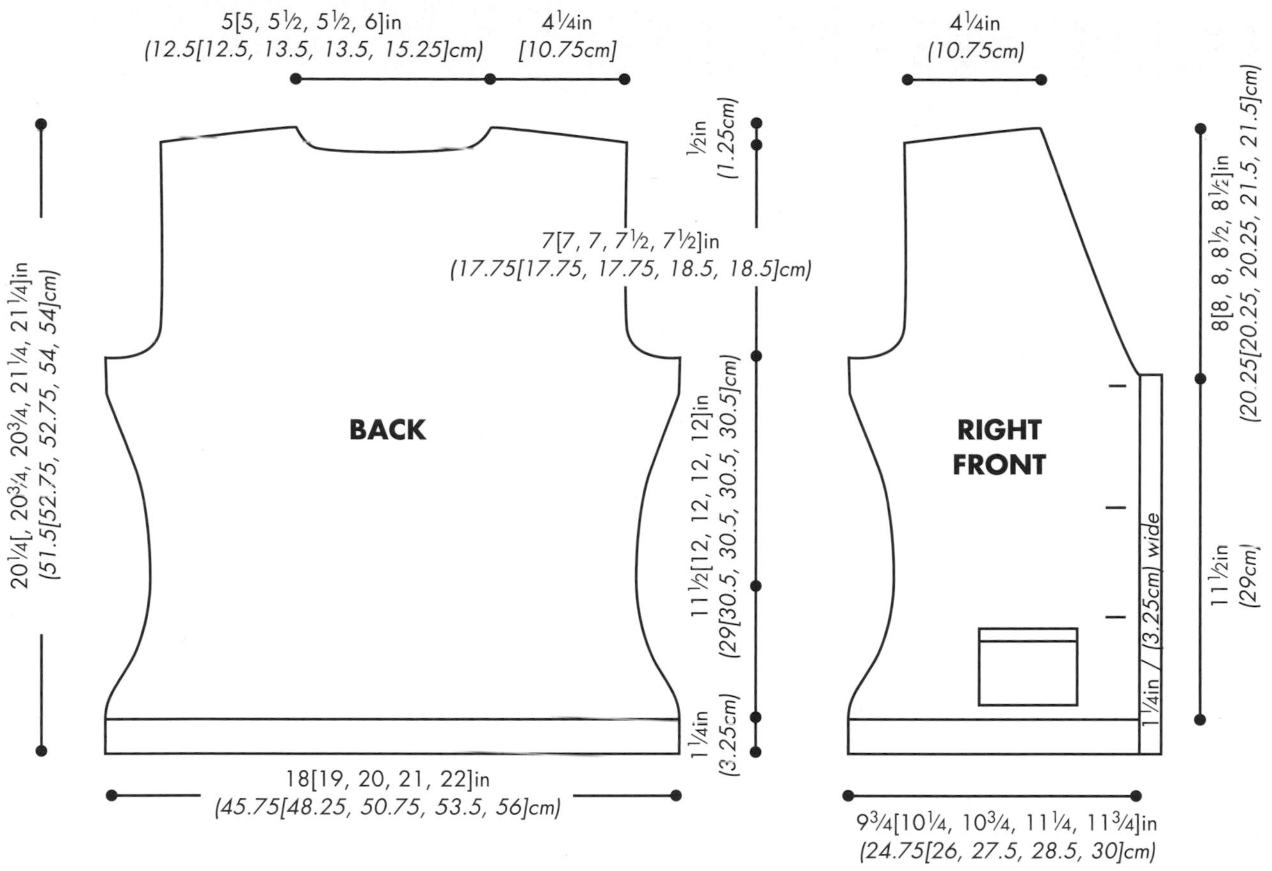
5[5, 5½, 5½, 6]in
(12.5[12.5, 13.5, 13.5, 15.25]cm)
4¼in
[10.75cm]
½in
(1.25cm)
7[7, 7, 7½, 7½]in
(17.75[17.75, 17.75, 18.5, 18.5]cm)
20¼[, 20¾, 20¾, 21¼, 21¼]in
(51.5[52.75, 52.75, 54, 54]cm)
BACK
11½[12, 12, 12, 12]in
(29[30.5, 30.5, 30.5, 30.5]cm)
1¼in
(3.25cm)
18[19, 20, 21, 22]in
(45.75[48.25, 50.75, 53.5, 56]cm)
4¼in
(10.75cm)
8[8, 8, 8½, 8½]in
(20.25[20.25, 20.25, 21.5, 21.5]cm)
RIGHT
FRONT
1¼in / (3.25cm) wide
11½in
(29cm)
9¾[10¼, 10¾, 11¼, 11¾]in
(24.75[26, 27.5, 28.5, 30]cm)

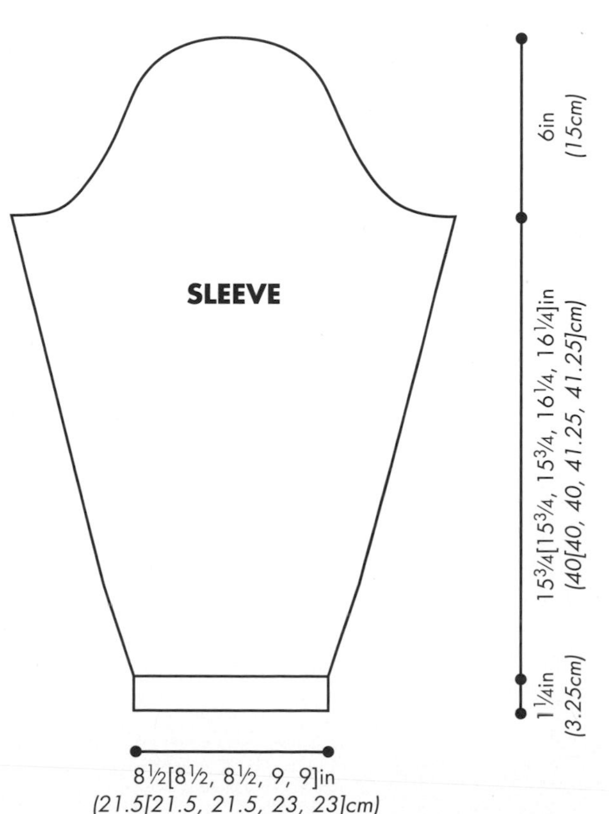
SLEEVE
6in
(15cm)
15¾[15¾, 15¾, 16¼, 16¼]in
(40[40, 40, 41.25, 41.25]cm)
1¼in
(3.25cm)
8½[8½, 8½, 9, 9]in
(21.5[21.5, 21.5, 23, 23]cm)

# TAMARA

Square up to both fairisle and sculptured stitches in this mandarin-collared jacket. Easier to knit than it looks, with the bonus of edge-to-edge frog fasteners dispensing with bands and buttonholes!

## SIZES

XS – to fit bust 32in (81cm),
S –(to fit bust 34in (86cm)
M – to fit bust 36in (91cm)
Large – to fit bust 38in (96cm)
XL – to fit bust 40in (101cm).
See schematic for actual measurements.

## MATERIALS

Jaeger Extra Fine Merino
137yd (125m) per 50g ball:
11[11, 12, 12, 13] balls Colour A Raspberry (943)
2[2, 2, 2, 2] balls Colour B Jet (951)
1[1, 1, 1, 1] balls Colour C Natural (937)
1[1, 1, 1, 1] balls Colour D Elderberry (944)
3.25 mm (US 3), 4mm (US 6),
Stitch holders
3 x frog fasteners

## TENSION

23 sts and 36 rows = 10 cms or 4" over checkerboard patt (Chart 2).

## STITCHES USED

**Stocking stitch**
**Moss st**

## STITCH KEY

■ Jet 951 (B)
■ Natural 937 (C)
■ Elderberry 944 (D)
□ Colour A – Raspberry (943)
Knit on RS and purl on WS – st st
⊡ Colour A – Raspberry (943)
Purl on RS and knit on WS – rev st st

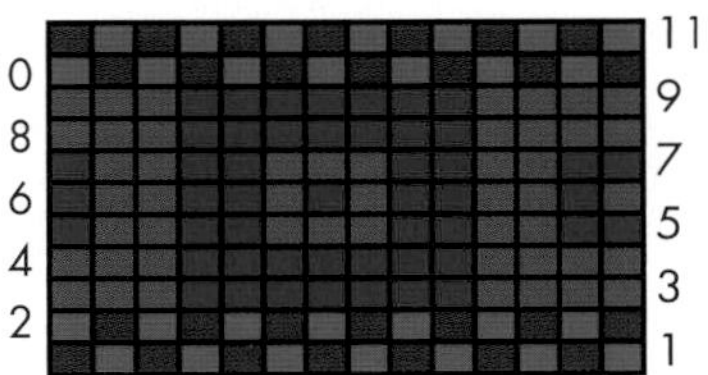


**Chart 1 (14 sts)**

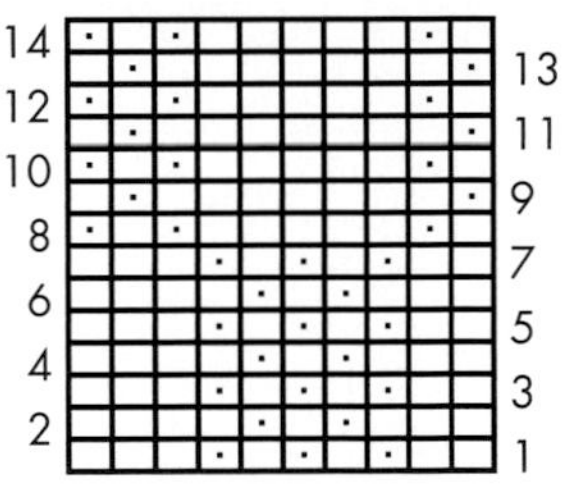


**Chart 2 (10 sts)**

### Back

Using smaller needles and Colour B, cast on 98[104, 110, 116, 122] sts and work in moss st until work measures 1¼in (3cm) from c.o.e, ending on RS row. Knit one row to form fold line, then change to larger needles and refer to Chart 1 and work the 11 rows, starting on RS row, centring the chart as foll:

**Row 1** Work the last 0[3, 6, 2, 5] sts of chart, work the 14 sts 7[7, 7, 8, 8] times, work the first 0[3, 6, 2, 5] sts.

**Row 12** Purl in Colour A.

When 12 rows are completed refer to Chart 2 and using Colour A rep the 14 rows to end of work, inc 1 st at both ends of 7th and ev foll 18th row until there are 106[112, 118, 124, 130] sts, centering the chart as foll:

**Row 1** Work the last 4[2, 0, 3, 1] sts of chart, work the 10 sts 9[10, 11, 11, 12] times, work the first 4[2, 0, 3, 1] sts.

When work measures 10½[10¾, 11, 11¼, 11½]in (26.5[27.25, 28, 28.5, 29]cm) from fold line (start of Chart 1) ending on WS row

**Shape armhole**

Cast off 5[5, 5, 6, 6] sts at beg of next 2 rows.

Dec 1 st at both ends of next and ev foll alt row 8[9, 11, 11, 13] times – 80[84, 86, 90, 92] sts.

Cont, keeping patt correct as set, until work measures 18½[19, 19½, 20, 20½]in (47[48, 49.5, 51, 52]cm) from fold line, then

**Shape neck and shoulder**
Patt 28[29, 29, 30, 30] sts., turn, leave rem 52[55, 57, 60, 62] sts on holder.
Work each side of neck separately.
Dec 1 st at beg of next row, patt to end.
Place 8[9, 9, 9, 9] sts at beg of next row on holder, patt to end.
Dec 1 st at beg of next row. patt to end.
Place 9 sts at beg of next row on holder, patt to end.
Patt 1 row.
Cast off across all 26[27, 27, 28, 28] sts.
With RS facing rejoin yarn to rem sts, leave centre 24[26, 28, 30, 32] sts on holder, patt to end. Work to match first side, reversing shapings.

## FRONTS

**Pocket linings** (make two)
Using larger needles and Colour A cast on 24 sts and, beg with a knit row, work 3in (7.5cm) in stocking stitch. Break yarn and leave sts on holder.

**Left front**
Using smaller needles and Colour B, cast on 49[52, 55, 58, 61] sts and work in moss st until work measures 1¼in (3cm) from cast on edge, ending on RS row. Knit one row to form fold line, then change to larger needles and refer to Chart 1 and work the 11 rows, starting on RS row, centring patt as foll:
**Row 1** Work the last 0[3, 6, 2, 5] sts of chart, work the 14 sts 3[3, 3, 4, 4] times, work the first 7sts.
**Row 12** Working in Colour A, cast on 7 sts for band (these sts to be worked in moss st to end), purl to end of row.
When 12 rows are completed refer to Chart 2 and using Colour A rep the 14 rows to end of work, inc 1 st at beg of 7th and ev foll 18th row until there are 60[63, 66, 69, 72] sts, centering the chart as foll:
**Row 1** Work the last 4[2, 0, 3, 1] sts of chart, work the 10 sts 4[5, 5, 5, 6] times, work the first 5[0, 5, 5, 0] sts, moss st 7 sts.
AT THE SAME TIME when work measures 3½in (9cm) (from start of Chart 2 ending on WS row

**Place pocket lining**
Patt 13[15, 16, 18, 19] sts, slip next 24 sts onto holder, patt across 24 sts of first pocket lining, patt 21[22, 24, 25, 27] sts.
When work measures 10½[10¾, 11, 11¼, 11½]in (26.5[27.25, 28, 28.5, 29.25]cm) from fold line (start of Chart 1) ending on WS row

**Shape armhole**
Cast off 5[5, 5, 6, 6] at beg of next row. Work 1 row in patt as set.
Dec 1 st at beg of next and ev alt row 8[9, 11, 11, 13] times – 47[49, 50, 52, 53] sts. When work measures 16.5[17, 17.5, 18, 18.5]in (42[43, 44.5, 45.75, 47]cm) from foldline ending on RS row

**Shape neck**
Cast off 14[15, 16, 17, 18] sts at beg of next row.
Dec 1 st at neck edge on next and ev alt row 7 times, keeping patt correct.
Cont in patt until work measures 18½[19, 19½, 20, 20½]in (47[48.25, 49.5, 50.75, 52]cm) from fold line.

**Shape shoulder**
Place 8[9, 9, 9, 9] sts on holder at beg of next row, patt to end. Work 1 row.
Place 9 sts on holder at beg of next row, patt to end.
Work 1 row.
Cast off across all 26[27, 27, 28, 28] sts.

**Right front**
Work as for left front, reversing all shapings and pocket placements and moss st centre band.

## SLEEVES (both alike)

Using smaller needles and Colour B, cast on 52[52, 54, 54, 56] sts. Work 1¼in (3cm) in moss st, ending on RS row. Knit one row to form fold line, then change to larger needles and refer to Chart 1 and work the 11 rows, starting on RS row, centering patt as foll:
**Row 1** Work last 5[5, 6, 6, 0] sts, work the 14 sts 3[3, 3, 3, 4] times, work first 5[5, 6, 6, 0] sts.
**Row 12** Purl in Colour A
When 12 rows are completed refer to Chart 2 and using Colour A rep the 14 rows to end of work, inc 1 st at both ends of ev 6th row 0[0, 0, 7, 10] times, then ev 7th row 2[14, 22, 16, 14] times, then ev 8th row 18[7, 0, 0, 0] times – 92[94, 98, 100, 104] sts. Centre chart:
**Row 1** Work the last 1[1, 2, 2, 3] sts of chart, work the 10 sts 5 times, work the first 1[1, 2, 2, 3] sts.
Cont in patt until work measures 20½[20¼, 20¼, 20¼, 20½]in (52[51.5, 51.5, 51.5, 52]cm) from foldline ending on WS row.

**Shape top of sleeve**
Cast off 5[5, 5, 6, 6] sts at beg of next 2 rows.
Dec 1 st at both ends of next and ev foll alt row 8[9, 11, 11, 13] times keeping patt correct.
Cast off rem 66 sts.

## FINISHING

Join shoulder seams. Turn the 7 sts of moss st at centre fronts onto inside and slip stitch in place.
POCKET TOPS
With WS facing slip sts from holder onto smaller needles, then using Colour A, purl 1 row to form foldline. Work 4 rows in st st and then cast off. Turn st st onto inside of pocket and slip stitch in place.
COLLAR
Using larger needles and Colour B, with RS facing and starting 2 sts in from right centre front neck edge, pick up and k 24[25, 26, 26, 27] sts to shoulder seam, 2 sts down back neck, 24[26, 28, 30, 32] sts from holder at centre back, 2 sts up other side back neck and 24[25, 26, 26, 27] sts down left side neck edge, ending 2 sts in from centre front edge – 76[80, 84, 86, 90] sts.
Refer to Chart 1 and work the 11 rows, starting on a WS row working from left to right. Centre chart as foll:
**Row 1** Work the last 3[5, 7, 8, 10] sts, work the 14 sts 5 times, work the first 3[5, 7, 8, 10] sts.
**Rows 12 & 13** Using Colour B knit to form foldline.

Change to smaller needles and work a further 1¼in (3cm) in moss st in Colour B and then cast off.
Fold collar down onto inside and slipstitch in place. Neatly slipstitch side edges of collar.
Insert sleeves. Join side and sleeve seams in one line. Turn hems onto inside and slipstitch in place. Sew side edges of hem together at each centre front edge, using Colour B.
Slip stitch pockets in place on inside.
Attach 3 frog fasteners, the first 1in (2.5cm) down from neck shaping at centre front, the third 6in (15cm) up from hem and the other spaced evenly between, taking care that patt is in line across the jacket.

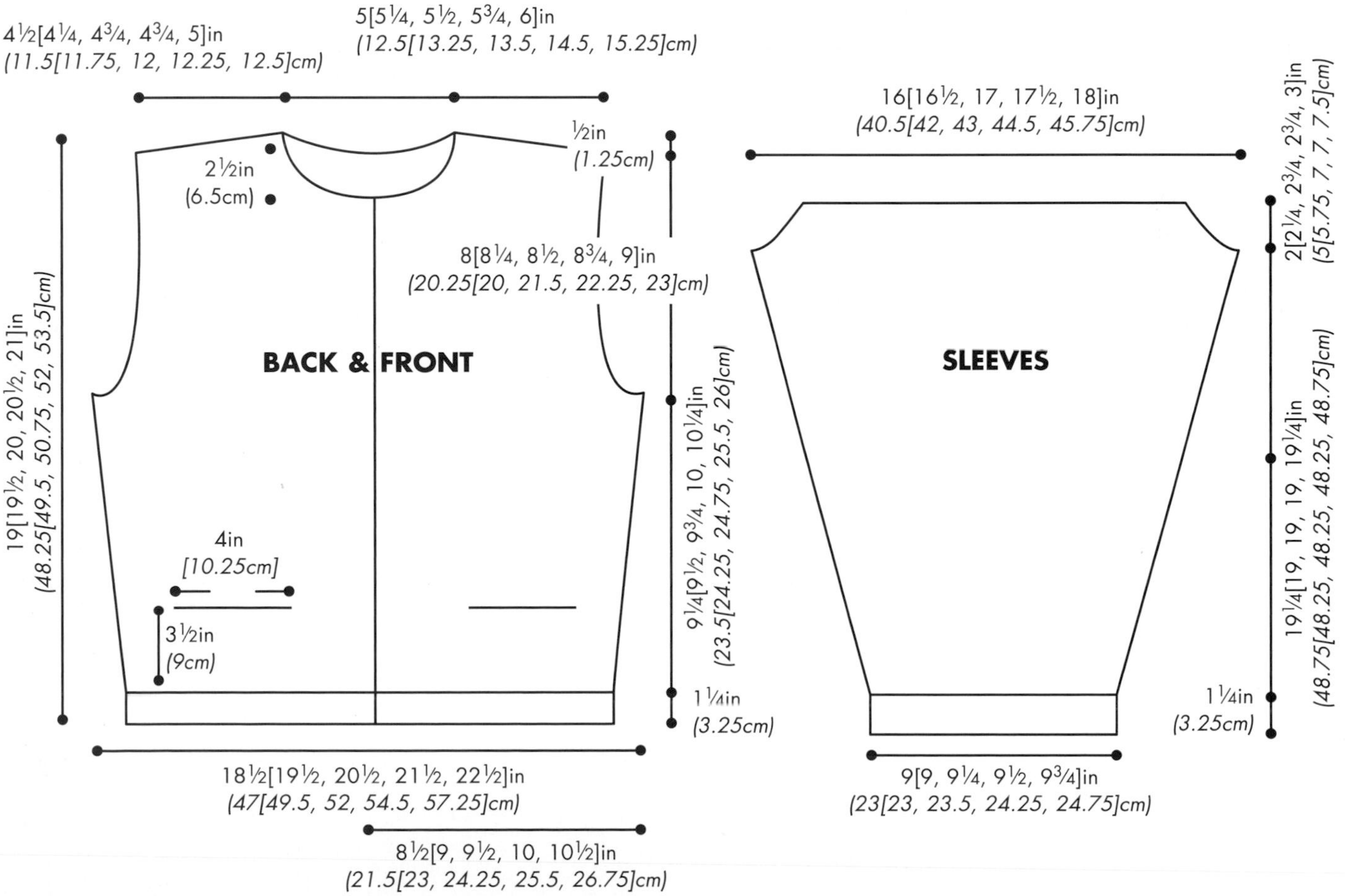

4½[4¼, 4¾, 4¾, 5]in
*(11.5[11.75, 12, 12.25, 12.5]cm)*

5[5¼, 5½, 5¾, 6]in
*(12.5[13.25, 13.5, 14.5, 15.25]cm)*

½in
*(1.25cm)*

2½in
(6.5cm)

8[8¼, 8½, 8¾, 9]in
*(20.25[20, 21.5, 22.25, 23]cm)*

**BACK & FRONT**

19[19½, 20, 20½, 21]in
*(48.25[49.5, 50.75, 52, 53.5]cm)*

9¼[9½, 9¾, 10, 10¼]in
*(23.5[24.25, 24.75, 25.5, 26]cm)*

4in
*[10.25cm]*

3½in
*(9cm)*

1¼in
*(3.25cm)*

18½[19½, 20½, 21½, 22½]in
*(47[49.5, 52, 54.5, 57.25]cm)*

8½[9, 9½, 10, 10½]in
*(21.5[23, 24.25, 25.5, 26.75]cm)*

16[16½, 17, 17½, 18]in
*(40.5[42, 43, 44.5, 45.75]cm)*

**SLEEVES**

2[2¼, 2¾, 2¾, 3]in
*(5[5.75, 7, 7, 7.5]cm)*

19¼[19, 19, 19, 19¼]in
*(48.75[48.25, 48.25, 48.25, 48.75]cm)*

1¼in
*(3.25cm)*

9[9, 9¼, 9½, 9¾]in
*(23[23, 23.5, 24.25, 24.75]cm)*

YOU ARE MY DESTINY

# ELLA

Get the 'wow factor' of fairisle with a fraction of the hassle. Minimal colourwork gives maximum impact with this fitted cardigan. However, if you're allergic to fairisle, substitute narrow stripes and trim the cuffs, hem and collar with a row of contrast.

## SIZES

XS – to fit bust 32in (81cm)
S – to fit bust 34in (86cm)
M – to fit bust 36in (91cm)
L – to fit bust 38in (96cm)
XL – to fit bust 40in (101cm).
See schematic for actual measurements.

## MATERIALS

Rowan Wool Cotton
123yd (113m) per 50g ball and
Rowanspun dk
219yd (200m) per 50g ball:
7[7, 8, 8, 9] balls Colour A
2[2, 2, 2, 2] balls Colour B
1[1, 1, 1, 1] ball Colour C
1[1, 1, 1, 1] ball Colour D
1[1, 1, 2, 2] ball Colour E
1[1, 1, 1, 1] ball Colour F
3mm (US 3); 3.75mm (US 5); circular
3mm (or size to obtain tension)
Stitch holders and markers
8 buttons

## TENSION

24 sts and 26 rows = 4in (10cm) over 2-colour stranded knitting (see page 121)
28 sts and 30 rows = 4in (10cm) over rib on larger needles.

## STITCHES

**2 x 2 rib**
**Stocking stitch**

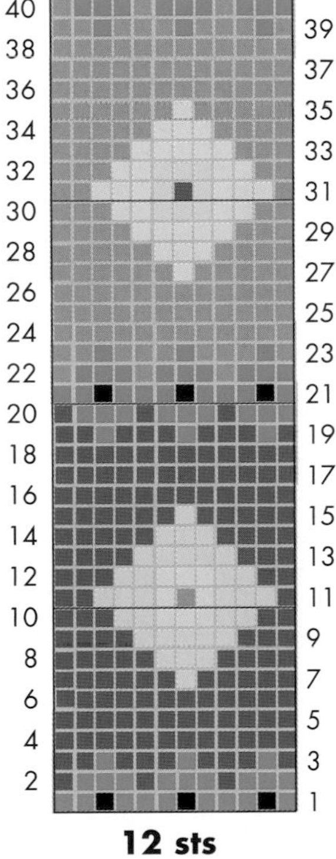


**Photographs show Colourway 2**

| Colourway 1 | Colourway 2 |
|---|---|
| Inky 908 (A) | Coffee Rich 956 |
| Flower 943 (B) | Rich 911 |
| Elf 946 (C) | Gypsy 910 |
| Ship Shape 955 (D) | Deepest Olive 907 |
| Bilberry Fool 959 (E) | Punch 731 (Rowanspun dk) |
| Aqua 949 (F) | Ship Shape 955 |

## Back

Using smaller needles and Colour A cast on 102[106, 114, 118, 126] sts and work in 2 x 2 rib for 7½[7½, 8, 8, 8]in (19[19, 20.25, 20.25, 20.25]cm) ending on WS row.
Change to larger needles and refer to chart and starting on Row 21, work rem rows to end, then rep the 40 rows to end of back, centring the chart as foll:
**XS** Work the last 3 sts, work the 12 sts 8 times, work the first 3 sts.
**S** Work the last 5 sts, work the 12 sts 8 times, work the first 5 sts.
**M** Work the last 3 sts, work the 12 sts 9 times, work the first 3 sts.

**L** Work the last 5 sts, work the 12 sts 9 times, work the first 5 sts.
**XL** Work the last 3 sts, work the 12 sts 10 times, work the first 3 sts.
Cont in patt as set until work measures 12[12, 12, 11½, 12]in (30.5[30.5, 30.5, 29.25, 30.5]cm) from c.o.e ending on WS row.

**Shape armhole**
Cast off 5[5, 5, 6, 6] sts at beg of next 2 rows. Then dec 1 st at both ends of next and ev foll alt row 7[6, 10, 9, 12] times in all, keeping patt correct – 78[84, 84, 88, 90] sts.
Cont in patt as set until work measures 19[19, 19½, 19½, 20]in (48.25[48.25, 49.5, 49.5, 50, 50.75]cm) from c.o.e. ending on WS row.

**Shape shoulder and neck**
Cast off 8[9, 8, 9, 9] sts at armhole edge on next 2 rows,
**Next row** (RS) Cast off 8[9, 9, 9, 9] sts at armhole edge, work 8[9, 9, 10, 10] sts in patt, place 30[30, 32, 32, 34] sts for neck on holder and place rem 24[27, 26, 28, 28] sts on holder.
**Next row** (WS) Work in patt as set
**Next row** (RS) Cast off rem 8[9, 9, 10, 10] sts.
Join second ball of yarn to other side and work in patt to end, reversing all shapings.

## Left Front
Using smaller needles and Colour A cast on 56[58, 62, 64, 68] sts and work in 2 x 2 rib for 7½[7½, 8, 8, 8]in (19[19, 20.25, 20.25, 20.25]cm) ending on WS row.
Change to larger needles and refer to chart and starting on Row 21, work remaining rows to end, then rep the 40 rows to end of back, centring the chart as foll:
**XS Row 1** Work the last 3 sts, work the 12 sts 3 times, work first 11 sts.
**Row 2** Work last 11 sts, work 12 sts 3 times, work first 3 sts
**S** Work the last 5 sts, work the 12 sts 3 times, work the first 11 sts.
**M** Work the last 3 sts, work the 12 sts 4 times, work the first 5 sts.
**L** Work the last 5 sts, work the 12 sts 4 times, work the first 5 sts.
**XL** Work the last 3 sts, work the 12 sts 4 times, work the first 11 sts.
AT THE SAME TIME on row 1 of chart place last 6 sts on holder for band – 50[52, 56, 58, 62] sts.
When work measures 11½[11½, 11½, 11, 11½]in (29.25[29.25, 29.25, 28, 29.25]cm) from c.o.e ending on WS row.

**Shape armhole**
Cast off 5[5, 5, 6, 6] sts at beg of next row. Work 1 row. Then dec 1 st at armhole edge of next and ev foll alt row 7[6, 10, 9, 12] times in all, keeping patt correct – 38[41, 41, 43, 44] sts. Cont in patt as set until work measures 17(17, 17.5, 17.5, 18)in (43[43, 44.5, 44.5, 45.75]cm) from c.o.e ending on RS row.

**Shape neck**
Cast off 6[6, 7, 7, 7] sts at beg of next row. Work 1 row in patt, then dec 1 st at neck edge on next and ev foll row 8[8, 8, 8, 9] times.
Cont in patt as set until work measures 19[19, 19½, 19½, 20]in (48.25[48.25, 49.5, 49.5, 50, 50.75]cm) from c.o.e. ending on WS row.

**Shape shoulder**
Cast off 8[9, 8, 9, 9] sts at armhole edge. Work 1 row.
Cast off 8[9, 9, 9, 9] sts at armhole edge. Work 1 row.
Cast off rem 8[9, 9, 10, 10] sts.

## Right Front
Mark position of 8 buttons on Left Front, first one ½in (1cm) up from bottom edge and 8th ¼in (.5cm) down from start of neck shaping and others spaced evenly between. Work as for left front reversing all shapings and inserting buttonholes opposite markers as below. Centre chart as foll:
**XS Row 1** Work the last 11 sts, work the 12 sts 3 times, work first 3 sts.
**Row 2** Work last 3 sts, work 12 sts 3 times, work first 11 sts
**S** Work the last 11 sts, work the 12 sts 3 times, work the first 5 sts.
**M** Work the last 5 sts, work the 12 sts 4 times, work the first 3 sts.
**L** Work the last 5 sts, work the 12 sts 4 times, work the first 5 sts.
**XL** Work the last 11 sts, work the 12 sts 4 times, work the first 3 sts.
AT THE SAME TIME insert buttonholes on RS rows to correspond to markers on Left Front as foll:
**Next row** Work 2 sts, cast off 2 sts, work to end of row.
**Next row** Work to last 4 sts, cast on 2 sts, work 2 sts.
Work in back of 2 cast on sts on foll row.
**NB** On row 1 of chart place first 6 sts on holder for band.

## Sleeves (both alike)
Using smaller needles and Colour A cast on 52(52, 52, 54, 54) sts and work in 2 x 2 rib for 3¼in (8.25cm) ending on RS row. Knit 1 row to form foldline.
Change to larger needles and refer to chart and starting on row 1, work 21 rows, centring the chart as foll:
Work the last 2[2, 2, 3, 3] sts, work the 12 sts 4 times, work the first 2[2, 2, 3, 3] sts.
**Next row** Using Colour A, purl, inc 8[8, 8, 10, 10] sts evenly across row 60[60, 60, 64, 64] sts.
Work to end in 2 x 2 rib, centring work as foll:
K1, *p2, k2, rep from *14[14, 14, 15, 15] times, p2, k1
AT THE SAME TIME inc 1 for sleeves as foll, keeping 2 x 2 rib correct:
**XS** Inc 1 st at both ends of ev 11th row 8 times, then ev 12th row once – 78sts
**S** Inc 1 st at both ends of ev 10th row 10 times – 80sts
**M** Inc 1 st at both ends of ev 8th row 13 times – 86sts
**L** Inc 1 st at both ends of ev 7th row 15 times – 94sts
**XL** Inc 1 st at both ends of ev 6th row 15 times, then ev 7th row twice – 98sts
Cont rib as set until work measures 21¼[21¼, 21¾, 21¾, 21¾]in (54[54, 55.25, 55.25, 55.25]cm) from c.o.e. ending on WS row.

**Shape sleeve cap**
Cast off 5[5, 5, 6, 6] sts at beg of next 2 rows. Then dec 1 st at both

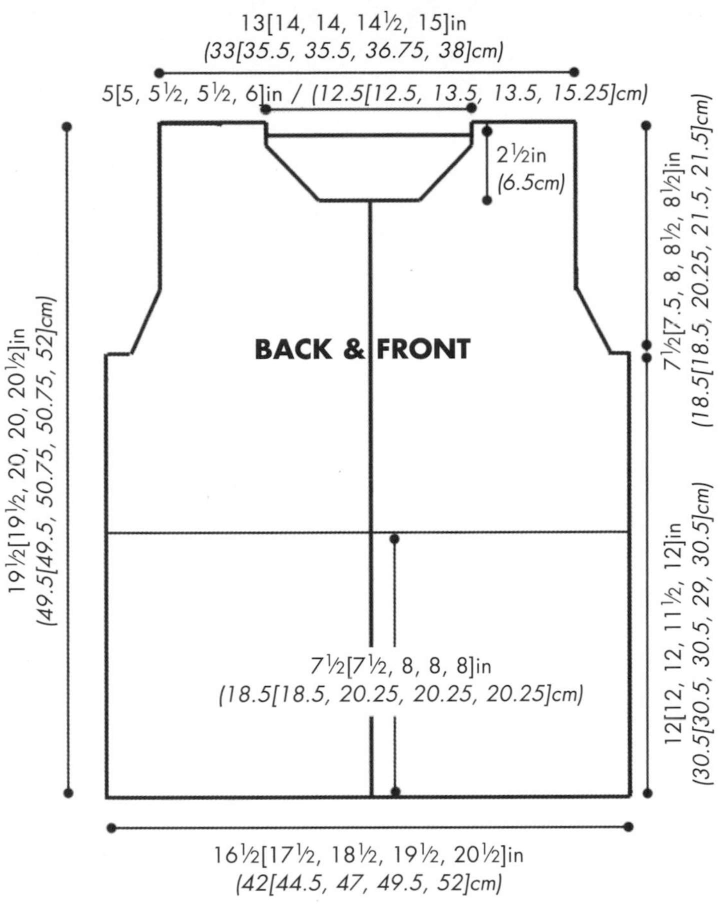


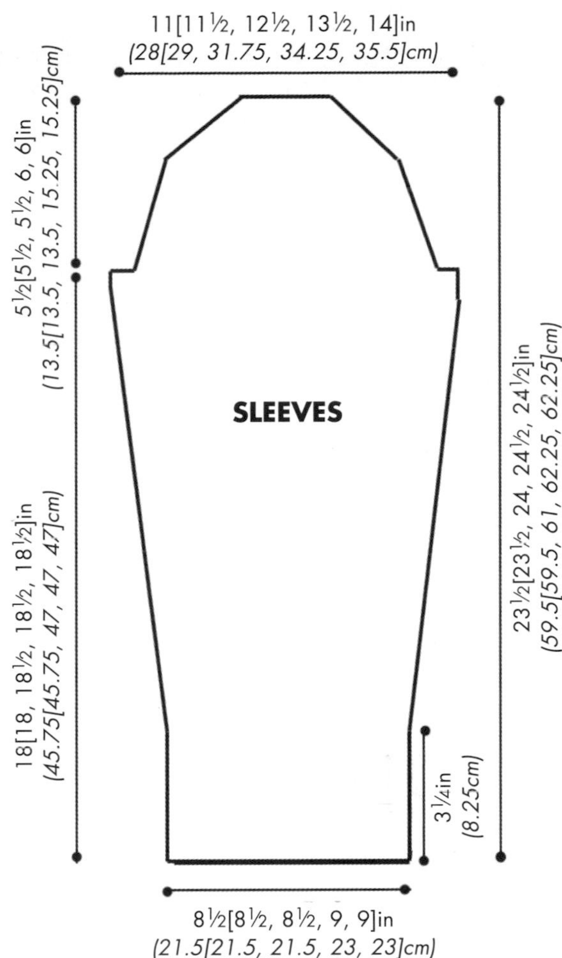


ends of next and then ev foll alt row 16[16, 14, 16, 15] times, then ev foll row 4(4, 8, 8, 10) times – 28[30, 32, 34, 36] sts.
Cast off 3 sts at beg of next 4 rows.
Cast off rem 16[18, 20, 22, 24] sts

## Finishing

Join shoulder seams. Insert sleeves placing any fullness evenly over top of sleeve cap. Join side and sleeve seams in one line. Turn sleeve facing back along foldline and slip stitch into place on inside.

BANDS

Using smaller needles, cont in Colour A until band reaches start of neck shaping at centre front, inserting the rem of buttonholes on Right Front to correspond with markers. Oversew bands to sweater as you knit.
Attach 8 buttons on button band opposite buttonholes.

COLLAR

Using smaller needles and Colour A, starting in centre of Right Front buttonhole band, pick up and knit 36[36, 37, 39, 40] sts to shoulder seam, 2 sts down back neck, 30[30, 32, 32, 34] sts from holder at centre back, 2 sts up other side back neck and 36[36, 37, 39, 40] sts around Left Front neck edge, ending in centre of button band – 106[106, 110, 114, 118] sts.
Working in 2 x 2 rib, work 1in (2.5cm) and then change to larger needles and work a further 2½in (6.5cm) and then cast off in rib patt.

# CAMILLA

Learn to knit with beads with this dramatic plunge-neck cardigan. If you don't relish the intarsia colourwork, work in monotone and pick out the zigzag pattern with contrasting beads.

## SIZES

XS – to fit bust 32in (81cm)
S – to fit bust 34in (86cm)
M – to fit bust 36in (91cm)
L – to fit bust 38in (96cm)
XL – to fit bust 40in (101cm).
See schematic for actual measurements.

## MATERIALS

Artesano Alpaca
131yd (120m) per 50g:
7[8, 9, 9, 10] balls Damson (53);
1 ball Cream (000); Fuchsia (57), Black (0012), Olive (402)
One pair each 3.25mm (US 3) & 3.75mm (US 5); circular 3.25mm (US 3); or size to obtain tension
Stitch holders
3 buttons
Approx 272(286, 290, 304, 312) small glass beads

## TENSION

24 sts and 32 rows = 4in (10cm) over st st.
24 sts and 26 rows = 4in (10cm) over fairisle

## STITCHES USED

**Stocking stitch**
**1 x 1 rib**
(**NB** For 2-colour stranded knitting and attaching beads see pages 121 and 122.)

## BACK

Using smaller needles and Colour A cast on 102[106, 114, 118, 126] sts and work in 1 x 1 rib for 5[5, 5½, 5½, 5½]in (12.75[12.75, 14, 14, 14]cm) ending on WS row. Change to larger needles and work in st st to end. When work measures 12[12, 12, 11½, 12]in (30.5[30.5, 30.5, 29.25, 30.5]cm) from c.o.e ending on WS row

**Shape armhole**

Cast off 5[5, 5, 6, 6] sts at beg of next 2 rows. Then dec 1 st at both ends of next and ev foll alt row 7[6, 10, 9, 12] times in all, keeping patt correct – 78[84, 84, 88, 90] sts. Cont in st st until work measures 15½[15½, 16, 16, 16½]in (39.25[39.25, 40.5, 40.5, 42]cm) from c.o.e ending on WS row, then refer to chart and work the 24 rows, threading 92[98, 98, 102, 104] beads onto Colour C yarn at beg.
**NB** Check row gauge.

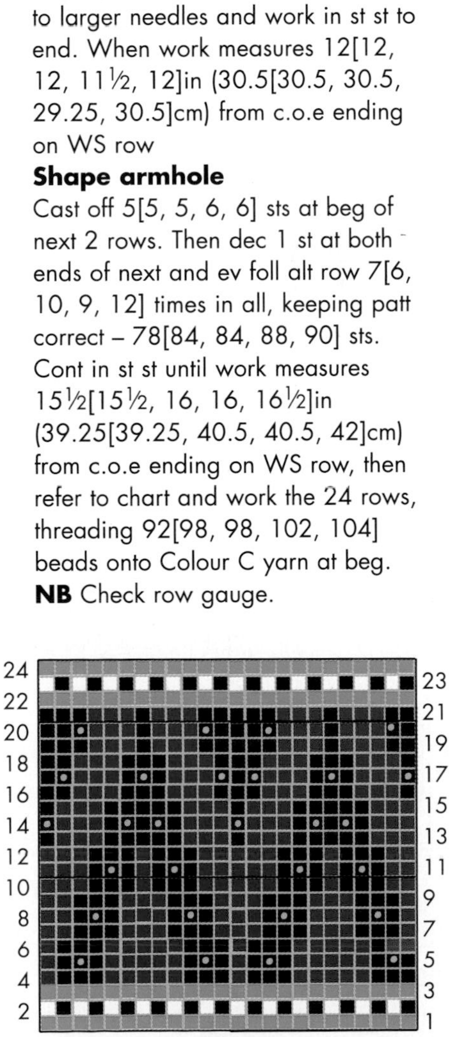

**24 sts**

Centre chart as foll: Work the last 3(6, 6, 8, 9) sts of chart, work the 24 sts 3 times, work first 3(6, 6, 8, 9) sts.

**Shape shoulder and neck**

In st st in Colour A:
Cast off 8(9, 8, 9, 9) sts at armhole edge on next 2 rows.
**Next row** (RS) Cast off 8(9, 9, 9, 9) sts at armhole edge, work 8(9, 9, 10, 10)sts in patt, cast off 30(30, 32, 32, 34) sts for neck and place rem 24(27, 26, 28, 28)sts on holder.
**Next row** (WS) Work in patt as set
**Next row** (RS) Cast off rem 8(9, 9, 10, 10)sts in Colour B.
Join second ball of yarn to other side and work in patt to end, rev all shapings.

## Left Front

Using smaller needles and Colour A cast on 57(59, 63, 65, 69) sts and work in 1 x 1 rib for 5[5, 5½, 5½, 5½]in [12.75(12.75, 14, 14, 14)cm] ending on WS row, first threading 10[10, 11, 11, 11] beads.

- Damson 53 (A)
- Olive Green 402 (B)
- Black 0012 (C)
- Place bead on Colour C background
- Cream 000 (D)
- Fuchsia 57 (E)

AT THE SAME TIME place one bead on first and ev 4th row (WS) on last st, so that it sits on edge of band. Change to larger needles and working in st st to end and placing last 7 sts on holder for band

**Start neck shaping**

50[52, 56, 58, 62] sts.

Dec 1 st at beg of next and then 6th row 4[4, 11, 11, 14] times, then ev 7th row 9[9, 3, 3, 1] times – 36[38, 41, 43, 46] sts.

AT THE SAME TIME when work measures 12[12, 12, 11½, 12]in (30.5[30.5, 30.5, 29.25, 30.5]cm) from c.o.e ending on WS row

**Shape armhole**

Cast off 5[5, 5, 6, 6] sts at beg of next row. Work 1 row. Then dec 1 st at armhole edge of next and ev foll alt row 7[6, 10, 9, 12] times in all, keeping patt correct.

AT THE SAME TIME when work measures 15½[15½, 16, 16, 16½]in (39.25[39.25, 40.5, 40.5, 42]cm) from c.o.e. ending on WS row, refer to chart and work the 24 rows, threading 28(32, 32, 34, 35) beads onto Colour C yarn at beg.

**NB** Check the row gauge is accurate.

Centre chart as foll:

Work the last 3[6, 6, 8, 9] sts of chart, work the rem 21[21, 20, 20, 19] sts.

**Shape shoulder and neck**

In st st in Colour A:

Cast off 8[9, 8, 9, 9] sts at armhole edge. Work 1 row.

Cast off 8[9, 9, 9, 9] sts at armhole edge. Work 1 row.

Cast off rem 8[9, 9, 10, 10] sts in Colour B.

## Right Front

Mark position of 3 buttons on Left Front, first one ½in (1cm) up from bottom edge and 3rd ¼in (0.5cm) down from start of neck shaping and other spaced evenly between. Work as for left front reversing all shapings and inserting buttonholes opposite markers as below.

Centre chart as foll:

Work the last 21[21, 20, 20, 19] sts of chart, work the first 3[6, 6, 8, 9] sts of chart.

AT THE SAME TIME insert buttonholes on RS rows beg at markers on Left Front as foll:

**Next row** Work 4 sts, turn, leave rem 3 sts on hold and work back. Work a further 2 rows on these 4 sts, then attach yarn to sts on hold and work 4 rows.

**Next row** Work across all 7 sts.

## Sleeves (both alike)

Using smaller needles and Colour A cast on 54[54, 54, 58, 58] sts and work in 1 x 1 rib for 3.25in (8.25cm) ending on WS row.

Change to larger needles and refer to chart (threading 27[27, 27, 30, 30] beads onto Colour C yarn at beg.) and starting on row 1, work 12 rows, then go back to row 1 and work rows 1–3 (15 rows in all) centring the chart as foll:

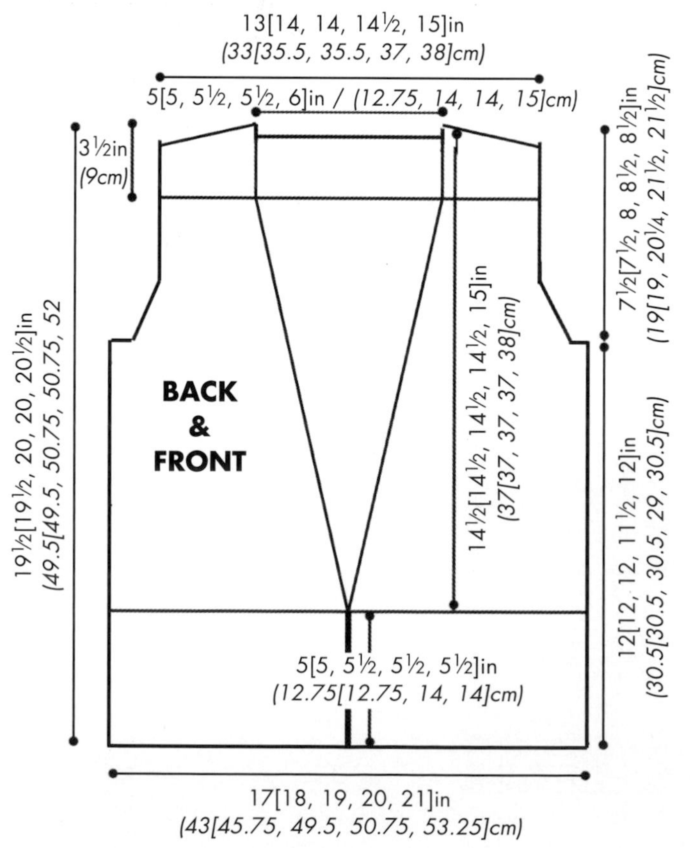


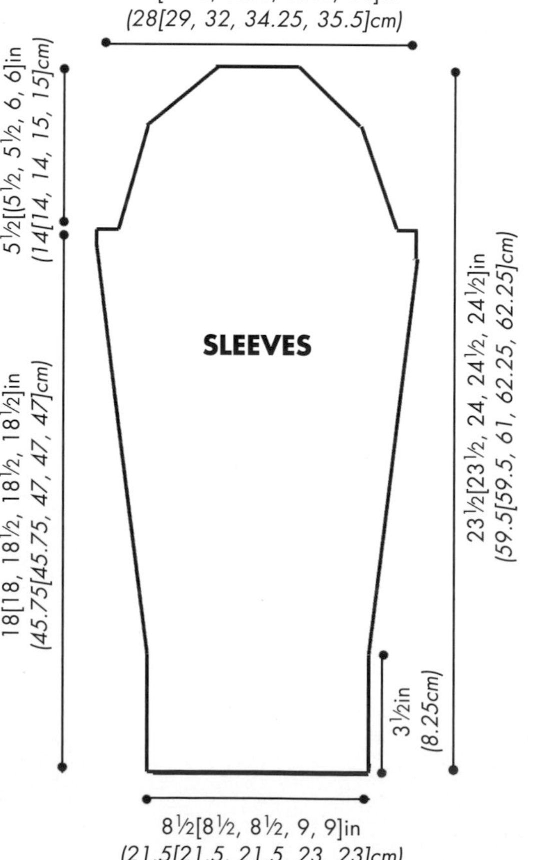

Work the last 3[3, 3, 5, 5] sts, work the 24 sts twice, work the first 3[3, 3, 5, 5] sts.
AT THE SAME TIME work sleeve shapings, keeping fairisle correct:
**XS** Inc 1 st at both ends of ev 17th row 4 times, then ev 18th row twice – 66sts
**S** Inc 1 st at both ends of ev 13th row 8 times – 70sts
**M** Inc 1 st at both ends of ev 9th row twice, then ev 10th row 9 times – 76sts
**L** Inc 1 st at both ends of ev 9th row 12 times – 82sts
**XL** Inc 1 st at both ends of ev 8th row 9 times, then ev 9th row 4 times – 84sts.
When colour work is completed cont in st st in Colour A to end. When work measures 18[18, 18½, 18½, 18½]in (45.75[45.75, 47, 47, 47]cm) from c.o.e end on WS row,

**Shape sleeve cap**

Cast off 5[5, 5, 6, 6] sts at beg of next 2 rows. Then dec 1 st at both ends of next and then ev foll 3rd row 7[3, 0, 3, 1] times, then ev alt row 8[14, 18, 16, 19] times, then ev foll row 0[0, 1, 0, 0] times – 24[24, 26, 30, 30] sts.
Cast off 2 sts at beg of next 4 rows. Cast off rem 16[16, 18, 22, 22] sts

## Finishing

Join shoulder seams. Insert sleeves placing any fullness evenly over top of sleeve cap. Join side and sleeve seams in one line.

**Bands**

Using smaller needles and Colour A, cont in 1 x 1 rib on 7 sts, threading approx 35[35, 37, 37, 39] beads at start and placing them ev 4th row until band reaches centre back. Cast off. Oversew bands to sweater as you knit. Sew bands together at centre back. Attach 3 buttons on button band opposite buttonholes.

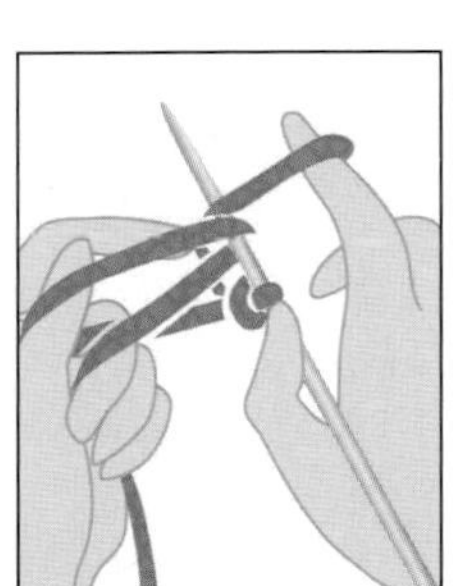

PART 5

# TECHNIQUES

## CASTING ON

I usually use the thumb method since, like the continental cast-on, it gives an elastic edge. If you have a tendency to cast on tightly then also use a needle one or two sizes larger than the pattern calls for. For cast on stitches in the middle of a row, I use a cable cast-on.

### Thumb method

**1**

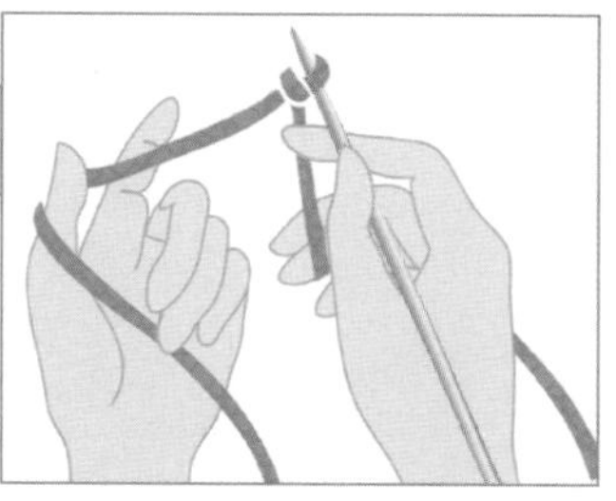

Make a slip knot 39in (1m) from the end of the yarn. Hold the needle in your right hand with the ball end of the yarn over your index finger. * Wind the loose end of the yarn around your left thumb from front to back.

**2**

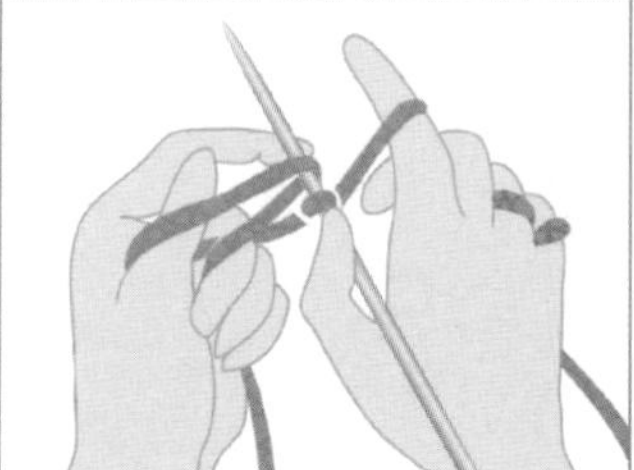

Insert the point of the needle under the first strand of yarn on your thumb.

**3**

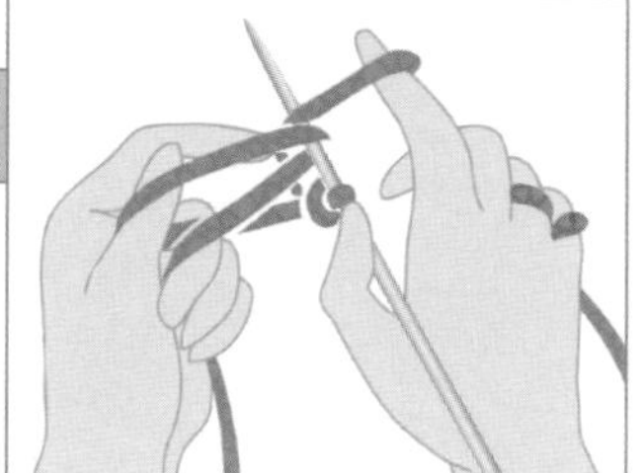

With your right index finger, take the ball end of the yarn over the point of the needle.

**4**

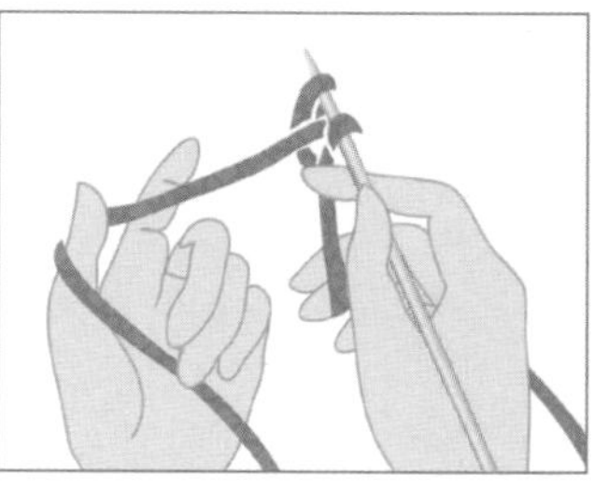

Pull a loop through to form the first stitch. Remove your left thumb from the yarn. Pull the loose end to secure the stitch. Repeat from * until the required number of stitches have been cast on.

### Continental cast-on

Make a slip knot for the initial stitch, at a distance from the end of the yarn of about 1¼in (3cm) for each stitch to be cast on.

**1**

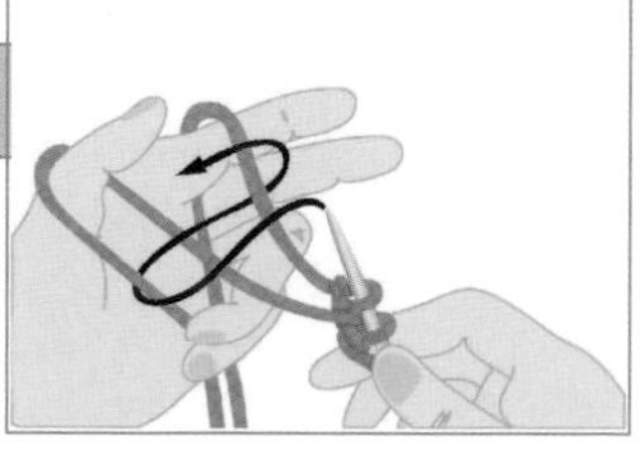

Arrange both ends of yarn in your left hand as shown. Bring needle under front strand of thumb loop, up over front strand of index loop, catching it...

**2**

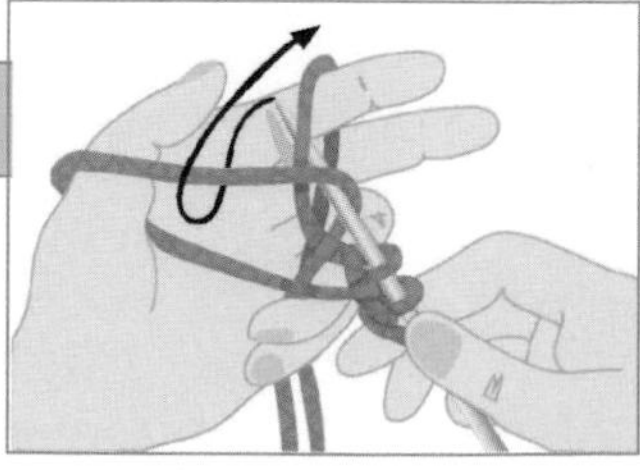

...and bringing it under the front of the thumb loop. Slip thumb out of loop, and use it to adjust tension on new stitch. One stitch cast on.

Repeat this process until all the stitches are cast on.

## Cable cast-on

This is a useful cast-on when stitches need to be added within your work.

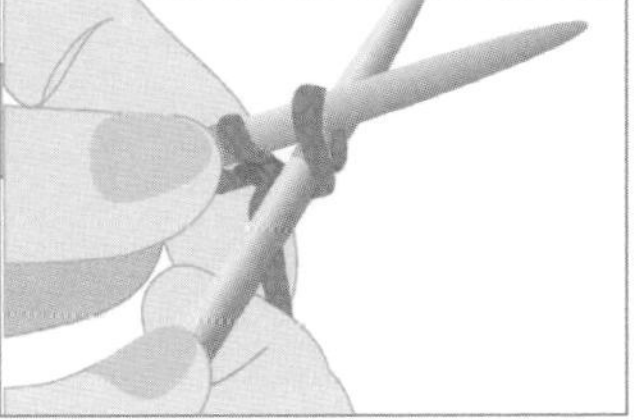

Make a slip knot on left needle, as for knit cast-on. When 2 sts are on the left needle, insert right needle between them.

2

Knit a stitch and place it on left needle.

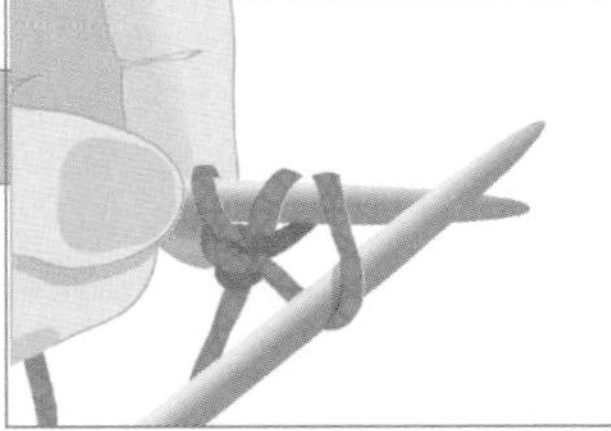

Repeat steps 2 and 3 for each additional st.

### Backwards loop cast-on

A simple cast-on, useful for casting on stitches in the middle of a row, made by making a backwards loop and placing it on the needle. It's also used for making a stitch between stitches.

1 With yarn held in right hand, place the thumb of the left hand over the yarn and then back up under it to form a loop.

2 Place the loop on the right-hand needle by inserting needle into this loop from the bottom of the thumb up.

3 Tighten to form a stitch.

Repeat from 1–3 until you have as many stitches as you require.

## CASTING OFF

I use the basic chain cast-off and always cast off in pattern, keeping knit, purl, yarn overs, decreases and so on correct. If you cast off on the wrong side, this will hide the chain edge. For projects like shawls or those that require the cast-on and cast-off edges to be the same width, the important thing to bear in mind is that it's often better to cast off using needles at least one size larger, especially if you have a tendency to knit tightly. Casting off using a crochet hook also helps solve this problem as you can more easily regulate the length of the stitches.

## Basic chain cast-off

Work 2 sts. Then with left-hand needle, lift the first stitch over the second stitch and off the needle. * Work another stitch and lift the previous stitch over it similarly. Repeat from * to last stitch.  Cut the yarn and pull through last loop.

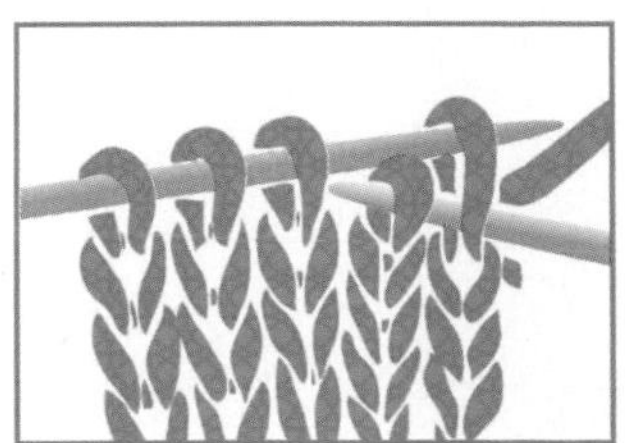

## Crochet cast-off

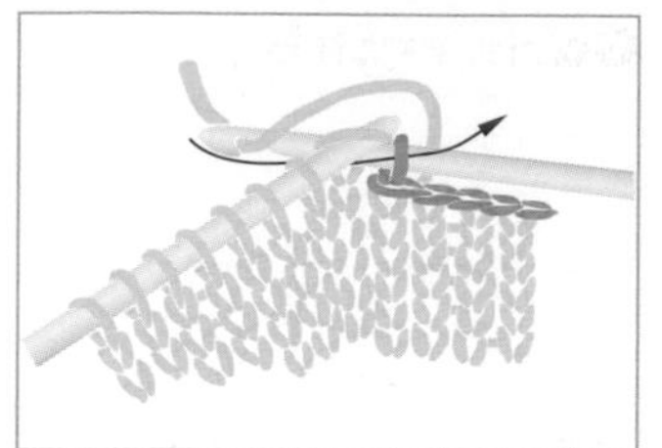

Holding yarn in left hand at back of work, slip 1 stitch purlwise onto hook. * Insert hook into next stitch and drop the stitch from left needle. Using hook, pull the yarn through the 2 stitches, which then leaves 1 stitch on hook. Repeat from *.

## Three-needle cast-off

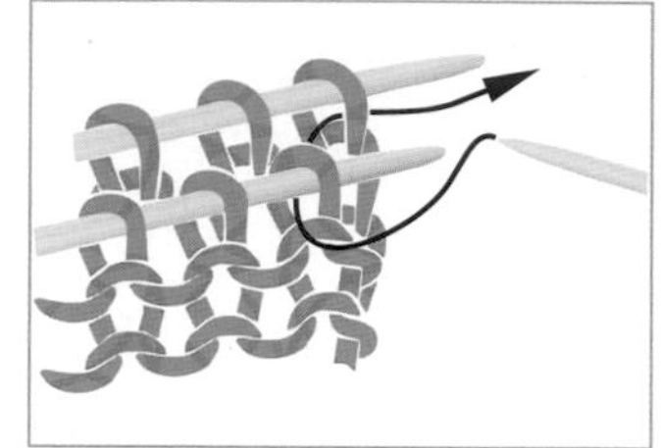

This is a neat way of joining seams on inside, or decoratively on outside, especially if the shoulder shaping is short-rowed.

Place right sides together, back sts on one needle and front sts on another. * Work 2 together (1 from front needle and 1 from back needle). Repeat from * once. Cast off first st over 2nd st. Continue to work 2 together (1 front st and 1 back) and cast off across.

## Picot point cast-off

Cast off 2 sts, *slip rem st on RH needle onto LH needle, cast on 2 sts, cast off 4 sts; repeat from * to end and fasten off rem st.

## STITCHES

There is nothing mystical or particularly difficult about any of the stitches in Couture Knits. Below is every stitch you'll ever need to knit every sweater in the book.

## 1 x 1 Rib

*k1, p1, rep across 1st row; on subsequent rows keep knit and purl sts correct.

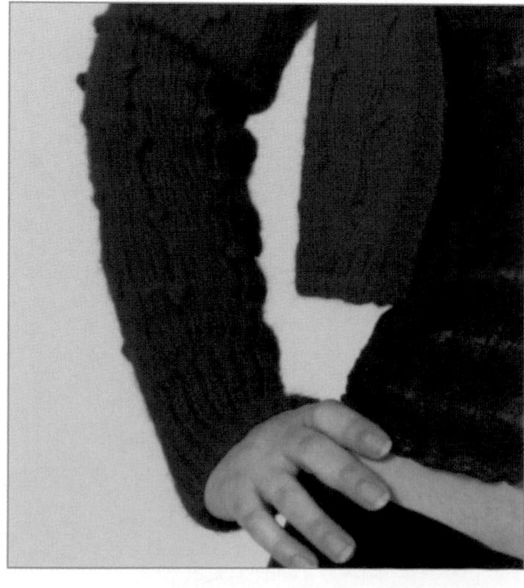

## 2 x 2 Rib

Multiple of 4 + 2
**Row 1** *k2, p2, rep from * to last 2 sts, k2
**Row 2** *p2, k2, rep from * to last 2 sts, p2
Repeat these 2 rows.

## Garter stitch

Knit every row

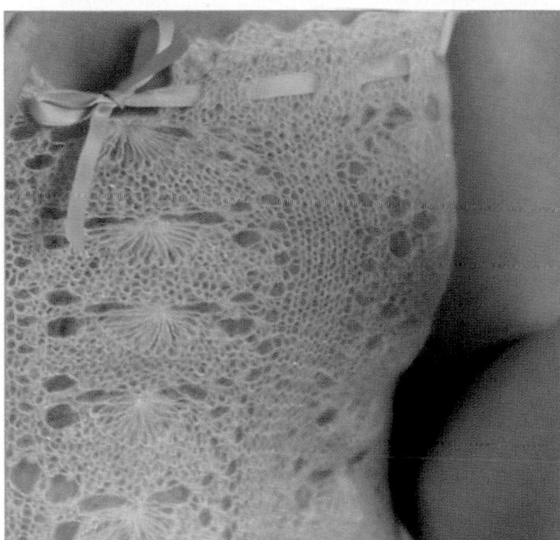

## Stocking stitch

Knit on right side rows and purl on wrong side rows.

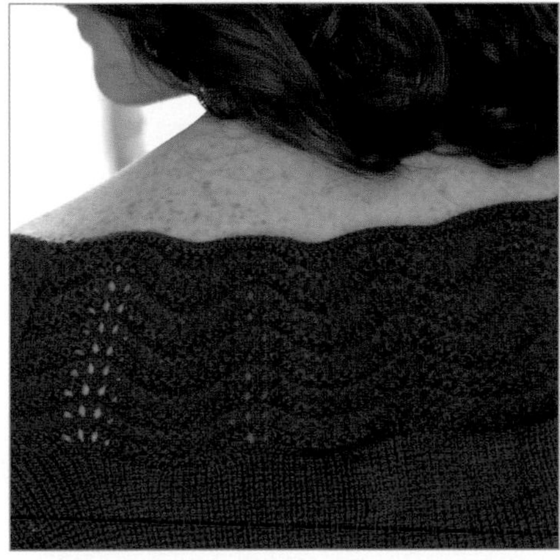

## Reverse stocking stitch

Purl on right side rows, knit on wrong side rows.

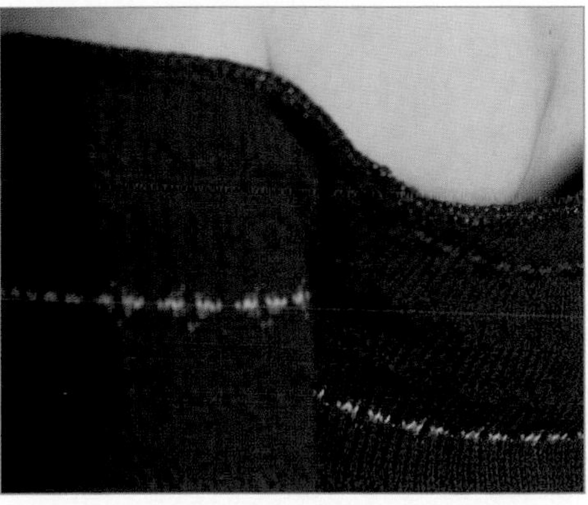

## Moss (or seed) stitch

**Row 1** *k1, p1; repeat from * to end
**Row 2** Knit the purl sts and purl the knit stitches
Repeat row 2.

## I-cord

A simple but versatile technique that creates a circular tube, like French knitting. It has many uses, from edgings to highlighting parts of a project. I-cord can obviously be used for tying, but with a little imagination you can easily construct flowers and other three-dimensional sculptural pieces with which to adorn your creations.

Using two dpns, cast on 3 sts, *slide these sts to the other end of the needle, and knit them (using the yarn from other end of row). Repeat from * to end.

## CABLES AND TWISTS

Many knitters are afraid of cables, but actually they're not difficult to master and are a great way of getting movement and texture into your knitting. The technique is simply a way of crossing one set of stitches over another set and looks best when worked against a contrasting background stitch; ie a stocking stitch cable on a reverse stocking stitch background. Basic cables are worked by placing the first set of stitches on a cable needle and holding them at the back or front of your knitting, depending whether you want the crossing to slope towards the right or left. Holding the stitches at the front will result in a left-sloping cable and holding them at the back will result in a right-sloping cable. By working a right- and then a left-sloping cable you'll get a symmetrical cable meeting at the centre.

### Cable 4 front (C4F) – left sloping

**1**

On a right side row, work to the position of the cable and slip the next two stitches onto the cable needle, leaving it at front of work.

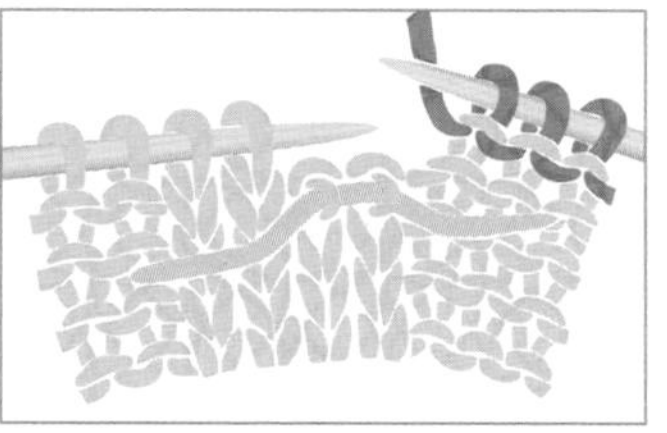

**2**

Working behind the cable needle, knit the two stitches from the left-hand needle.

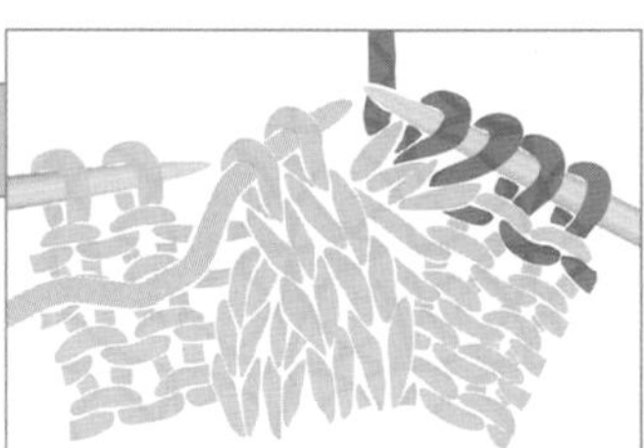

**3**

Now knit the two stitches from the cable needle to produce a crossover to the left.

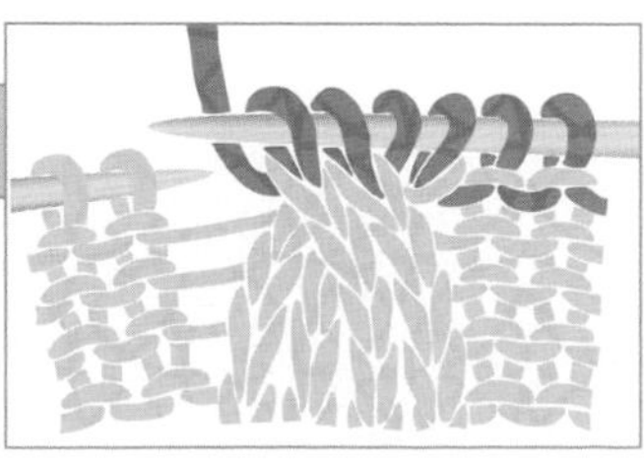

Twists achieve the same effect as a cable but are usually worked over fewer stitches and don't use a cable needle. The principle is the same though, ie crossing one stitch (or stitches) over another, creating a travelling stitch or stitches. Twists are made by working the second stitch on the left-hand needle first, without slipping it off the needle. The first stitch is then worked and both stitches slipped off the needle together. There are many variations on cables and twists but once you have the basic concept you should find them easy to follow.

## Twist 2 Back (T2B)

Work to one stitch before the knit stitch. Miss the first stitch, then knit the second (the knit) stitch through the front of the loop.

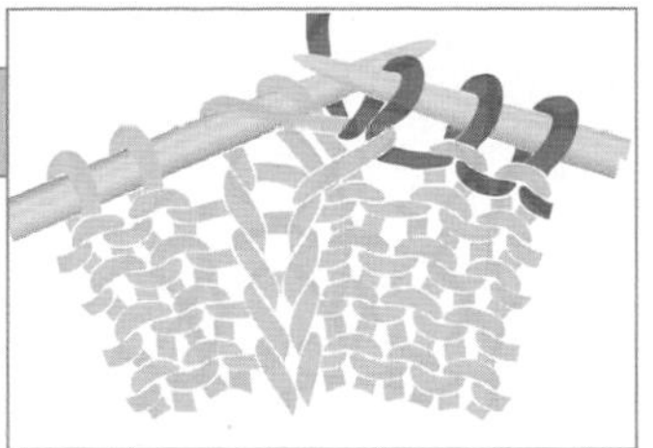

2

Without slipping the worked stitch off the needle, bring the yarn to the front and purl the missed stitch through the front of the loop, then slip both stitches off the left-hand needle together.

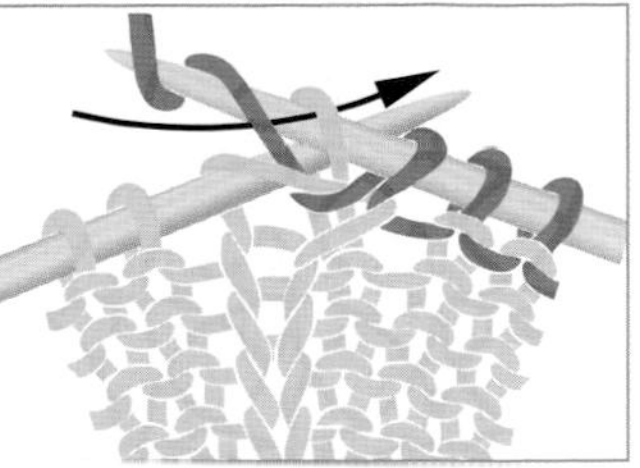

## Twist 2 Front (T2F)

Work to the knit stitch. Miss the first (the knit) stitch, then purl the second stitch through the back of the loop, working behind the first stitch.

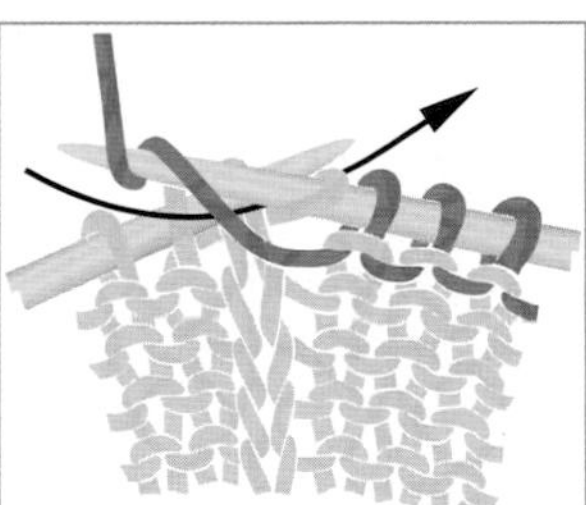

2

Without slipping the worked stitch off the needle, take the yarn back and knit the missed stitch through front of loop, then slip both stitches off the left-hand needle together.

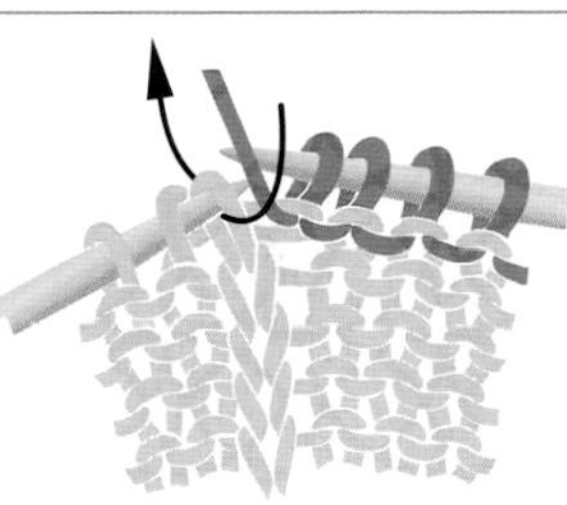

# CROCHET

## Double crochet (US single crochet)

Work slip stitch to begin.

Insert hook into next stitch.

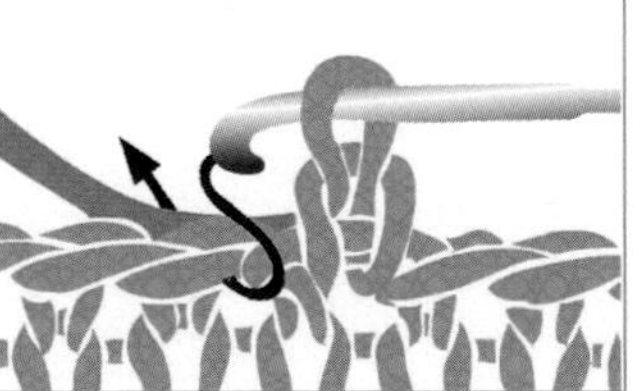

2

Yarn over and through stitch; 2 loops on hook.

3

Yarn over and through both loops on hook; double crochet completed. Repeat steps 1–3.

## Treble crochet (US double crochet)

**1**

Pass yarn round hook, miss 2 chain, insert hook under 2 top threads of 3rd chain from hook, pull a loop through, (3 loops on hook), pass yarn round hook, pull through 2 loops, (2 loops on hook).

**2**

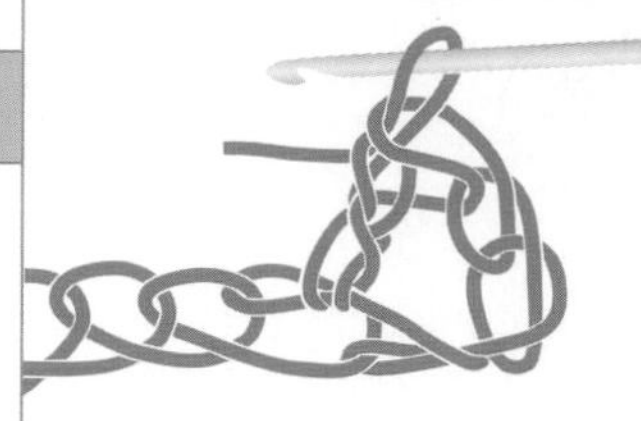

Pass yarn round hook, pull loop through remaining 2 loops, leaving 1 loop on hook.

## BRIOCHE RIB

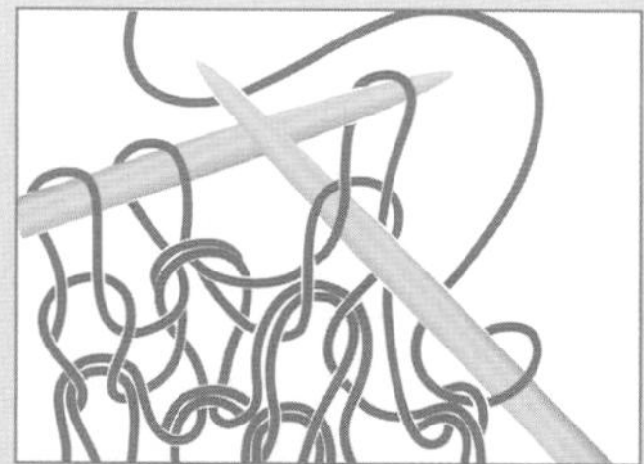

I love brioche ribs because they create a fabric that is reversible but use no purl stitches, usually using slipped stitches and yarn overs instead. They're really easy to knit once you get the hang of k1 (below) – insert needle through centre of stitch below next stitch on needle and knit this in the usual way, slipping the stitch above off the needle at the same time.

**Multiple of 2 sts**

**Foundation row** – knit
**Row 1** *k1, k1 below (insert needle through centre of st below next st on needle and knit this in the usual way, slipping the stitch above off the needle at the same time); rep from * to last 2 sts, k2.
**Repeat row** 1 throughout.

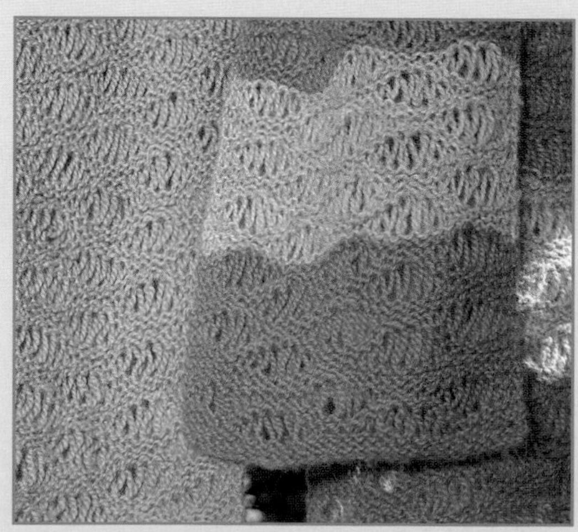

## SELVEDGES

Always work a selvedge on every row when possible. This helps prevent curl and makes finishing easier (especially when using mattress stitch) as the resulting notches can be matched. There are many different selvedge stitches, but old habits die hard and I usually use the beaded selvedge my grandmother taught me: slip the first stitch knitwise and knit into the back of the last stitch on every row. Another good one is the chain selvedge, which is great for backstitch seams and also helps when picking up stitches or working crochet edges:
**RS rows:** slip first stitch knitwise, knit last stitch
**WS rows:** slip first stitch purlwise, purl last stitch
Take time to experiment and find the selvedge that works for you.

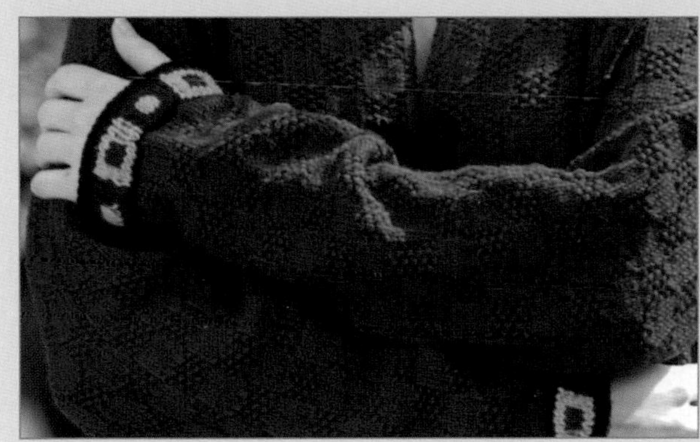

## TWO-COLOUR STRANDED KNITTING

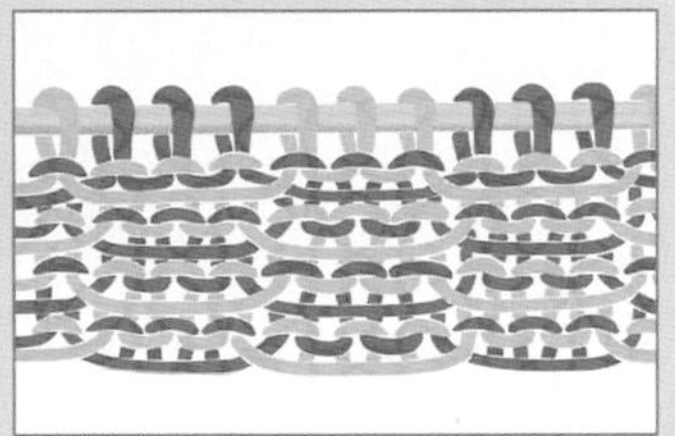

Many knitters remain in awe of this technique, but once you have mastered stocking stitch, it's just a matter of organizing your yarn and making sure you don't pull the yarn too tightly.
Carry the contrast yarn loosely on the wrong side, either weaving it in or stranding it. Do not strand the yarn over more than 3 stitches.

## WEAVING

The two-handed method, illustrated top, involves being able to work simultaneously with the British method (throwing the yarn) in the right hand and the Continental method (picking the yarn) in the left hand. This produces an even, pleasing effect but many knitters have problems with tension on the purl side. A good alternative is to use either circular or double-pointed needles and work across the row, knitting every colour A stitch and slipping (purlwise) every colour B stitch. Do not turn the work at the end of the row, but slide the stitches back to the right-hand point of the needle, drop A, pick up B and work sts, slipping sts previously worked in A. Turn the work and proceed with purl side.

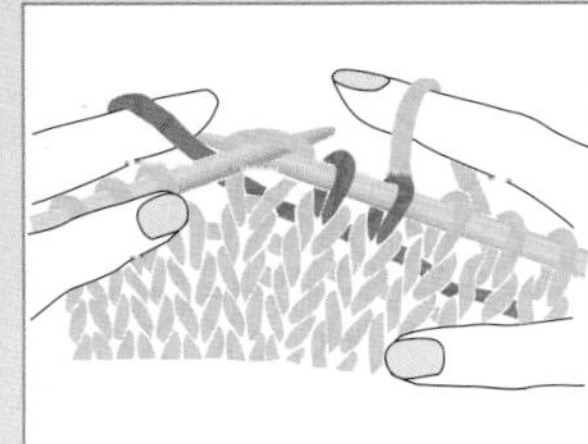

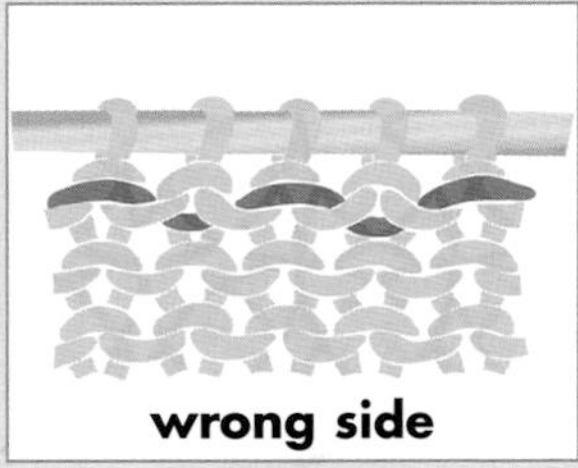

**wrong side**

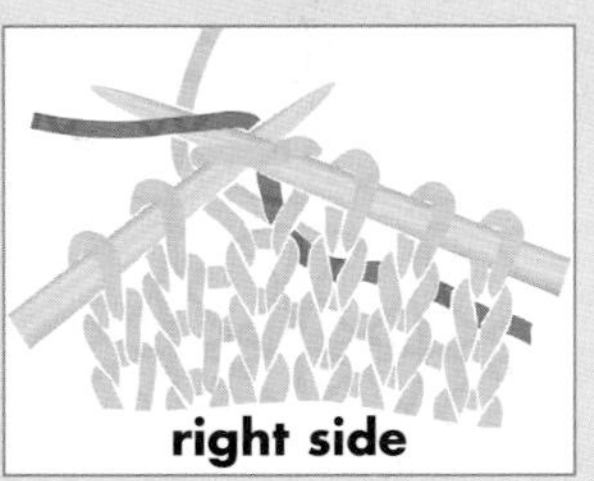

**right side**

## READING KNITTING CHARTS

When knitting back and forth, charts are read from right to left on right-side rows and from left to right on wrong-side rows. Charts can begin with a right-side or wrong-side row, this will be indicated by where row 1 is situated on the chart. For instance if row 1 is on the left, then the chart starts with a wrong-side row, if it is on the right, it starts with a right-side row. In circular knitting all rows are right-side rows and every row is read from right to left. Every square (or rectangle) represents one stitch horizontally and one row vertically. The symbols represent either stitches (knit, purl, cable etc) or colours (in intarsia or two-colour stranded knitting). When working with several colours it's good to tape a small reeling of each colour alongside its symbol so you have a constant reminder of which yarn to use. Use a line finder or alternatively make one yourself: take a strip of card or plastic the width of the chart and cut a long slit into it, approximately the size of a row. This can then be moved up the chart as you knit, masking the rows you've knitted and highlighting the one you're working on. Charts in books are notoriously small, so if this is a problem for you make an enlarged photocopy before you start.

## READING KNITTING PATTERNS

Throughout the book, figures in parenthesis relate to S, M, L and XL sizes respectively. When there is only one figure, this relates to all.

## INTARSIA KNITTING

Not my favourite type of knitting any longer over a whole sweater, but small bursts can create excitement and add impact to a project. If your design has a background colour then use seperate balls for each of the contrast colours and strand or weave the main colour behind. This cuts down on the number of ends and gives the contrast colours a slightly raised effect, which helps define the pattern. For intarsia with random shapes, use a separate length of yarn for each colour every time it occurs, twisting the two colours around each other at start and finish to avoid holes. To eliminate tangles, either wrap each length around a separate peice of card with a small slit along the side edge to secure yarn and dangle on back of work, or treat yourself to the readymade version available in most yarn shops. Alternatively use short lengths of yarn (no longer than 24in (61cm) and straighten at end of row.

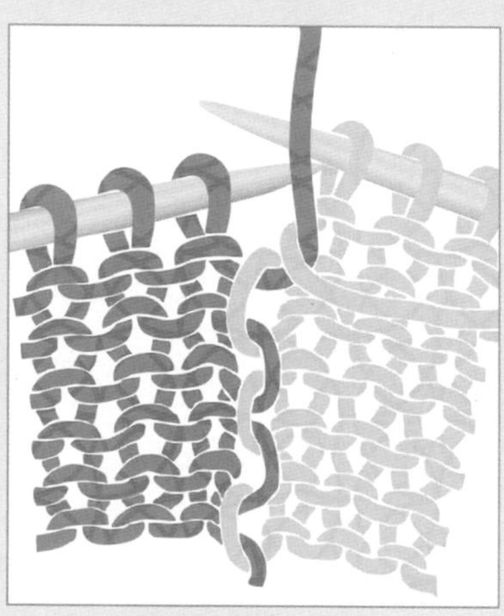

## ATTACHING BEADS

The Big Eye needle is wonderful for threading the beads. As its name suggests, it's one gigantic flexible eye. I've only ever seen these in the States, but it may have crossed the pond by now or be available online. If you can't get hold of one, then thread a fine needle with about 8in (20cm) of cotton and knot the two ends together. Thread the yarn through the loop of cotton and off you go. For attaching the beads I prefer the following slip stitch method as it ensures that the bead stays on the right side of the work.

On a RS row, work to the position of the beaded stitch. Bring the yarn forward to front of work and push a bead down the yarn so that it lies against the needle at the front of the work. Slip the next stitch purlwise, leaving the bead in front of the slipped stitch. Take the yarn to the back and continue to work as normal.

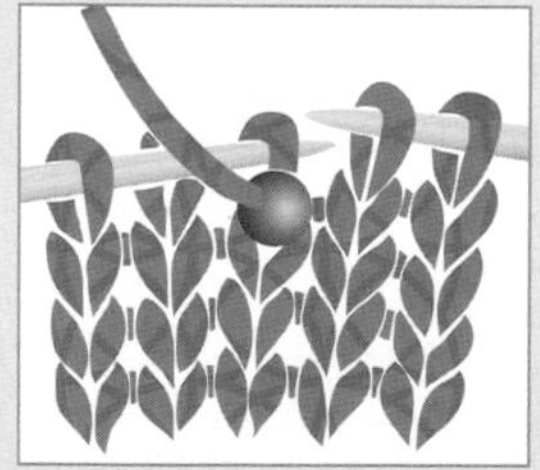

On a WS row, work to the position of the bead, take the yarn to the back of the work and place the bead so that it lies on RS of work against the needle. Slip the next stitch purlwise, leaving the bead behind the slipped stitch.Take the yarn to the front and continue to purl as set.

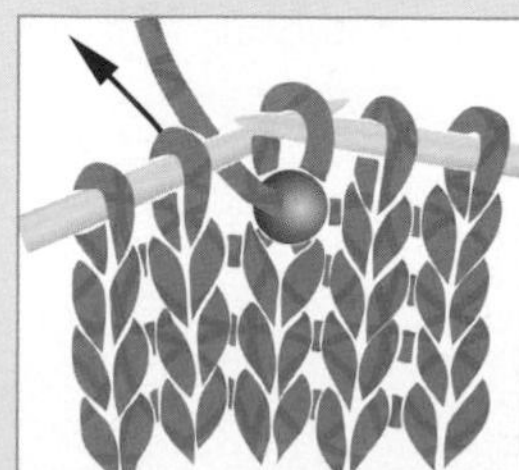

## WRAPPING STITCHES

This is an indispensable tool in any knitter's kit, helping to give work a professional finish. Useful for short-row shaping of darts, shoulders, necklines, hat tops, adding flair to a skirt, curved edges, creating a pouch, or anything which requires live stitches to be left for picking up later.

### On a knit row

**1**

With yarn in back, slip the next stitch as if to purl. Bring yarn to front of work and slip stitch back to left needle. Turn the work.

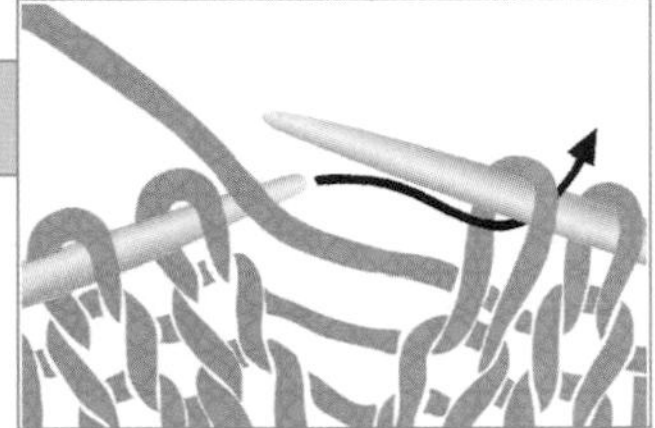

**2**

When you come to the wrap on the following knit row, make it less visible by knitting the wrap together with the stitch that it wraps.

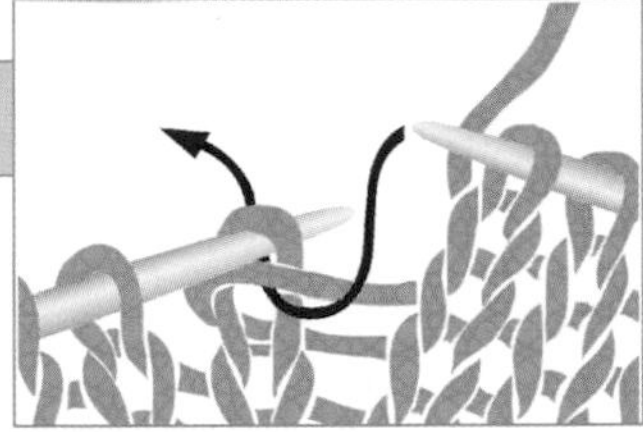

### On a purl row

**1**

With yarn in front, slip next stitch as if to purl. Bring yarn to back of work and slip stitch back to left needle. Turn the work.

**2**

When you come to the wrap on the following purl row, make it less visible by inserting right needle under wrap, placing the wrap on the left needle and purling it together with the stitch that it wraps.

## YARN OVERS

Essential for lace knitting, the array of seemingly different yarn overs creates panic in many knitters. Basically the various abbreviations mean the same thing; ie make a stitch by placing the yarn over the needle.
The following yarn overs (to make new stitch) all achieve the same result ie; make a lacy stitch or eyelet. The different abbreviations reflect where the yarn is starting from ie either at the back or the front of the knitting. If you are doing a yarn forward after knitting the last stitch and the next stitch is a purl, then nothing is needed other than to purl the next stitch without bringing the yarn to the front of the work (yo).

**yfrn** yarn forward round needle (rather than taking it underneath first)
**yrn** yarn round needle (following on from above, do the same again)
**yon** yarn over needle (following on from above, do the same again)
**yo** yarn over

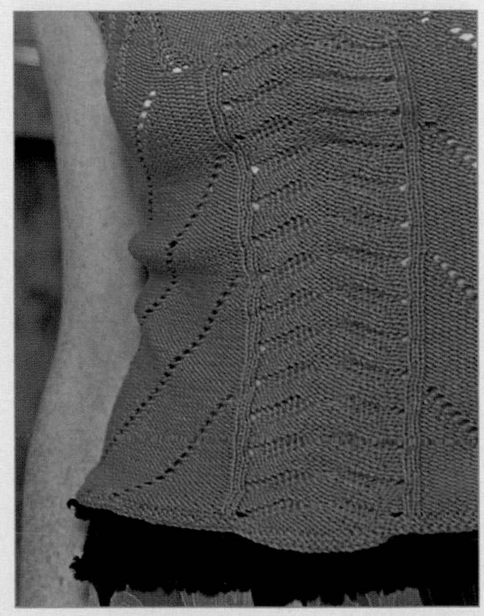

## Between two knit stitches

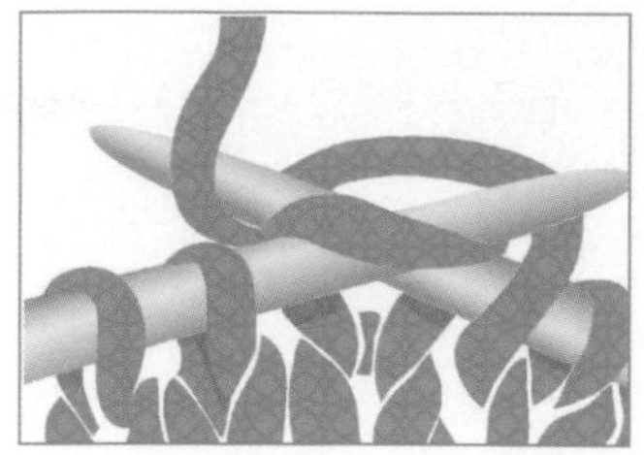

Bring yarn from back to front of work between the two needles.
Knit next st, bringing yarn to back over right needle.

## Between a knit and a purl stitch

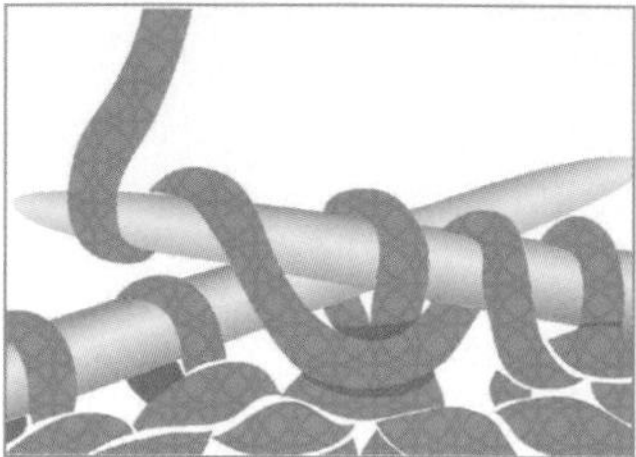

Bring yarn from back to front between the two needles,
then to back over right needle and to front again. Purl next stitch.

## Between a purl and a knit stitch

Leave yarn at front of work. Knit next stitch, bringing yarn to back over right needle.

## Between two purl stitches

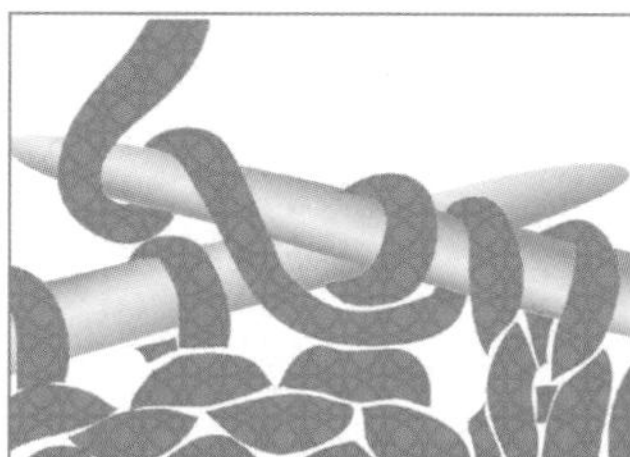

Leave yarn at front of work. Bring yarn to back over right needle and to front again.
Purl next stitch.

## At beginning of a knit row

Keep yarn at front of work. Insert right needle knitwise into first stitch on left needle. Bring yarn over right needle to back and knit next stitch, holding the yarn over with the thumb if necessary.

## At beginning of a purl row

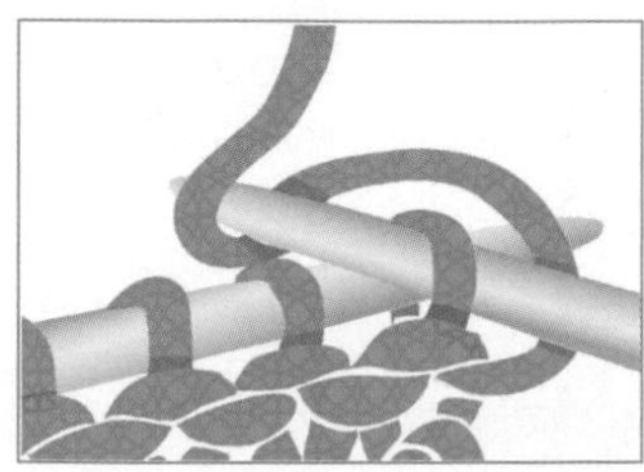

Keep yarn at back of work. Insert right needle purlwise into first stitch on left needle and purl the stitch.

## DECORATIVE INCREASES AND DECREASES

These always add class to a garment. Simply work the shaping as set, but do it any number of stitches in from the edge, to give a smooth line. For instance, to run a cable up the edge of a neckline, make all the neckline decreases on the inside of the edging cable. Use paired increases and decreases; eg ssk at beginning of right-side rows (to slope to the left) and k2tog at end of right-side rows (to slope to the right). Very good for raglan sleeves, neck edges, darts and godets.

## GODETS

I regularly use godets, or gores, in my sweaters and love the way they bring instant feminine shape. Simply cast on an extra number of stitches for each godet, then decrease the extra stitches regularly in pairs where each godet occurs, until all the extra stitches are decreased. Decorative decreases can be used to accent the godets.

## SHOULDER SHAPING

I like to work shoulder shaping by leaving stitches on hold (short rows with wraps) rather than casting them off, so that on the final row there is a straight cast off edge with no jags.

## PICKING UP STITCHES AROUND A NECKLINE

To get a professional finish on a neckline it's really important to pick up and knit evenly, with no bunching or stretching of stitches. Sometimes, due to the design of the sweater, stitches are left live at back and/or centre front, but unless the pattern calls for this, it's generally best to cast off. The reason for this is that all the stress of the sweater when worn will be falling away from centre back neck, therefore necklines tend to stretch and become bigger than intended. One way of countering this is to do a firm cast-off at centre back/front neck.

## How to pick up a stitch

Hold the knitting with the right side toward you, insert the needle under an edge stitch, take the yarn around and pull a loop through to make a stitch. When you have picked up enough stitches, remember the next row will be a wrong-side row.

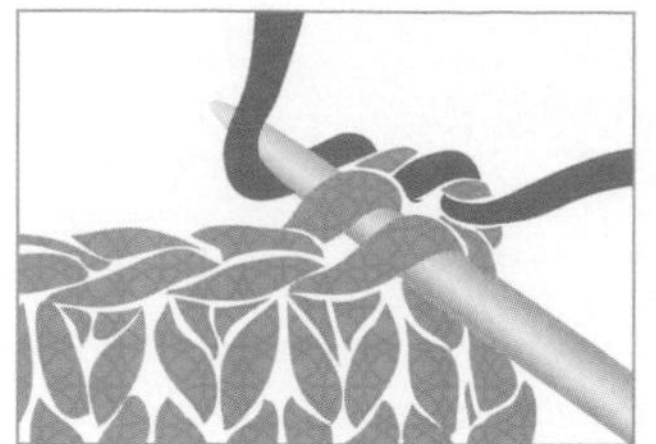

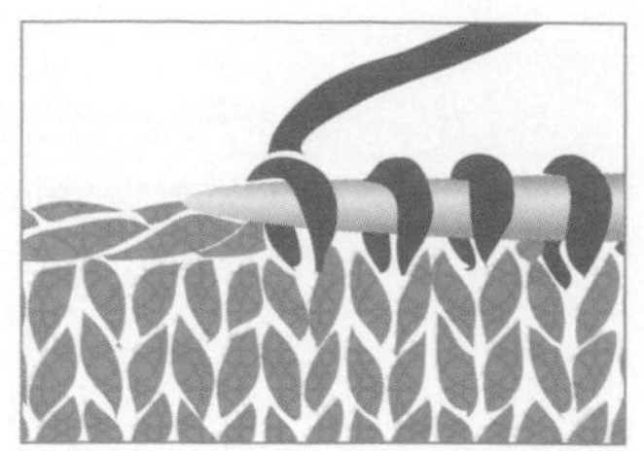

### TURNING RIDGES

A turning ridge is a row worked when the hem is the required length, at the lower or the upper edge. It demarcates the edge making a clean line. My favourite turning ridge is a purl row, but I do sometimes use a picot ridge or a slipstitch ridge, depending on the design. The right-side pattern always begins on the next RS or WS row, depending on the pattern.

## Purl

Knit the sts through the back of loops on WS, so forming a purl ridge on RS.

## Picot

Worked over an even number of sts on RS row:
K1, *k2tog, yarn over; rep from * end k1.

## Slip stitch

Worked over an odd number of stitches on RS row:
*k1, with yarn at front, slip 1, k1; repeat from * to end.

## EDGINGS

Frills and interesting edgings can transform a plain garment into a stunning one. You can substitute a decorative edging for a boring rib, or if your pattern has an edging which does nothing for you, replace it with one you love. You'll soon see what a huge difference this can make. Just make sure that the new pattern repeat fits the number of stitches in the pattern – it's an easy introduction to designing/customising your own sweaters!

## POCKETS

It's always worth taking extra care with pocket tops. Make sure they don't bag (if they do then use smaller needles) and that the side edges are attached neatly. Use an invisible slipstitch on the inside to secure pocket tops and linings, making sure that the latter are square and lined up with rest of knitting.

## BANDS

I hate to see all the hard work and craft which goes into a handknit being wasted because of ill-fitting bands. This is a most important element in producing a professional-looking jacket or cardigan – the bands should fit snugly when stretched slightly and never be longer than the edge to which they are attached. Take care that bands fit well, it really isn't so difficult once you know how. Horizontal bands should be sewn on as you knit to ensure a snug fit. Overstitch in place on wrong side, matching notches made by selvedge stitch. As the band will usually be worked on smaller needles than the fronts, this should stretch the band slightly.

If a band is applied horizontally by picking up stitches, the number of stitches will be given in your pattern, but read your knitting and if the band seems at all wavy or to have too many stitches, go with what you see and either use smaller needles or pick up fewer stitches. Some knitters advise picking up one stitch for every row on the fronts, but whilst it's a good way of calculating approximately how many stitches, I find this usually results in too many stitches and is dependent on the ratio of row to stitch gauge.
I prefer to take a measurement around the fronts and neck edge and then multiply by the stitch gauge.
As the band is worked on smaller needles this usually results in a well-fitting band.

## BUTTONS AND TRIMMINGS

Beautiful buttons, fasteners and trimmings will endow an otherwise ordinary garment with the wow factor. My favourites are glass, mother-of-pearl, silver, copper and ceramic. I'm always on the lookout for unusual hand-crafted buttons and I love vintage buttons. Also the idea of recycling old ones from second-hand sweaters bought for practically nothing in thrift shops really appeals to me. I usually prefer shanks to holes since it's easier to focus on the design of the button. Colour is important, and if you can't get an exact match to the yarn, then often it's better to go for a complete contrast.

Also consider scale when buying buttons. The balance of the sweater will be thrown out of kilter if you get this is wrong. If you have a bold design in chunky yarn you need big buttons to complement the design, as small ones would look lost and be impractical. Buttons need to be up to the job of fastening the garment and thick yarn will produce holes which will be too large for small buttons. Also take yarn into account. A fine silk yarn will never look elegant with heavy wooden buttons dragging it down, a light mother-of-pearl would work better. Never skimp on trimmings, choose them carefully to complement your sweater, which has taken lots of your valuable time to knit. If you just can't find what you're looking for, make your own knitted ones. Knots or bobbles will work for some projects or alternatively buy button blanks and cover them with knitted fabric.

## BUTTONHOLES

Buttonhole spacing is really important in achieving a professional finish. Do not place the first and last buttonholes too close to the edge, but neither should there be acres of gaping space. A good rule is that the button when fastened should finish ¼in (0.6cm) from the edge. Patterns often call for spacing the remainder evenly. This is where your creativity can kick in. You can do just that taking care to space them evenly, or you could decide that you would like to create a totally different buttonhole spacing. Try placing the buttonholes in groups of twos or threes – this would usually mean using smaller buttons with larger spacing between the groups. If I have a longish rib or border, I like to place extra buttonholes on the rib to keep it from gaping.

The one row buttonhole is a fabulous technique. As it's as strong as it's neat, no further reinforcing is needed. The lower buttonhole is worked from the right side and the upper slightly neater one is worked from the wrong side.

**1**

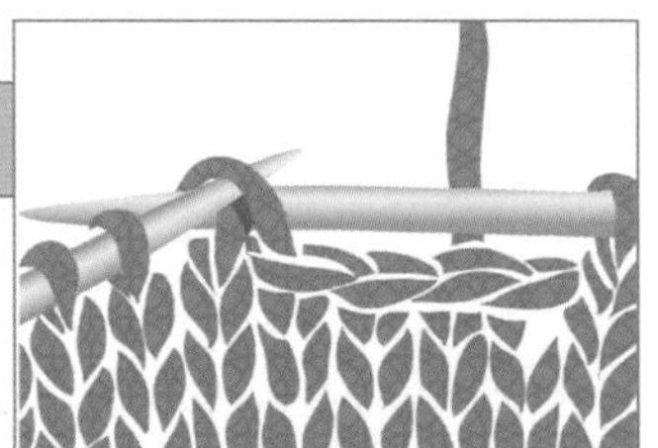

Work to buttonhole, bring yarn to front, slip a st purlwise. Yarn to back, *slip next st from LH needle, pass the first slipped st over it. Repeat from * for the number of sts to be cast off for buttonhole, keeping yarn at back. Slip last cast off stitch to LH needle and turn work.

**2**

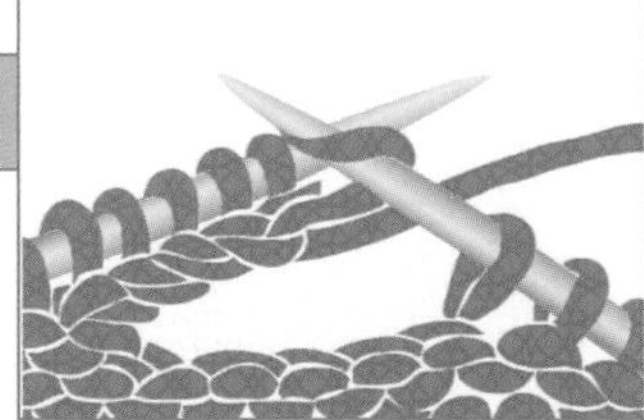

With yarn at back, cast on one more st than the number you cast off using the cable cast on: *insert RH needle between the first and second sts on LH needle, draw up a loop and place it on LH needle. When all sts are cast on, turn the work.

**3**

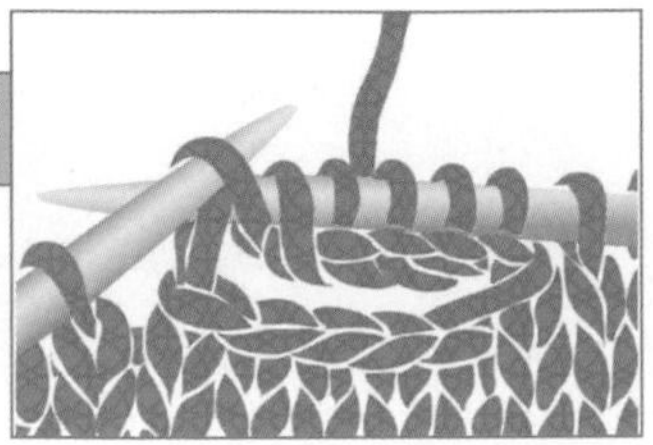

With yarn at back, slip the first stitch from the LH needle and pass the extra cast on st over it to close the buttonhole.

## BLOCKING AND PRESSING

Never underestimate the power of blocking and pressing! Small mistakes often become invisible when the overall impression of a piece is spruce and well presented. Not that you should be worrying about mistakes – the important thing is that you've completed a handknit project, so take a bow and view any variations as bonuses which make it unique and special.

First, neaten selvedges by sewing/weaving in all the ends along sides or along colour joins where appropriate. Then, using pins, block out each piece of knitting to shape. Next, gently press each piece, omitting ribs, using a warm iron over a damp cloth. Take special care with the edges, as this will make sewing up easier.

## BACKSTITCH SEAM

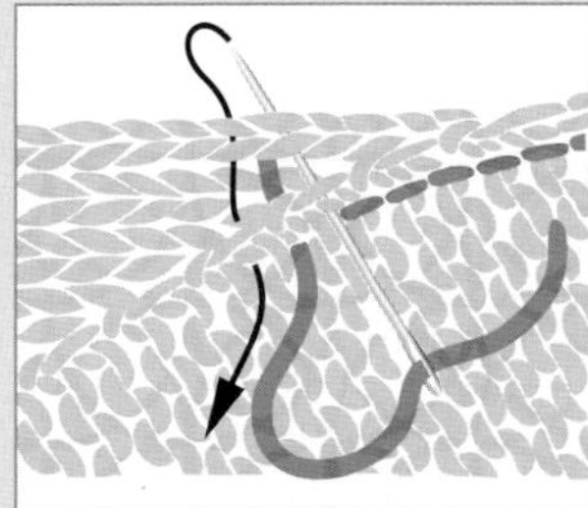

Place right sides together and insert needle from back to front between first and second rows. Pull yarn through, then insert needle from front to back between first row and cast on edge, then from back to front between second and third rows. Pull yarn through, then *insert needle from front to back at end of last stitch (one row back), then from back to front two rows forward. Pull yarn through. Repeat from * to end.

## SLIPSTITCH SEAM

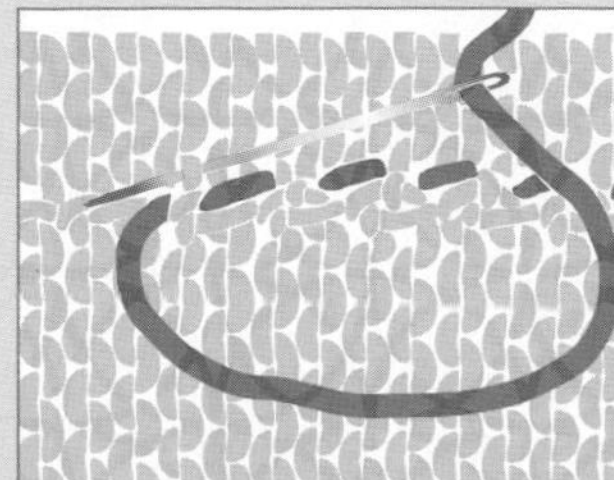

Worked with the two wrong sides facing you, catch one or two strands from the top piece and then the same from the other edge. Don't pull the yarn too tightly.

## SEWING UP

Poor finishing will ruin a beautifully knitted sweater, so it's worth taking extra care. Keep areas of pattern and texture in line across sweater, matching the notches made by the selvedge stitches. Take time to pin the garment first and, before sewing, make sure you're satisfied with the way the pieces are fitting together. I usually use a small neat backstitch on the inside of the selvedge stitch for all main seams as this creates a very stable, strong seam. I join the ribs and neckband with a slip stitch so that they lie flat. This method is suitable for all but bulky yarn. In this case I use mattress stitch. Experiment with your seams, you'll soon learn which finishing method works best for you.

## MATTRESS STITCH

Thread blunt needle with yarn. Working between the selvedge and the next stitch, pick up 2 bars. Cross to matching place in opposite piece and pick up 2 bars. * Return to first piece, go down into the hole you came out of, and pick up 2 bars. Return to opposite piece, go down into the hole you came out of, and pick up 2 bars. Repeat from * across, pulling thread taut as you go.

# ABOUT **JEAN MOSS**

Jean Moss grew up close to a Bolton cotton mill where many of her family worked as weavers, spinners or carders. The knitting spark was kindled at the age of five when her grandmother taught her to knit, but otherwise Jean is entirely self-taught in knit design and fashion. Always a firm believer that you can make a success of anything, she had been, before the knitting took off, a singer/songwriter, busker, goat breeder, beekeeper, newsagent, painter, decorator and wholefood shop owner.

Her professional knitting career started in the 1970s through chance and necessity. Living the good life with her family and an arkful of animals in a remote, rambling Yorkshire farmhouse, it was difficult to make ends meet without travelling long distances. Jean finally hit upon the idea of buying a knitting machine to design and make sweaters to sell in local markets and London boutiques. Soon she took the plunge and showed her collections in London and it was at one of these trade shows that her original fairisles caught the eye of Ralph Lauren. Within months she was designing and manufacturing (with a team of two thousand knitters) most of the Polo handknits coming out of the UK. Working for the Ralph Lauren empire was a steep learning curve; Jean's trademark styling and meticulous shaping owe a lot to the exacting demands of this period. Subsequently, Jean went on to work with many other fashion houses including Calvin Klein, Laura Ashley and Benetton, as well as to design and sell her own handknit collections internationally.

Jean is now recognised as one of Britain's leading knit designers. Her innovative combinations of intricate textures, striking colourways and sophisticated styling have been widely influential over the years. Rowan, *Vogue Knitting* and *Knitting* magazine regularly publish her designs. At present she is the principal designer for Artesano Alpaca. Her five books include *Designer Knits Collection* (1991), *Knits for All Seasons* (1993) and *Sculptured Knits* (2000). Her monthly column 'Ask Jean', in *Knitting* magazine, grapples with knitters' questions on topics ranging from exotic Tunisian crochet to how knitters can cope with Carpal Tunnel Syndrome.

***Top:*** *On the road in Monticello, Wisconsin, 2006 US tour*
***Below:*** *Spanish Village, Balboa Park, San Diego*
***Left:*** *Knitting in Venice*
***Top left:*** *In-store book signing*

As well as handknit design her other passions include gardening and music. A trained garden designer, Jean is fascinated by the cross-overs between knitting and gardening. Her experience as a colourist is expressed in the one-off, imaginative gardens she has designed for clients in Yorkshire.

Music is in Jean's blood: one-time singer, guitarist and spoons player in the professional folk duo Scarlet Vardo, she collects songs with textile themes and has recorded some on her roots CD *More Yarn Will Do the Trick*. She gardens obsessively (if recklessly), dotes on her cats and is a committed vegetarian, enjoying a reputation for her tasty, organic food.

With her partner Philip Mercer she hosts tours for knitters visiting the UK. Based in the Lakes, Edinburgh, Wales or York, international participants take workshops from Jean and other leading designers, visit glorious gardens and places of textile interest, and get a taste of the British knitting scene. She teaches and lectures in Europe and North America and is always thrilled to share ideas with other members of the global knitting village.

**For more on Jean visit www.jeanmoss.com**

***Left:*** *In her garden in Artists Valley, Wales*
***Top:*** *Early days in York market*
***Below:*** *Learn-to-knit workshop at St. Peter's School, York*

# ABBREVIATIONS

**RH** right-hand
**LH** left-hand
**WS** wrong side
**RS** right side
**L** left
**R** right
**yfrn** yarn forward round needle
**yrn** yarn round needle
**yon** yarn over needle
**yo** yarn over
**cn** cable needle
**ssk** Slip sts knitwise then knit them together
**Ssp** Slip sts knitwise then purl them together
**dpn(s)** double pointed needle(s)
**C4F** Cable 4 front
**Cr3L** Cross 3 left
**Cr3R** Cross 3 right
**tbl** through back of loop
**mb** make bobble

**dc** double crochet
**ch** chain
**st(s)** stitch(es)
**k** knit
**p** purl
**ss** slip stitch
**st st** stocking stitch
**cont** continue
**inc** increase (increasing)
**dec** decrease (decreasing)
**alt** alternate
**rep** repeat
**foll** following
**ev** every
**beg** beginning
**rem** remaining
**patt** pattern
**c.o.e.** cast off edge

# NEEDLE **SIZE** CONVERSION **TABLE**

| METRIC | OLD UK | US |
|---|---|---|
| 2 | 14 | 0 |
| 2.25 | 13 | 1 |
| 2.5 | – | – |
| 2.75 | 12 | 2 |
| 3 | 11 | – |
| 3.25 | 10 | 3 |
| 3.5 | – | 4 |
| 3.75 | 9 | 5 |
| 4 | 8 | 6 |
| 4.5 | 7 | 7 |
| 5 | 6 | 8 |
| 5.5 | 5 | 9 |
| 6 | 4 | 10 |
| 6.5 | 3 | 10.5 |
| 7 | 2 | 10.5/11 |
| 7.5 | 1 | 10.5/11 |
| 8 | 0 | 11 |
| 9 | 00 | 13 |
| 10 | 000 | 15 |
| 12 | – | 17 |
| 15 | – | 19 |
| 20 | – | 35/36 |

# DISTRIBUTORS

## Artesano distributors

**UK AND EUROPE** (except France, Denmark)
Artesano Ltd
28 Mansfield Rd
Reading
Berkshire
RG1 6AJ
44 (0)118 9503350
www.artesano.co.uk for stockists lists

**DENMARK AND SCANDINAVIA**
Markno
Marianne Knorborg
Hoejbovej 9
DK-7620 Lemvig
Denmark
www.marknodesign.dk

**FRANCE**
Distrilaine
Gwenola Kerhornou
5 Rue Thomas Edison
44470 Carquefou
France
Tel: (33) 08 73 65 44 06
www.distrilaine.com

**US**
Royal Yarns International
404 Barnside Place
Rockville
MD 20850
Tel: (1 202) 215 2300
www.royalyarns.com

**CANADA**
Wool Needlework
PO Box
Station Main
Salmon Arm
V1E 4P9
British Columbia
Tel: (1 888) 408 3777
www.woolneedlework.com

## Rowan and Jaeger distributors

**AUSTRALIA:** Australian Country Spinners, 314 Albert Street, Brunswick, Victoria 3056
Tel: (61) 3 9380 3888 Fax: (61) 3 9387 2674
E-mail: sales@auspinners.com.au

**BELGIUM:** Pavan, Meerlaanstraat 73, B9860 Balegem (Oosterzele).
Tel: (32) 9 221 8594 Fax: (32) 9 221 8594
E-mail: pavan@pandora.be

**CANADA:** Diamond Yarn, 9697 St Laurent, Montreal, Quebec, H3L 2N1
Tel: (514) 388 6188

Diamond Yarn (Toronto), 155 Martin Ross, Unit 3, Toronto, Ontario, M3J 2L9
Tel: (416) 736 6111 Fax: (416) 736 6112
E-mail: diamond@diamondyarn.com www.diamondyarn.com

**DENMARK:** Coats Danmark A/S, Mariendlunds Alle 4, 7430 Ikast
Tel: (45) 96 60 34 00 Fax: (45) 96 60 34 08
Email: coats@coats.dk

**FINLAND:** Coats Opti Oy, Ketjutie 3, 04220 Kerava
Tel: (358) 9 274 871 Fax: (358) 9 2748 7330
E-mail: coatsopti.sales@coats.com

**FRANCE:** Coats France / Steiner Frères, 100, Avenue du Général de Gaulle, 18 500 Mehun-Sur-Yèvre
Tel: (33) 02 48 23 12 30 Fax: (33) 02 48 23 1240

**GERMANY:** Coats GMbH, Kaiserstrasse 1, D-79341 Kenzingen
Tel: (49) 7644 8020 Fax: (49) 7644 802399
www.coatsgmbh.de

**HOLLAND:** de Afstap, Oude Leliestraat 12, 1015 AW Amsterdam
Tel: (31) 20 6231445 Fax: (31) 20 427 8522

**HONG KONG:** East Unity Co Ltd, Unit B2, 7/F Block B, Kailey Industrial Centre, 12 Fung Yip Street, Chai Wan
Tel: (852) 2869 7110 Fax: (852) 2537 6952
E-mail: eastuni@netvigator.com

**ICELAND:** Storkurinn, Laugavegi 59, 101 Reykjavik
Tel: (354) 551 8258
E-mail: malin@mmedia.is

**ITALY:** D.L. srl, Via Piave, 24 – 26, 20016 Pero, Milan
Tel: (39) 02 33910 180 Fax: (39) 02 33914661

**JAPAN:** Puppy Co Ltd, T151-0051, 3-16-5 Sendagaya, Shibuyaku, Tokyo
Tel: (81) 3 3490 2827 Fax: (81) 3 5412 7738
E-mail: info@rowan-jaeger.com

**KOREA:** Coats Korea Co Ltd, 5F Kuckdong B/D, 935-40 Bangbae- Dong, Seocho-Gu, Seoul
Tel: (82) 2 521 6262 Fax: (82) 2 521 5181

**LEBANON:** y.knot, Saifi Village, Mkhalissiya Street 162, Beirut,
Tel: (961) 1 992211. Fax: (961) 1 315553
E mail: y.knot@cyberia.net.lb

**NEW ZEALAND:** Please contact Rowan for details of stockists

**NORWAY:** Coats Knappehuset AS, Pb 100 Ulste, 5873 Bergen
Tel: (47) 55 53 93 00 Fax: (47) 55 53 93 93

**SINGAPORE:** Golden Dragon Store, 101 Upper Cross Street 02-51, People's Park Centre, Singapore 058357
Tel: (65) 6 5358454 Fax: (65) 62216278
E-mail: gdscraft@hotmail.com

**SOUTH AFRICA:** Arthur Bales PTY, PO Box 44644, Linden 2104
Tel: (27) 11 888 2401 Fax: (27) 11 782 6137

**SPAIN:** Oyambre, Pau Claris 145, 80009 Barcelona.
Tel: (34) 670 011957 Fax: (34) 93 4872672
E mail: oyambre@oyambreonline.com

**SWEDEN:** Coats Expotex AB, Division Craft, Box 297, 401 24 Grteborg
Tel: (46) 33 720 79 00 Fax: (46) 31 47 16 50

**TAIWAN:** Laiter Wool Knitting Co Ltd, 10-1 313 Lane, Sec 3, Chung Ching North Road, Taipei
Tel: (886) 2 2596 0269 Fax : (886) 2 2598 0619

**US:** Westminster Fibers Inc, 4 Townsend West, Suite 8, Nashua, New Hampshire 03063
Tel: (1 603) 886 5041 / 5043 Fax (1 603) 886 1056
E-mail: rowan@westminsterfibers.com

**UK:** Rowan, Green Lane Mill, Holmfirth, West Yorkshire, England HD9 2DX
Tel: 44 (0)1484 681881 Fax: 44 (0)1484 687920
E-mail: mail@knitrowan.com www.knitrowan.com

For stockists in all other countries please contact Rowan for details.

# PROJECT **INDEX**

This is a recent retrospective. Some patterns have appeared published under different names.

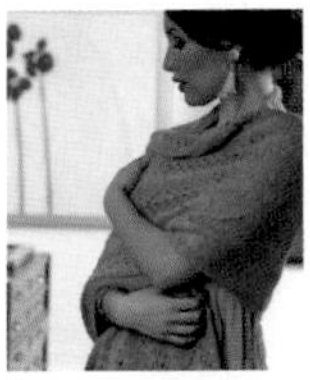

# ACKNOWLEDGEMENTS

Making a book is both magical and mysterious. The co-operation and talents of many people are paramount in creating something which, at its best, will amount to more than the sum of its parts. However, each and every part is vital and my grateful appreciation goes to everyone involved.

I especially wish to thank my knitters, in particular Ann Banks, Mary Coe and Glennis Garnett, without whose extraordinary skills there would be no sweaters. Thanks also to Tom Coomber of Artesano, both for his gorgeous yarn and for approaching GMC originally with the idea. Also to Rowan and Jaeger for their inspiring yarns and efficient support in producing the samples. Peggy Brodie at the Modern Artists Gallery generously let us free-range in her home and gallery whilst shooting the Artesano pieces. Warm thanks to her and also to Freya Berry, my favourite model.

The GMC team have been great to work with. Thanks to Gerrie Purcell for her enthusiasm and belief in the project, the editorial department and all involved with design, photography and art direction. Also a big thank-you to Kate Taylor, editor of *Knitting* magazine, which has done so much to inspire and invigorate the British knitting scene.

Thanks to Philip Mercer, behind-the-scenes unsung (not really) hero who keeps the show on the road, cheerfully turning his hand to anything. Also to Sandra Reston for providing a quiet space and support when things got tough. Lastly I'd like to thank my wonderful family of non-knitters, who don't understand what all the fuss is about.

We got there in the end. Big hugs all round!

Modern Artists Gallery, High Street, Whitchurch on Thames, Nr. Pangbourne, Reading, Berkshire. RG8 7EX 0118 984 5893
**www.modernartistsgallery.com**

GMC Publications would like to thank the following for their help in creating this book:

**Lansdowne Place Hotel** (www.landsdowneplace.co.uk) for providing the photoshoot location for projects on pages 13, 51, 55, 73, 77, 95.

**Pelham House (www.pelhamhouse.com)** for providing the photoshoot location for projects on pages 21, 33, 45, 59, 87, 105, 109.

**Harriet Hoff** for styling of projects on pages 13, 21, 33, 45, 51, 55, 59, 73, 77, 87, 95, 101, 105, 109.

**Jan Hansen** for hair and make-up for projects on pages 13, 21, 33, 45, 51, 55, 59, 73, 77, 87, 95, 101, 105, 109.

**Models** Anna Moody and Rosie Williams at MOT Models, and Freya Berry.

**Jean Moss** for the art direction and styling of images on pages 16, 19, 27, 28, 42, 48, 68, 111, 112.

**Philip Mercer** for images on pages 130-134

**Felix Mercer Moss** for images in Venice on pages 130-131

# INDEX

# INDEX

# INDEX

To place an order, or to request a catalogue, contact:
GMC Publications, Castle Place, 166 High Street,
Lewes, East Sussex BN7 1XU, United Kingdom
**Tel:** 01273 488005 **Fax:** 01273 402866
**Website:** www.gmcbooks.com
Orders by credit card are accepted